Paramilitarism

Paramilitarism

*Mass Violence in the Shadow
of the State*

UĞUR ÜMIT ÜNGÖR

OXFORD
UNIVERSITY PRESS

OXFORD
UNIVERSITY PRESS

Great Clarendon Street, Oxford, OX2 6DP,
United Kingdom

Oxford University Press is a department of the University of Oxford.
It furthers the University's objective of excellence in research, scholarship,
and education by publishing worldwide. Oxford is a registered trade mark of
Oxford University Press in the UK and in certain other countries

Published in the United States of America by Oxford University Press
198 Madison Avenue, New York, NY 10016, United States of America

British Library Cataloguing in Publication Data
Data available

Library of Congress Control Number: 2020931722

ISBN 978–0–19–882524–1

Printed and bound in Great Britain by
Clays Ltd, Elcograf S.p.A.

Links to third party websites are provided by Oxford in good faith and
for information only. Oxford disclaims any responsibility for the materials
contained in any third party website referenced in this work.

Acknowledgments

This book argues that paramilitarism is a historical and contemporary phenomenon that has existed across cultures, nations, regime types, and political systems, but always in the shadow of the state. It examines how pro-government militias relate to politics, crime, and communities, and looks into their roles in violent conflicts such as civil wars and genocides. The book makes a substantial intervention into the debate on paramilitarism, by providing the first wide-ranging historical and sociological analysis of how and why states outsource the perpetration of mass violence against civilians. The goal of this book is not to follow particular individuals, profile or prosecute certain paramilitary groups, dispute a particular theory, stake an activist claim, or to confuse analytical categories. Rather, I hope to provide an overview of a complex phenomenon, for which there are no comparative, wide-angled overviews. I offer a modest synthesis that aims to lay the foundation for further case studies on paramilitarism.

This book is at once sequel and prequel. It grew organically out of a research project on the violent aftermath of World War I, hosted at University College Dublin's Centre for War Studies. I spent a year at that institution in the eminent company of fine colleagues such as Robert Gerwarth, John Paul Newman, Tomas Balkelis, William Mulligan, and Julia Eichenberg. Our valuable, elaborate discussions on paramilitarism during that period prompted me to launch this project, which represents a clear shift in my intellectual focus and interests: from a historian working on the late Ottoman Empire, I have expanded geographically, temporally, and thematically, toward studying modern and contemporary mass violence through a more social-scientific lens. At the same time, this book is a prolegomenon: when the Syrian uprising began in 2011, the Assad regime unleashed a host of murderous pro-government militias to repress it, and I immediately realized this was a typical case of paramilitarism. As I was mulling over the structure of this book, I decided to include a chapter on Syrian paramilitarism. However, the

Syrian conflict increasingly engrossed me and before I knew it, that chapter outgrew its original bounds and mission, and is well on its way to becoming a separate monograph on Assad's militias. In this book, the introductory pages provide a glimpse of their profoundly brutal world.

This book was made possible by a generous grant from the Dutch Research Council (NWO), which provided me with a few years' leave to conduct research, supervise PhD students, and write the manuscript. This grant allowed me to assemble a team of graduate students at Utrecht University, a very special group of young scholars, without whom the project would not have succeeded. I am very grateful for their enthusiasm, commitment, and input in this project and this book. Ayhan Işık and Ali Aljasem have demonstrated that one can be both an eyewitness and a researcher of paramilitarism, and their forthcoming publications on Turkey in the 1990s and Syria in the 2010s will prove indispensable to anyone interested in political violence in those countries. The indefatigable Iva Vukušić has proven that with her strong work ethic and unique knowledge, she is set to make an indelible impact on the literature on the Serbian paramilitaries of the 1990s. Finally, the talented Amir Taha's terrific work on Iraqi paramilitarism in the 2000s was published even before he graduated, his article being downloaded and viewed thousands of times. Their work testifies to the relevance of the topic, their participation endowed this project with greater depth and credibility, and I am deeply grateful.

Working at the intersections of such disparate research fields, area studies, disciplines, and specializations means that I have incurred many professional and personal debts over the years. In the course of researching and writing this book, I have had the privilege of working with and benefitting from a great number of inspiring individuals and institutions. The stimulating academic environment at the Department of History of Utrecht University has been remarkably supportive of me, and has refined this research project in countless ways. Maarten Prak, Jolle Demmers, Annelien de Dijn, Geraldien von Frijtag, Pepijn Corduwener, Lars Behrisch, Remco Raben, the late Ralph Sprenkels and the Conflict Studies group, the support staff including Jan Welling, and especially Ido de Haan, have been tremendously generous with their time and attention. Susanne Knittel is an exemplary scholar and it has been a pleasure to cooperate with her on the Perpetrator Studies

Network and the *Journal of Perpetrator Research*. The unique intellectual community of the NIOD Institute in Amsterdam, too, has offered stalwart support over the years: Wichert ten Have, Marjan Schwegman, Frank van Vree, and Nanci Adler, Karel Berkhoff, and Ismee Tames as notable colleagues. I have benefitted from the collegiality and friendship of Thijs Bouwknegt and Kjell Anderson, often over a steaming pot of delicious *ugali*. What has made these institutions such inviting places to work is the level of attention given to work–life balance, a true privilege that only makes for better academics and better humans.

This book has been on quite a journey throughout the years. Whereas my home base has been and continues to be the Netherlands, this book was incubated, researched, discussed, presented, revised, and written on at least four continents. A series of visiting fellowships made possible an exceptionally gratifying academic experience that doubtlessly has enriched this book. In the autumn of 2014, I spent a few months as visiting researcher at the University of British Columbia in Vancouver. My discussions at that splendid campus with Erin Baines and Philippe Le Billon were very helpful in thinking through the initial phase of the book. In the autumn of 2016, I was fortunate enough to spend two very productive months at Central European University, where Tolga Esmer and Vladimir Petrović offered a blend of collegiality, friendship, and hospitality that is unparalleled. To a large extent, this book owes its existence to many late-night discussions with Vladimir on the similarities and differences between Serbian and Turkish paramilitarism in the 1990s. I spent the spring of 2019 in the Armenian capital Yerevan, finalizing the book in the outstanding company of Vahakn Keshishian, Gohar Khachatryan, Anahit Ghazaryan, Mikael Zolyan, Öndercan Muti, Tamar Sarkissian, Hovig Keshishian, and occasionally a number of retired paramilitaries now driving taxis. Finally, the second half of 2019 was one of my most satisfying experiences as I spent it as a visiting professor at the Department of History of the University of California Los Angeles. Michael Rothberg, Yasemin Yıldız, Sebouh Aslanian, Houri Berberian, Aslı Bâli, Margaret Jacob, Lynn Hunt, Daniel Ohanian, Salih Can Açıksöz, Zeynep Korkman, Kaya Menteşoğlu, Liana Grancea, Laurie Hart, Michael Provence, Wael Sawah, Jay Abdo, Fadia Afashe, Wolf Gruner, Manuk Avedikyan, and many others have all been grand in receiving me in their communities. A very special thanks goes out to two terrific scholars and individuals: Geoffrey Robinson and Benjamin Madley, whose warm hospitality made me feel home on UCLA campus.

This project has also benefitted immensely from the input of a host of scholars at a number of workshops that I organized. These include Ton Robben, Alette Smeulers, Joost Jongerden, Kerem Öktem, Şemsa Özar, Tomislav Dulić, James Gow, Ariel Ahram, Romain Malejacq, Weronika Grzebalska, Bart Luttikhuis, Abdul Wahid, Reinoud Leenders, Wil Pansters, Corinna Jentzsch, Rebecca Bryant, Dirk Moses, Alexander Hinton, Erwin van Veen, and a special word of thanks goes out to Christian Axboe Nielsen. Invited lectures took place at Warwick University, the Zentrum Moderner Orient in Berlin, the National University of Singapore, King's College, Central European University, University of Siena, University of Michigan, University of Oxford, the Center for Studies of the Holocaust and Religious Minorities in Oslo, Leicester University, University of Winchester, and the Peace Palace in The Hague. My heartfelt gratitude goes out to Stephanie Ireland and Cathryn Steele at Oxford University Press, to Dharuman Bheeman at SPi Global, and to freelance copy editor Brian North, for their scrupulous work.

Writing on political violence is a stressful process that is prone to all kinds of professional deformations—as my friends and family will confirm. At some point during the writing of this book, I typed in the word "parliamentary" and my word processor autocorrected it to "paramilitary." In our private WhatsApp group, we made jokes about paramilitarism that were hilarious to us but would be quite inaccessible to outsiders. During a costume party with graduate students, someone may or may not have dressed up as a paramilitary. And finally, one researcher's mother was first puzzled and then concerned that her son was listening to dozens of Iraqi paramilitary anthems night after night. But all of this was for a good cause: keeping each other sane while simultaneously generating more and better knowledge on the phenomenon of paramilitarism. I'd also like to acknowledge the support of a number of special people: Akram, Amr, Ararat, Artemy, Arwen, Bedross, Enno, Farid, George, Jacek, Lidija, Magda, Nisan, Ous, Özgür, Raz, Rênas, Roschanack, Samrad, Sherwan, Solange, Tayfun, Ton, Yassin, Yektan, and many others. Special thanks goes out to Kris, Tina, and Preta for their unwavering friendship, whether on the streets of Berlin or in the mountains of Alberta. And finally, particularly special thanks go to Annsar Shahhoud and Mohammad Kanfash, whose resilience and friendship always offers inspiration and consolation.

Coming from a large extended family, it would be impossible to thank everyone here, but my grandparents, as well as Polat amca and Kudret hala, deserve a special tribute for their lifetime interest in my education. They are with me in mind and spirit. The credit is due mostly to my loving parents Halil Üngör and Gönül Turan, and my unique sister and friend Devran.

This book is dedicated to Ayşenur, my loving and supporting wife, soulmate, partner, friend, colleague, and much more. She has been there for me during my lowest moments and my highest peaks, and I am truly blessed to be on this journey with her.

Contents

List of Abbreviations

AAA	Argentine Anti-Communist Alliance [or Triple A]
AUC	Autodefensas Unidas de Colombia [Colombia]
CDR	Coalition for the Defence of the Republic [Rwanda]
CIA	Central Intelligence Agency [United States]
CUP	Committee for Union and Progress [Turkey]
DAS	Administrative Department of Security [Departamento Administrativo de Seguridad, Colombia]
DOSAAF	Volunteer Society for Cooperation with the Army, Aviation, and Navy [Soviet Union]
DOSO	Voluntary Organization for Assisting Defense [Bulgaria]
DSNM	Dimitrov Union of People's Youth [Bulgaria]
ELN	National Liberation Army [Colombia]
FARC	Revolutionary Armed Forces of Colombia [Colombia]
FRY	Federal Republic of Yugoslavia [Yugoslavia]
GRU	Main Intelligence Directorate [Russia]
ICC	International Criminal Court
ICTY	International Criminal Tribunal for the Former Yugoslavia
IDP	internally displaced person
IRA	Irish Republican Army [Ireland]
JATD	Unit for Anti-Terrorist Action [Serbia]
JİTEM	Gendarmerie Intelligence and Counter-Terrorism Organization [Turkey]
JNA	Yugoslav National Army
JPRA	Peronist Youth of the Argentine Republic
JSP	Peronist Trade Youth [Argentina]
JUSMMAT	Joint United States Military Mission for Aid to Turkey
KdA	Combat Groups of the Working Class [*Kampfgruppen der Arbeiterklasse*, German Democratic Republic]
KGB	Committee for State Security [Soviet Union]
LCA	Argentine Civic Legion [Legión Civica, Argentina]
MHP	Nationalist Action Party [*Milliyetçi Hareket Partisi*, Turkey]
MICT	Mechanism for International Criminal Tribunals [United Nations]
MLN	National Liberation Movement [Guatemala]

MRND	National Republican Movement for Democracy and Development [Rwanda]
MUP	Interior Ministry [Serbia]
MUP	Ministry of Interior [Serbia]
NDF	National Defense Forces [Syria]
NGO	non-governmental organization
NKAO	Nagorno-Karabakh Autonomous Oblast [Azerbaijan]
NSDAP	National Socialist German Workers' Party [Nazi Party, Germany]
ÖHD	Special Warfare Department [*Özel Harp Dairesi*, Turkey]
ÖK	Special Forces [*Özel Kuvvetler*, Turkey]
ÖKK	Special Forces Command [*Özel Kuvvetler Komutanlığı*, Turkey]
OSA	Open Society Archives [Central European University, Budapest]
PKK	Kurdistan Workers' Party
PMF	Popular Mobilization Forces [Iraq]
PRI	Institutional Revolutionary Party [Partido Revolucionario Institucional, Mexico]
PRU	Provincial Reconnaissance Units [United States]
PSS	Paramilitary Staff Section [CIA, United States]
RPF	Rwandan Patriotic Front [Rwanda]
RSF	Rapid Support Forces [Sudan]
SCIRI	Supreme Council for Islamic Revolution in Iraq
SDB	State Security Service [Serbia]
SDG	Serb Volunteer Guard
SDS	Serb Democratic Party
SFRY	Socialist Federal Republic of Yugoslavia
SPS	Socialist Party of Serbia
SRS	Serbian Radical Party
SSJ	Party of Serbian Unity
STK	Mobilization Research Council [*Seferberlik Tetkik Kurulu*, Turkey]
Svazarm	Union for Cooperation with the Army [*Svaz pro spolupráci s armádou*, Czechoslovakia]
UÇK	Albanian Kosovo Liberation Army
UDA	Ulster Defence Association [Northern Ireland]
UDBA	Yugoslav secret service
UDR	Ulster Defence Regiment [British Army, Northern Ireland]
UN	United Nations
UPA	Ukrainian Insurgent Army
UVF	Ulster Volunteer Force [Northern Ireland]
VRS	Bosnian Serb Army

1

Introduction

Old Wine in New Bottles?

Syrian Preface: A Murder in Latakia

On the night of Thursday August 6, 2015, the 19-year-old Suleiman al-Assad, first nephew of Syrian President Bashar al-Assad, was driving his black SUV with black tinted windows through the coastal city of Latakia. According to eye witnesses, Suleiman's car was overtaken by another car at a roundabout. Suleiman followed the other vehicle to al-Azhara roundabout, swerved his car around it, got out holding an AK-47, and after a brief altercation shot the driver dead with seven bullets to the chest. He then got back into his car and fled the murder scene. The victim died on the spot. Amid a brutal civil war that was claiming the lives of dozens of people every day, one might suppose that a murder such as this one would hardly have been noticed, but the incident took an unexpected turn due to the identities of the perpetrator and victim, and what unfolded afterward.

Suleiman had long been known in Syria as the *enfant terrible* of the Assad family, and a scion representing a new generation of "Shabbiha," the thuggish criminal gangs with political connections that had been terrorizing the coast for decades.[1] Apart from being related to the president, Suleiman relied on another major source of power: his father Hilal al-Assad had headed the pro-regime paramilitary National Defense Forces (NDF) (قوات الدفاع الوطني) in Latakia before he died in March 2014 in clashes with rebels near Kessab. Suleiman himself was also a member of the NDF, which grew out of pro-regime militias that emerged in 2011 as a tool of repressing the Syrian uprising. The victim was identified as

---

[1] See my book: *Shabbiha: Assad's Militias and Mass Violence in Syria* (forthcoming, 2021).

Hassan al-Sheikh, a prominent colonel of the Syrian Air Force. Al-Sheikh had studied engineering in Syria and Bulgaria, and was off duty that night to visit his family, ardent pro-regime loyalists who lived in Latakia and were steeped in the tradition and milieu of the Syrian army. The victim's two children and his brother Nasser were also with him in the car on the night of the murder and witnessed it, suffering deep trauma that affected their mental and physical health. The story of the murder and its aftermath then took an interesting turn, as it became a national scandal and exacerbated the tensions within the Syrian loyalist camp, in particular among the coastal Alawite communities.

In the immediate aftermath of the murder, Nasser al-Sheikh filed a legal complaint with the military police in Latakia, but as soon as they realized the accused was Suleiman al-Assad, they silenced Nasser, claiming that he must have been traumatized and had not gotten a proper look at the perpetrator. The incredulous and disillusioned Nasser then took his case to social media in a public appeal. On August 8, he posted his brother's military ID on his Facebook page and turned directly to the head of state: "Dear Mr. President Bashar al-Assad: my brother the officer, colonel, and engineer was not killed by ISIS or by Jabhat al-Nusra, my brother was killed by the coward, perfidious traitor of the nation, the terrorist Suleiman al-Assad. I would have celebrated if my brother had been killed by ISIS, but please advise me what to do."[2] His post was liked over 3,000 times, with 700 comments and 600 shares. The same day, an emotional Nasser called for a public demonstration on Ziraa roundabout. The demonstration drew over 1,000 residents, who held a vigil and chanted for the arrest and execution of Suleiman, whose whereabouts were still unknown.

In response to the public unrest, the governor of Latakia, General Ibrahim Kheder al-Salem, hastened to give an interview with Sham FM Radio but committed two gaffes: first, he tried to suppress the information on the victim's military rank and identity, claiming that the killer had committed his crime without knowing the identity of the victim. This was not true, as Hassan al-Sheikh had identified himself to Suleiman as a colonel in the air force, and also led to an outburst of public outrage across the country as knowledge of the victim's credentials spread.

---

[2] See https://www.facebook.com/naser.alnaser.942/posts/1630196373928263.

Second, the governor did not call the victim "martyr" (*shaheed*), thereby depriving him of his dignity. He did promise to arrest Suleiman.[3] Meanwhile, Suleiman taunted the authorities and demonstrators online, posting a photo on his Facebook page, smirking, slouched on a sofa, a hookah in his hand, with a threatening caption that "the dogs" who were demonstrating would meet their fate in good time. He also denied the murder, claiming that he had been in Beirut at the time, despite dozens of eyewitness accounts to the contrary.[4]

Suleiman was not arrested until August 10, 2015 at 9:00 am, at a farm in Kilmakho village where he was hiding, near the Assads' ancestral village of Qardaha. He was handed over to the military police and military prosecutors, and charged with three breaches of the law, plus the murder. On August 14, the governor triumphantly explained on the national television channel al-Ikhbariyeh that "the law in Syria applies to everyone without exception to anyone, and the capture of Suleiman proves that the law is enforced." But he committed another gaffe by mispronouncing the victim's name (Husam instead of Hassan) and urging his family to have faith in the law and not stir "sedition" (*fitna*).[5] However, the legal process would suffer from several problems and peculiarities. Since Hassan al-Sheikh had not been killed by enemy forces and Suleiman al-Assad had not officially been on active duty, there were two major consequences: al-Sheikh was not designated as a "martyr" (which deprived him of status and his family of a pension), and al-Assad would not be tried by a military field tribunal (by which he escaped summary execution). The jurisdiction was now placed at the Military Court in Homs, where the first hearing was held on October 28. After an arduous legal process lasting several months, the Military Court sentenced Suleiman al-Assad to twenty years' imprisonment on January 21, 2016;

[3] Sham FM Radio, August 8, 2015, at https://www.facebook.com/watch/?v=851286051591357 (accessed April 23, 2019). When Nasser then emphasized his brother's credentials, a sardonic Facebook user quickly commented: had he not been an officer but an ordinary citizen, would it have been acceptable to kill him? See https://www.facebook.com/naser.alnaser.942/posts/1630193787261855 (accessed April 23, 2019).
[4] See https://www.facebook.com/%D8%B3%D9%84%D9%8A%D9%85%D8%A7%D9%86-%D9%87%D9%84%D8%A7%D9%84-%D8%A7%D9%84%D8%A3%D8%B3%D8%AF-1656521291259611/ (accessed April 23, 2019). Suleiman has since removed the post.
[5] *Al-Ikhbariyeh*, August 14, 2015, at https://www.facebook.com/watch/?v=1105441376150120 (accessed April 23, 2019).

Nasser posted the verdict on his Facebook page.[6] However, Suleiman's lawyer appealed the decision, and the case was referred to the Military Court in Latakia, which accepted his appeal on July 1, 2016 and annulled the sentence for a bizarre technicality: according to the judge, the killer could not have been Suleiman al-Assad, because the car was not registered under his name. Obviously, the car was stolen and this was a travesty of justice.[7] Subsequently, Nasser al-Sheikh's lawyer appealed to the Military Supreme Court in Damascus, which was supposed to deliver the final decision, but it kept delaying the session for two years. At the time of writing, the last court session was on March 25, 2019, which Suleiman did not attend.

The regime's efforts of damage control were in vain: it sent mediators to reconcile with the al-Sheikh family, but, embarrassingly on camera, both the mother and the brother refused. Nasser even offered a sharp public rebuttal of the rumors that they had taken "blood money" (*fidye*) of 50 million or 30 million Syrian pounds, writing angrily: "I'm tired of all these lies, and I don't know who is benefitting from these lies. I will tell you the millionth time that we will never bargain with the blood of the dear martyr even if they gave me all the money in the world."[8] Even Suleiman's mother Fatima Massoud al-Assad admitted that her son was responsible for the crime, and on August 16 she paid a humble visit to the al-Sheikh family to apologize on behalf of her son. But civil and military regime officials pressured the family to drop the case. Finally, none other than Qasem Suleimani, Major-General of the Revolutionary Guards, commander of the Iranian Quds Force, and main Iranian sponsor of the NDF, traveled to Qardaha in an effort to quell the ever-growing national scandal.[9]

---

[6] See   https://www.facebook.com/naser.alnaser.942/posts/1688890771392156   (accessed April 23, 2019).

[7] According to one account, when the Latakia court threw out the case and freed Suleiman, he went on a killing rampage, shooting two more people: Waddah Yousef (head of Sham FM Radio) and Nabil Hamdan (a Latakia engineer who led demonstrations against him). However, this could not be confirmed: see *The New Arab*, "Syria's Suleiman al-Assad reportedly kills two critics" (August 26, 2015), at https://www.alaraby.co.uk/english/politics/2015/8/27/syrias-suleiman-al-assad-reportedly-kills-two-critics (accessed April 23, 2019).

[8] See   https://www.facebook.com/naser.alnaser.942/posts/1637593566521877   (accessed April 23, 2019).

[9] "والدة سليمان الأسد تتبرأ منه وتتراجع عن تهديداتها", *Akhbarak* (August 14, 2015), at http://www.akhbarak. net/news/2015/08/14/7045236/articles/19514225/%D9%88%D8%A7%D9%84 D8%AF%D8%A9-%D8%B3%D9%84%D9%8A%D9%85%D8%A7%D9%86-%D8%

But the damage had been done, as attested to by the undertones of easily perceptible public discussions. On pro-regime social media, debates of the case had now shifted to broader discussions on the "internal ISIS" (داعش الداخل), a euphemism for the Shabbiha and their behavior and violence, of which the Suleiman al-Assad case was but one example.[10] Opposition groups snickered, but pro-regime circles asked themselves: How could a 19-year-old punk kill an air force colonel in broad daylight and get away with murder, while the country was suffering under the pressure of a war, and countless young men were risking life and limb on the fronts every day? Most social media comments by soundly pro-regime commentators were nonetheless sardonic about any member of the Assad family ever being held accountable to the law. The widespread expectation was that he would sit out his sentence in the relative comfort of house arrest or a hotel. In many private interviews with both Nasser al-Sheikh and Suleiman al-Assad, conducted through the Internet, I perceived a highly explosive mix of suppressed rage and narcissistic wound, respectively. Nasser regularly ranted against the Assad family, "the internal ISIS," who were ruining the country and never cared for the ordinary man in the street, while never broadening his critique to the entire regime or, God forbid, endorsing the opposition. Suleiman was paranoid and enraged, glowering at the "impudence" of the demonstrators, who he accused of "treason" and "ungratefulness" for everything the Assad family had done for Syria. But at the same time, he was afraid the regime would eliminate him, since his father was no longer there to protect him.[11]

In one of the few instances in which both opposition and pro-regime groups were vindicated, the expected happened. Suleiman al-Assad did not show up for his final two court sessions. In March 2019, photographs emerged of Suleiman in Romania, free as a bird.

A7%D9%84%D8%A3%D8%B3%D8%AF-%D8%AA%D8%AA%D8%A8%D8%B1%D8%A3-%D9%85%D9%86%D9%87-%D9%88%D8%AA%D8%AA%D8%B1%D8%A7%D8%AC%D8%B9-%D8%B9%D9%86-%D8%AA%D9%87%D8%AF%D9%8A%D8%AF%D8%A7%D8%AA%D9%87%D8%A7 (accessed April 23, 2019).

[10] See, for example, https://www.facebook.com/doa3sh.alda5l/ (accessed April 23, 2019).
[11] Interviews conducted with Nasser al-Sheikh, August 26 and 27, 2018. Interviews conducted with Suleiman al-Assad, September 26, October 1 and 2, 2018.

This one murder in Syria encapsulates, in a microcosm, a broad range of issues and problems relating to violent conflict, civil war, crime, the state, and paramilitarism. Paramilitarism has great importance for understanding the processes of violence that are played out during civil wars, such as in Syria, which often see the formation of paramilitary forces that conduct counter-insurgency operations, hold immense power beyond the state's official security organs, and inflict violence on civilians.[12] Paramilitaries have appeared in violent conflicts in very different settings and have been responsible for widespread violence against civilians and transformations of the states in which they operate. Preliminary investigation of paramilitaries reveals two puzzling patterns: they maintain close links with political elites including heads of state, and they are heavily involved in the social milieu of organized crime. This book examines paramilitarism through the prism of the interpenetration of paramilitaries and the state, as well as the interplay between organized crime and the state. It looks at how and why paramilitaries are related to both worlds, and how their violence has had a profound impact on a large number of different countries, but which nevertheless shared similar dynamics, rationales, and logics of paramilitarism. A thorough understanding of these dynamics can clarify the direction and intensity of violence in wartime and peacetime. The book approaches paramilitarism through a historical and sociological lens, using both close analysis of primary documents, such as non-governmental organization (NGO) reports, newspaper articles, social media posts, leaked files, interviews conducted during ethnographic fieldwork, and a wide range of secondary sources. The combination of these perspectives is useful for studying paramilitarism, as it is a process that leaves traces across different spaces and bureaucracies, and deserves a flexible and multi-faceted approach.

Unpacking Paramilitarism

What is "paramilitarism"? This book conceptualizes paramilitarism as a system in which a state has relationships with irregular armed

---

[12] The Pro-Government Militias Database identifies over 300 pro-government militias between 1981 and 2007. See https://militias-guidebook.com (accessed April 24, 2019).

organizations that carry out violence. These armed groups have different forms and types of relationships with the state, but nevertheless are linked to it.

In this book, paramilitaries are taken to be synonymous with "state-sponsored militias" or "pro-government militias," and various other characterizations used to denote the same phenomenon: pro-state, armed groups.[13] But rather than a binary categorizing of which groups exactly *are* and *are not* paramilitaries, or attempts at precise pinpointing of essential features or exclusive differences, it is more useful to bound the concept by placing two buoys in the conceptual landscape along an axis of state involvement. Paramilitarism can then be conceived of as an umbrella concept that covers a broad continuum, distinguished by levels of state involvement.[14] At the left end of this spectrum, there are spontaneous, bottom-up initiatives such as local vigilantes, lynch mobs, and self-defense groups, and on the other end of the continuum stand the much more organized, top-down, professional paramilitary units of the state. In between, from left to right we can place vigilantes, such as neighborhood patrols well-known in gated communities—tacitly condoned but not necessarily actively organized by the state. Moving right, we would see off-duty police/army paid by businessmen or politicians—not institutionally supported but "connected." Next along would be covertly organized and supported armed groups whose affiliation with the state is denied and concealed to various degrees—such as death squads and proxy militias that are "astroturfed"—surreptitiously supported but made to appear autonomous and grassroots. Another step right and we can find officially sanctioned civil defense forces, irregular forces, and civil militias that function, for example, as auxiliaries in violent conflicts. Finally, at the very right of the spectrum are the paramilitary armies of a

---

[13] A subtle distinction needs to be drawn here between paramilitary and para-police forces in terms of their insertion in, informal links to, and knowledge of the state and society. Some units under discussion in this book are strictly seen as para-police forces: they operate under the auspices of Interior Ministries, not Defense Ministries, their acts and tasks are often operationally different (swarming, detention, torture, disappearance), they are often more independent, and they are often financed by various societal actors. Finally, it is the police that have the most contacts with criminals, therefore a focus on (organized) crime is crucial (see Chapter 3).

[14] For a somewhat similar approach, see Martha Huggins, "Vigilantism and the State: A Look South and North," in Martha Huggins (ed.), *Vigilantism and the State in Modern Latin America: Essays on Extralegal Violence* (Westport, CT: Praeger, 1991), 1–18.

state: special operations forces of the police or army, of which virtually every state disposes. The latter group operates explicitly in the name of the state and is generally accountable to the government and (democratic) oversight, but nevertheless enjoys special status. The continuum mostly pertains to the key issue of levels of state involvement, but also levels of organization, professionalism, mobility, and firepower—all in all, their capacity. All of these groups are taken as different expressions of the same analytical category, and are thus under examination in this book.

The major distinction between paramilitarism and militias is that the former contains the prefix "para," which means "beside" as well as "on behalf of" or "beyond," and suggests its dynamic and relational proximity to the state. The suffix -ism denotes wider societal and political implications, but not an ideology. The insular term "militias" focuses myopically on an armed group of men in relative isolation, and also includes those armed groups that fight for decidedly non-state groups, such as rebel groups in general, but also political parties or unions in democracies, neighborhood vigilantes in societies with the right to bear arms, and others, without ties to the state. Therefore, this book centers not only on paramilitaries or pro-government militias per se, but on their changing assemblages and evolving constellations with the state. It departs from the assumption that ambiguity is part and parcel of defining paramilitarism both analytically and descriptively.[15] Whereas it accepts this ambiguity, there are two problems in defining paramilitarism: excessive definitionalism, and over-ambitious theorizing. First and foremost, defining paramilitarism requires a dual strategy: on the one hand avoiding excessive hair-splitting and a drive for absolute precision, and on the other hand adopting a modest working definition and running with it. The argument that research on militias suffers from "the politics of naming, leading to a proliferation of different terms to describe similar activities and functions"[16] is not a problem per se. Conceptual proliferation simply attests to the fact that paramilitarism can emerge in different political and cultural contexts. These concepts should reflect

---

[15] Then again, no scholarly field is ever unfragmented or uncontested: this assumption is just as valid for research on paramilitarism and militias as it is for the study of contested academic concepts such as "revolution," "feminism," or "genocide."

[16] Clionadh Raleigh, "Pragmatic and Promiscuous: Explaining the Rise of Competitive Political Militias across Africa," *Journal of Conflict Resolution* 60:2 (2016), 283–310, at 287.

the processual nature of the phenomenon rather than just sketching structures. On the other hand, descriptive definitions veer too close to emic notions of paramilitarism (such as "Freikorps," "Black and Tans," "JİTEM," "Triple A," "Četniks," "Kamajor," "Basij," "Rondas Campesinas"). Second, theories of paramilitarism that are too ambitious and maximalist run the risk that the model overtakes the empirics. Too many studies (especially journal articles) draw on a single case and hastily theorize from a narrow empirical basis. Paramilitarism must be recognized as a broad umbrella phenomenon that cannot be captured in the confines of one theoretical approach or single-case exemplification. However, despite the variety and diversity of the phenomenon, the key point is that it cannot be understood without the state, as the state precedes both anti-state groups and pro-state groups.

The diversity of approaches to paramilitarism and paramilitaries is evidenced by varying definitions of them.[17] Mary Kaldor defines paramilitary groups as "autonomous groups of armed men generally centered on an individual leader."[18] Kay Warren describes paramilitaries as death squads composed of former members of the army and police, which operate with impunity and benefit from direct or indirect logistical institutional support of the state.[19] For Joshua Lund, "paramilitarism has to do with the franchising out of the state's monopoly of violence."[20] Jasmin Hristov calls them "armed groups, created and funded by wealthy sectors of society, with military and logistical support provided unofficially by the state."[21] Julie Mazzei defines paramilitary groups as "anti- and counter-revolutionary armed groups."[22] Carey, Mitchell, and Lowe define

---

[17] For two comprehensive bibliographic overviews on the cognate and overlapping phenomena, see Romain Malejacq, "Pro-Government Militias" (July 26, 2017), *Oxford Bibliographies*, at http://www.oxfordbibliographies.com/view/document/obo-9780199743292/obo-9780199743292-0213.xml; Benjamin Beede, "Semi-Military and Paramilitary Organizations" (March 28, 2018), *Oxford Bibliographies*, at http://www.oxfordbibliographies.com/abstract/document/obo-9780199791279/obo-9780199791279-0100.xml (both accessed June 1, 2018).

[18] Mary Kaldor, *New and Old Wars* (Cambridge: Polity, 2006), 98.

[19] Kay Warren, "Death Squads and Wider Complicities: Dilemmas for the Anthropology of Violence," in Jeffrey Sluka (ed.), *Death Squad: The Anthropology of State Terror* (Philadelphia: University of Pennsylvania Press, 2000), 226.

[20] Joshua Lund, "The Poetics of Paramilitarism", *Revista Hispánica Moderna* 64:1 (2011), 61–7, at 64.

[21] Jasmin Hristov, *Paramilitarism and Neoliberalism: Violent Systems of Capital Accumulation in Colombia and Beyond* (London: Pluto, 2014), 4.

[22] Julie Mazzei, *Death Squads or Self-Defense Forces? How Paramilitary Groups Emerge and Challenge Democracy in Latin America* (Chapel Hill: University of North Carolina Press, 2009), 5.

pro-government militias as armed, organized groups that are identified as pro-government or sponsored by the government (national or subnational), but not as being part of the regular security forces.[23] Jentzsch, Kalyvas, and Schubinger conceive of militias as "armed groups that operate alongside state security forces or independently of the state, aiming to shield local populations from rebel demands or depredations and seeking to acquire its loyalty or collaboration," and focus on their anti-insurgent dimension.[24] In a wide-ranging analysis of militias, Kan conceptualizes them as "local guardians that use violence to fill a variety of political, social, and security gaps in a state." He sees them as paramilitary due to their "blurring of lines between what constitutes the public and private use of force," but does not see the state as essential either in their direct formation, tacit condoning, or indirect influence.[25]

These definitions focus on different elements of paramilitarism, including their military and political functions, aims and objectives, and especially the nature of their relationships with the state. This book focuses especially on the state, because paramilitaries' arrangements with the state are not necessarily placed front and center in the wider literature on paramilitarism. Some have even argued that pro-government militias in fact have a lot in common with anti-government rebels, as they defect back and forth. However, the centrality of the state has been recognized by many experts on paramilitarism. Hristov offers a typology of different paramilitary actors (death squads, vigilantes, warlords) and argues that "the steady features across the different cases is the paramilitary groups' pro-state stance—in other words their favourable attitude towards the state or the political party in power—as well as the state's tolerance, support or promotion of these groups."[26] Kalyvas and Arjona treat paramilitarism as a complex and multifaceted phenomenon, defined as follows: "Paramilitaries are armed groups that are directly or indirectly with the state and its local agents, formed by the state or

---

[23] Sabine Carey, Neil Mitchell, and Will Lowe, "States, the Security Sector, and the Monopoly of Violence: A New Database on Pro-Government Militias," *Journal of Peace Research* 50:2 (2013), 249–58.

[24] Corinna Jentzsch, Stathis Kalyvas, and Livia Schubiger, "Militias in Civil Wars," *Journal of Conflict Resolution* 59:5 (2015), 755–69.

[25] Paul Rexton Kan, *The Global Challenge of Militias and Paramilitary Violence* (Cham: Palgrave, 2019), 6.

[26] Hristov, *Paramilitarism and Neoliberalism*, 38.

tolerated by it, but that are outside its formal structure."[27] They identify four types of paramilitarism (vigilantes, death squads, home guards and militias, and paramilitary armies) and conceptualize two dimensions as crucial: the resources of the state, and the height of the threat. Their principal argument is that paramilitarism is related to state-building, in that the emergence of paramilitaries depends on the complex interplay between state resources and threat levels.[28] These qualitative discussions are confirmed by elaborate quantitative examinations: for example, Böhmelt and Clayton examine a wide range of cases of paramilitarism between 1981 and 2007, and conclude that state capacity was crucial for sustaining paramilitaries in all of the cases.[29]

Like many other studies, this book too departs from still widespread, common understandings of the state as a static and uniform Weberian construct. In that traditional interpretation, these types of armed groups are seen as the discordant "lumps in the dough" of the state's otherwise ostensibly smooth and homogeneous monopoly of violence. Clearly, the state/non-state dichotomy has limited use: state formation ("statification" and "de-statification") is a process, and state sovereignty is always a patchwork of interlocking, overlapping, and competing agencies and apparatuses of coercion. Only a focus on these intra-state dynamics can elucidate paramilitarism. Therefore, a more promising line of research is not only to look at the militias themselves, but take a broader view and examine their institutional environment and embeddedness in the state. Many scholars have recognized that the institutional environment and political interests are vital to identifying and understanding militias.[30] Staniland has taken the argument even farther, arguing that instead of approaching militias as a discrete, apolitical phenomenon isolated from their institutional environment, a better understanding can only be pursued by integrating research in a host of interconnected themes such

---

[27] Stathis Kalyvas and Ana Arjona, "Paramilitarismo: Una Perspectiva Teórica," in Alfredo Rangel (ed.), *El Poder Paramilitar* (Bogotá: Planeta, 2005), 25–45: "Los paramilitares son grupos armados que están directa o indirectamente con el Estado y sus agentes locales, conformados por el Estado o tolerados por éste, pero que se encuentran por fuera de su estructura formal."

[28] Ibid., 34.

[29] Tobias Böhmelt and Govinda Clayton, "Auxiliary Force Structure: Paramilitary Forces and Progovernment Militias," *Comparative Political Studies* 51:2 (2018), 197–237.

[30] Bettina Engels, "Mapping the Phenomenon of Militias and Rebels in Africa," in Wafula Okumu and Augustine Ikelegbe (eds), *Militia, Rebels and Islamist Militants: Human Insecurity and State Crisis in Africa* (Pretoria: Institute for Security Studies, 2010), 69–87.

as insurgencies, electoral violence, and state building, and examining "armed politics."[31] This book follows this strategy, because ultimately paramilitarism is about politics: the distribution of intra-societal power.

When following this road map, two important pitfalls need to be avoided: approaching the state as a monolith, and seeing paramilitaries as a static phenomenon. For example, Aliyev's distinction between "state-parallel" and "state-manipulated" paramilitaries offers a snapshot of two types of militias that simply have differing political and institutional distance to the state at a certain moment of time, but paramilitaries can shift in their relative position to the state.[32] Therefore, these static distinctions disappear if one takes a processual, continuous approach. Arnaut rightly claims that militias benefit from "proximity to the regular defence and security forces," by which he indicates "physical co-presence during training, on the front lines, and aspirations of the youngsters—as holders of secure employment and as icons of social success."[33] But "proximity" cannot be a static given, as violent conflict continuously restructures the constellation of the militias and the state. Second, the undifferentiated use of the terms state, regime, and government, postulates the state as a monolith instead of a processual, fluctuating set of networks in which particular agencies, institutions, or informal alliances are involved in organizing paramilitaries. Another example is Staniland's useful distinction of four strategies that states can deploy relating to militias: suppression, containment, collusion, and incorporation.[34] However, "the state" is no monolith: whereas one arm of the government can suppress certain militias, another can expend resources to covertly or overtly support militias. Tactical operations are often run by different agencies, institutions, and levels of the state, which should not be homogenized but aggregated and problematized. The result is that a state can be at war with itself, or successive governments can deal differently with the (nominally same) paramilitary group. The underlying problem with

---

[31] Paul Staniland, "Armed Groups and Militarized Elections," *International Studies Quarterly* 59:4 (2015), 694–705.

[32] Huseyn Aliyev, "Strong Militias, Weak States and Armed Violence: Towards a Theory of 'State-Parallel' Paramilitaries," *Security Dialogue* 47:6 (2016), 498–516.

[33] Karel Arnaut, "Corps Habillés, Nouchis and Subaltern Bigmanity in Côte d'Ivoire," in Mats Utas (ed.), *African Conflicts and Informal Power: Big Men and Networks* (London: Zed, 2012), 81.

[34] Paul Staniland, "Militias, Ideology, and the State," *Journal of Conflict Resolution* 59:5 (2015), 770–93.

some of these conceptualizations is that the nature of paramilitary–state relationships is highly dynamic, even volatile, and snapshot distinctions between "informal" or "semi-official" ties disregard their historical and changeable nature. Paramilitaries and militias are social groups with "biographies" that can extend over decades. What can begin as a rebel group, can transform into an informal militia, and become regimented and formalized within a state's security sector.

Studying Paramilitarism: Approaches and Limits

All in all, paramilitarism can be seen as a form, phase, and dynamic of state formation, because their activities extend to beyond mere murder, and include property dispossession, intelligence, security provision, and other state functions. But the nature of paramilitarism is still a hotly debated topic: *how* are paramilitaries connected to states? What type of complex, symbiotic relationship are we talking about? Classical principal–agent approaches have been developed and critiqued, and by now both case studies and comparative research have taught us a lot about the types of relationships that exist. Carey and Mitchell's typology of pro-government militias distinguish the links to the state into informal and semi-official militias, and sketch eight different types of militias. According to them, relationships with the state can be local, community-driven, ideological/political, and non-civilian.[35] Gerlach argued that genocide requires a coalition of violent forces in a society, and recognized the importance of mass participation in militias to commit violence and carry master cleavages into the countryside.[36] These coalitions can be contingent or structural, can predate a conflict or emerge during it, but in most cases are ad hoc and volatile. For Amar, a paramilitary group is "an armed band commissioned by the state and elite actors to perform illegal acts of enforcement, coercion, and punishment, often acting as vigilantes preserving national security and protecting the impunity of those in power." He argues that paramilitaries are linked to the state

---

[35] Sabine Carey and Neil Mitchell, "Pro-Government Militias," *Annual Review of Political Science* 20 (2017), 127–47.
[36] Christian Gerlach, *Extremely Violent Societies: Mass Violence in the Twentieth-Century World* (Cambridge: Cambridge University Press, 2010), 193–200.

through a set of "parastatal coalitions" that forge "a parallel realm of reduced accountability and unregulated power."[37] Civico's innovative ethnographic work has taken the Italian term *intreccio* as a metaphor for the types of relationships that are forged between paramilitaries and state officials (see Chapter 4).[38] Utas and Jörgel have argued that patrimonial systems of informal power, as a "parallel" or "shadow" state, have given birth to militias, especially in Central African countries.[39] Dowdle's research dovetailed nicely with this approach; he argued that paramilitaries result from clientelistic politics and a trade-off between resources for paramilitaries and security for political leaders.[40] Since they are defined by various levels of informality, these relationships are almost always characterized by ambiguity. In a similar vein, Reno developed the helpful argument that weak states can consist of dense private networks, and that militias are a result and indicator of weak formal political institutions, but strong informal political networks.[41] Finally, Jenss' research on Colombia has emphasized opacity and blurred boundaries, and an arrangement that was threefold in that country: coexistence, complementarity, and confrontation.[42]

State–militia links are complex and no conclusive, single theory has yet been formed, but most scholars agree on the impact that paramilitarism has on the state, arguing that militias can reinforce state power as well as undermine it. Delegating violence to extend the state's reach is a gamble: if it works, it obviates a threat, but if it does not work, it can backfire if reintegration or demobilization fails. Centralization might run the risk of failure, but decentralization runs the risk of autonomy. In any case, states always face a trade-off between a militia's capacities and its ability to control it; the result is a dynamic and delicate process of

[37] Paul Amar, *The Security Archipelago: Human-Security States, Sexuality Politics, and the End of Neoliberalism* (Durham, NC: Duke University Press, 2013), 18.

[38] Aldo Civico, *The Para-State: An Ethnography of Colombia's Death Squads* (Berkeley: University of California Press, 2016).

[39] Mats Utas and Magnus Jörgel, "The West Side Boys: Military Navigation in the Sierra Leone Civil War," *Journal of Modern African Studies* 46:3 (2008), 487–511. See also the informative volume, Utas, *African Conflicts and Informal Power*.

[40] Andrew Dowdle, "Civil Wars, International Conflicts and Other Determinants of Paramilitary Strength in Sub-Saharan Africa," *Small Wars & Insurgencies* 18:2 (2007), 161–74.

[41] William Reno, *Warlord Politics and African States* (Boulder, CO: Lynne Rienner, 1999).

[42] Alke Jenss, "From Coexistence and Complementarity to Confrontation? Colombian Paramilitaries, their Successors and their Relation to the State," *Sicherheit und Frieden/Security & Peace (S+F)* 33:4 (2015), 206–11.

balancing interests.[43] In a similar vein, Pereira has pointed out that "state capacity to centralize coercive control appears to be the result of intricate, contingent, inter- and intrainstitutional political bargains that are frequently renegotiated."[44] Therefore, paramilitarism is often volatile, because the temporary or permanent devolution of official military and police tasks is a process with ups and downs. The state's monopoly of force is temporary and reversible, and "management" or "oligopoly" has often been used as a better alternative to "monopoly."[45] This book takes this argument farther and argues that paramilitarism is much like a *business*: deals are struck between partners who might have no prehistory of engagement, and can even be strange bedfellows, but for the duration of the deal respect the arrangement, until it is renegotiated. Since no single puppet master is in control of these deals, and there is often no "market control" (supra-state coercion), paramilitarism often leaves indelible, long-term marks on the state that cannot be easily reversed or expunged. Indeed, some states have experienced a tradition or culture of paramilitarism that has persisted through different governments, regime types, and conflicts.[46] Historically, irregular armed forces have shaped the trajectory of many states, just as much as states have created paramilitaries. Just as state formation is a "blind process" (a process with a clear direction but not necessarily with a steersman), subcontracting violence can be as well: the authorities can never be 100 percent certain what the outcome will be, and how they will be able to control the consequences of their outsourcing.[47]

Having defined paramilitarism and briefly surveyed the ways in which it is set up, another main topic in the literature is motive. *Why* do states employ militias and paramilitaries outside their formal structures? Here, too, the literature offers a broad diversity of theories and arguments. Staniland argued that states avail themselves of militias due to

[43] Yelena Biberman, *Gambling with Violence: State Outsourcing of War in Pakistan and India* (Oxford: Oxford University Press, 2019).

[44] Diane Davis and Anthony Pereira (eds), *Irregular Armed Forces and their Role in Politics and State Formation* (Cambridge: Cambridge University Press, 2003), 388.

[45] Mutahi Ngunyi and Musambayi Katumanga, *From Monopoly to Oligopoly of Violence* (Nairobi: UNDP, 2014).

[46] Ariel Ahram, *Proxy Warriors: The Rise and Fall of State-Sponsored Militias* (Stanford, CA: Stanford University Press, 2011); Mazzei, *Death Squads or Self-Defense Forces?*, 209.

[47] Vanda Felbab-Brown, "Hurray for Militias? Not So Fast: Lessons from the Afghan Local Police Experience," *Small Wars & Insurgencies* 27:2 (2016), 258–81.

their ideological fit with the regime, and their operational value as combatants.[48] Schneckener's argument that states employ militias for the purposes of "counter-insurgency," "counter-crime," and "counter-rival," closely echoes Rosenbaum and Sederberg's triple notion of "crime control," "social group control," and "regime control."[49] For Jentzsch, Kalyvas, and Schubiger, the critical motive is the "anti-rebel dimension" of paramilitary groups, for Hristov the elimination or neutralization of individuals or groups that constitute "a threat or obstacle to the interests of those with economic and political power," and for Mazzei, "a strategy used to counter reform efforts."[50] In other words, they emerge to defend and preserve the political status quo, and most authors agree that paramilitary violence is directed outward against the forces threatening the political elites in command of the state.

Another way to think about paramilitarism is a functionalist view: what type of violence do they commit, and what social, political, cultural functions and impacts does this violence have? After all, it is often the "tasks" at hand that structure paramilitary group formation membership in the first place. We know that paramilitaries produce death, terror, fear, confusion, and many other effects in their efforts to suppress threats to the status quo. Even though paramilitary coercion tends to be applied in an ad hoc way, paramilitary violence is set up to target particular social groups in a categorical, systemic, and sustained way. That violence affects the state in many ways: it hinders the process of institution-building, and de-institutionalizes the state in at least three ways. First, paramilitary violence is not accountable and traceable up a chain of command, which affects the formal hierarchies of the state and sows confusion and conflict among state officials. Second, the victims cannot claim their rights through the compromised courts that fear prosecuting paramilitaries, which weakens the judicial branch. Finally, political parties that oppose paramilitarism are also in a bind, as publicizing and campaigning against paramilitary violence is risky and might not even yield votes. The net result is that the range and depth of the state's symbiotic ties with the paramilitaries becomes increasingly entrenched.

---

[48] Staniland, "Militias, Ideology, and the State."

[49] Jon Rosenbaum and Peter Sederberg, "Vigilantism: An Analysis of Establishment Violence," *Comparative Politics* 6:4 (1974), 541–70.

[50] Jentzsch, Kalyvas, and Schubiger, "Militias in Civil Wars," 756; Mazzei, *Death Squads or Self-Defense Forces?*, 17; Hristov, *Paramilitarism and Neoliberalism*, 4.

Therefore, as much as it seems like looking into the wrong end of a telescope, by looking closely at paramilitary violence we can understand paramilitary arrangements and constellations within the state.

Paramilitaries have been commonly approached as the outcome of a weak state, as purely criminal actors, as subcontractors of state terror, as reactionary capitalists, and in the context of path-dependent histories of problematic states.[51] This book takes the position that even though all of these approaches are partially useful and valid, the research landscape so far is still too uneven to draw broader conclusions about explanatory models. Only further comparative research that deepens and broadens our knowledge will yield more sophisticated concepts and toolboxes to understand paramilitarism in a more fine-grained manner. What this book does assume is that in all cases *history* matters, *crime* matters, and the *state* matters. Hence, the three central chapters in this book revolve around those themes.

Yet researching paramilitarism has clear limits. How can we study something that does not want to be studied? Paramilitarism is set up, through organizational ambiguity and plausible deniability, not to leave any political, physical, and legal traces, neither in the present, and nor in the future. Studying the iceberg while only looking at the tip will reproduce the confusion, silence, and intrigue that are widespread in public perceptions and discussions on paramilitarism. It is commonsensical that strolling into, say, the Russian government's offices and demanding a full disclosure of its dealings with paramilitaries in Ukraine would not yield any meaningful results. Scheper-Hughes therefore makes the compelling argument that research on secretive phenomena that are deliberately obfuscated and hidden by powerful actors requires unusual ethnographic methods, including "undercover" modes of approaching and interviewing respondents.[52] Studies like Huggins' examination of Brazilian death squads rely on works of immersive (and risky) journalism, government investigations, Freedom of Information Act requests, and careful interviews with

---

[51] For a thorough overview, see Hristov, *Paramilitarism and Neoliberalism*, 44–60. See also Joshua Lund and Anna Mahler, "Men with Guns: Cultures of Paramilitarism and the Modern Americas" (Symposium held at the University of Arizona, November 12–13, 2015), described at https://lasa.international.pitt.edu/members/special-projects/docs-archive/LundJoshua_prop. pdf (accessed April 22, 2019).

[52] Nancy Scheper-Hughes, "Parts Unknown: Undercover Ethnography of the Organs-Trafficking Underworld," *Ethnography* 5:1 (2004), 29–73.

perpetrators and survivors.[53] Adapting intelligent ethnographic methods to examine paramilitarism requires a separate discussion, but it suffices to state here that triangulating and inferring are complementary techniques to unearth possible links and hidden collusion.[54]

The same critical attitude is required for dealing with archival sources. Only a serious political transition accompanied by a massive declassification of state archives would expose the full range and implications of paramilitarism in these societies. There are few examples of these deluges of source material. The Guatemala and Mexico projects, including the Chiquita Papers at the National Security Archive website, and the 2019 release of the US State Department papers on Argentina have demonstrated the extent to which US governments and officials colluded with paramilitarism in Latin America. The International Criminal Tribunal for the Former Yugoslavia (ICTY) has collected millions of pages of material, many of which are secret files from Serbian and Bosnian-Serb archives that shed light on paramilitarism in the 1990s. But we lack similar access in other cases. The Ergenekon court case in Turkey, or the Truth and Reconciliation Commission in Colombia, the Commission for Historical Clarification in Guatemala, or regime change in Kenya, Indonesia, Iraq, or Pakistan, has so far failed to sufficiently clarify the paramilitary systems in those countries. Therefore, leaks and informers must be used as supplementary sources for a deeper appreciation of paramilitarism. The problems posed by archival scarcity and ethnographic obstacles, as well as their interplay, should also be topics for separate methodological discussions.[55]

What This Book Tries To Do

This is a wide-angled and synoptic book that departs from an empirical complication, the puzzle of paramilitarism. It does not offer one single

[53] Martha Huggins, "Modernity and Devolution: The Making of Police Death Squads in Modern Brazil," in Bruce Campbell and Arthur Brenner (eds.), *Death Squads in Global Perspective* (New York: Palgrave Macmillan, 2000), 203–28.

[54] I will deal with this problem in a separate book: *Shabbiha: Assad's Paramilitaries and Mass Violence in Syria* (forthcoming, 2021).

[55] Carolyn Nordstrom and Antonius Robben (eds), *Fieldwork Under Fire: Contemporary Studies of Violence and Culture* (Berkeley: University of California Press, 1995); Parvis Ghassem-Fachandi (ed.), *Violence: Ethnographic Encounters* (New York: Berg, 2009).

overarching theory, as the variety of the phenomenon is simply too broad. The reader will not find any datasets, regression analyses, or linear models, nor is the book based on reductive analysis, poststructuralist discursive frameworks, or overreliance on either nomothetic or ideographic approaches. Thus, this is neither a purely empirical historical treatise, nor a narrowly comparative politics perspective on paramilitarism. Researching the shadowy, hidden vectors of paramilitarism requires open-minded thinking, interpretive experimentation, and any hasty attempt to reach conclusive precision is likely to fail. The book fills empirical gaps and exposes theoretical oversights by employing theory to clarify history, and using history to build theory. This study also aims to build bridges between communities. There are currently significant gaps between civil war studies and genocide research, and then between paramilitarism studied in authoritarian regimes versus that in democracies. Furthermore, there are a large number of case studies that require further dialogue and integration, in order to emancipate some of the heavily emic understandings of paramilitarism from country-specific contexts. The book takes an intellectual risk by offering a tolerant, inclusive perspective that is open to new directions. As the discussion moves through individual regional or cultural histories and develops a global argument about the nature of paramilitarism, we cannot dispense with the nuances between the many cases. In other words, the book attempts to deepen, broaden, but especially solidify through synthesis and comparison.

The book connects with a host of literatures, including that on armed groups, perpetration of violence, organized crime, and others. It is based on a wide and attempted proportionate reading of paramilitarism in different national contexts, since the scholarship on paramilitarism is rich, but suffers from at least two problems. First, it is uneven and patchy: whereas the literature on Latin America can count on an incredibly rich body of knowledge and that on Southeast Asia has also developed a broad variety of publications, that on Southeastern Europe is not as well developed, and despite the relevance of the phenomenon in the Middle East, there is a relative scarcity of research output. Second, the scholarship is often too self-referential, in that empirical and conceptual expertise circulates within area studies communities, with little cross-fertilization. As Turkey experts have mulled over the notion of the "deep state" (*derin devlet*), Colombia specialists have developed sophisticated understandings of "parapolitics" (*parapolítica*). Scholars of Serb paramilitaries have looked into those groups' relationships with political parties, and colleagues examining Indonesian militias have focused on their links with the army. Africanists have analyzed Nigerian vigilantes' attitudes to crime, whereas others have attempted to understand the influence of organized crime on Mexican paramilitaries. Even if we admit that these are culturally different societies with dissimilar sociopolitical orders, only a serious attempt at accounting for the variety of paramilitarism and conceptualizing it in comparative, synthetic perspective can push the debate further. The close focus of specific historiographies and scholarly traditions has offered profound expertise, but has also brought a certain myopia and produced diverging literatures. We can gain the most from a broad, inclusive, and tolerant understanding of paramilitarism. From a bird's eye view, these studies are attempting the same thing: understanding paramilitarism.

The book consists of three main chapters that can be read separately, but offer an integrated perspective on paramilitarism. Chapter 2 is a historical overview of paramilitarism in the modern age. It traces the historical context of modern paramilitarism by developing an explicitly global review of these vastly different scenarios, but nevertheless arriving at the twin conclusion that the state was always central in its formation, and that the organization of the violence showed striking similarities across cases. Chapter 3 elaborates on the complex and multi-dimensional relationships between states, organized crime, and paramilitarism. Despite appearing in many discussions on paramilitarism, there exists no broad discussion of how crime is related to it, how criminals benefit from paramilitarism, and how paramilitarism often engenders crime. The chapter offers conclusions on the management of violence, and the problem of intertwinement between the state and crime. Chapter 4 examines the organization of paramilitarism by focusing on the place and influence of the state, since the web of paramilitary life is spun in and beyond the container of the state. It delves into the commission of violence against civilians including several massacres, and the central problem of plausible deniability. The chapter concludes by portraying paramilitarism as a form of violent performance. These three broad topics are not treated in a definitive way, but are meant to integrate and contrast existing views and perspectives.

2

Paramilitarism's Long Twentieth Century

Introduction: A Long Prehistory

How did paramilitarism develop in the modern age? The twentieth century has seen forms of paramilitarism ranging from the *Freikorps* in Germany early on in the century, to the Sudanese Janjaweed militias a century later, and a myriad of examples and episodes in between. Although these militias all originated under differing conditions and in different societies, their functions, logics, and dynamics demonstrate compelling similarities and instructive differences. This chapter traces the historical context of modern paramilitarism by developing an explicitly global review of these scenarios. As such, the chapter rejects culturalist explanations that paramilitarism is a phenomenon limited to exotic, inherently violent regions such as "the Balkans," "the Caucasus," or "Latin America." On the contrary, it is a truly global phenomenon. Even if no justice can be done to each and every single case of pro-state paramilitarism in the modern age, this chapter will offer a panoramic view of the major cases in the long twentieth century. It will also illustrate how paramilitarism changed from case to case and across time, illuminating key similar issues in different historical contexts.

Modern paramilitarism has a long prehistory. From the oldest cases of state formation to the Islamic State, state-building always required monopolies of violence and taxation. These monopolies of violence were never unchallenged but fluctuated over time and shifted shape. As argued by Charles Tilly in several of his works on the state and warfare, irregular armed forces were necessary to the consolidation of the early modern European state, which used irregular forces for the sake of military conscription, inter-state war, and later even citizenship. As an (unintended) consequence, the nascent nation states expanded their institutions and capacities. Before we move on to the rise of modern paramilitarism in the twentieth century and beyond, it is useful to take a glance at premodern paramilitaries.

The "Night Watch" (De Nachtwacht) is an imposing 1642 painting by the famous Dutch Golden Age painter Rembrandt van Rijn (1606–1669), prominently displayed in the Rijksmuseum in Amsterdam.[1] It depicts Amsterdam's Kloveniers or schutterij, the local civic militia guard or town watch consisting of volunteer citizens, tasked to protect and defend their town or village in the event of an external attack and to maintain order in the event of revolt, fire, or prominent visit. Captain Frans Banning Cocq (1605–1655), mayor of Amsterdam, lawyer, lord of castle, and head of the Kloveniers, commissioned the Nachtwacht around 1639. In the painting, Cocq stands in the center foreground of the company with a walking stick and orders the seventeen members of his company to march. Whereas the painting might look and feel majestic, the militia members initially were discontented about Rembrandt's portrayal of the group milling about randomly, instead of appearing as a tightly disciplined regiment. But Rembrandt's sharp eye had seen it well: the elements of the schutterij depicted in the Nachtwacht are typical for paramilitary self-portrayal. The painting depicts bold masculinity (the only woman is a mascot girl), weapons are brandished, a coat of arms and flag is prominently visible, and all of this accompanied by bombastic music. In a way, the Nachtwacht is the original paramilitary selfie, the likes of which we have seen many more times from around the world. Indeed, the schutterij is an excellent example of an early modern "paramilitary" vigilante group: it provided a military support system for the local civic authorities, was based on prominent volunteers, was sectarian (as only Dutch Reformed were allowed to join), and gradually gained a sociopolitical dimension. The meeting halls of the schutterij also came to be used by its members to discuss and decide on matters of local politics, as well as to organize relief for needy and sick members. The schutterij was abolished by decree on 1901, appropriately and symbolically as the

---

[1] The official name of the painting is "De compagnie van kapitein Frans Banninck Cocq en luitenant Willem van Ruytenburgh maakt zich gereed om uit te marcheren" ("The company of Captain Frans Banninck Cocq and Lieutenant Willem van Ruytenburgh gets ready to set out").

Netherlands entered the twentieth century. Nowadays, the men of the Night Watch proudly stand as a set of brass statues on Rembrandt Square in central Amsterdam.

The emergence of civil militias was in no way unique for the Netherlands in the early modern period. As the Italian city states of the Renaissance, Venice, Florence, and Genoa, experienced economic growth in the fourteenth century, the need for defense and security increased, and the ruling notables hired mercenaries for the job. The military-service terms and conditions were specified in a "contract" (*condotta*) for the enlisted men, whose captain became the *condottiere*. The *condottieri* were foreign to the land and fought mostly for financial gain (although they also had group loyalties and other motives) through the terms of the contract.[2] The *condottieri* have had a reputation as a brutal, rapacious, and unprincipled mercenary force that were no more than guns for hire, largely due to the influential contemporaneous works of Nicolo Machiavelli, who excoriated them as more a liability than an asset to their Florentine employers.[3] But more critical historical research depicts them as no inferior to armies in terms of their style of warfare and economic and political motives. After all, the word soldier derives from the Latin *soldarius* ("one having pay"). Furthermore, by the late fifteenth century, *condottieri* gradually transformed into permanent forces, much like standing armies, as their *condotti* increasingly acquired permanence and they settled down on land, inhabited palaces, acquired citizenship, and in a way became citizens of their city state.[4] As a political and cultural phenomenon of the Renaissance, "outsourcing" violence to mercenaries can be seen as an early, primitive form of paramilitarism.

Further east, the Florentine mercenaries had their Ottoman counterparts. From the *Akıncılar* to the *Serdengeçti*, irregular warfare was an important aspect of Ottoman military history. In nearly all wars irregulars fought on the battlefield and played political roles on the home front.[5] The symbol par excellence of Ottoman warfare were the Janissaries, the

[2] Janice Thomson, *Mercenaries, Pirates, and Sovereigns: State-Building and Extraterritorial Violence in Early Modern Europe* (Princeton, NJ: Princeton University Press, 1994), 27.

[3] Niccoló Machiavelli, *The Prince* (London: Norton, [1513] 1992), 34.

[4] Michael Mallett, *Mercenaries and their Masters: Warfare in Renaissance Italy* (London: The Bodley Head, 1974), 83–93.

[5] Mesut Uyar and Edward Erickson, *A Military History of the Ottomans: From Osman to Atatürk* (Santa Barbara, CA: ABC-CLIO, 2009), 59.

elite infantry units of the Ottoman army and bodyguards of the Sultan, manned by converted Christian boys who had been taken from the Balkans and trained in Anatolia to fight for the empire. By 1400, they were less than 1,000 men, but they grew steadily and by the early eighteenth century they numbered almost 70,000.[6] Their stereotypes of oriental brutality formed a source of both terror and admiration in the West. But the Janissaries shared with the *condottieri* the characteristic that they could also pose a liability, in this case for their Ottoman rulers. Two aspects of the development of the Janissaries echo some of the later paramilitaries. First, as they gained prestige and power, the Janissaries began capturing significant parts of the Ottoman state, hindering, mutinying, and dictating their will on it, including attempting palace coups. Second, they began to gain influence in non-military areas of Ottoman society, such as landholding and trade. They had become "an independent public corporation."[7] By the early nineteenth century, the Janissaries had become a serious threat to the Ottoman order: militarily inconsequential, resistant to reform, and a bloated membership caused a downward spiral. In 1826, Sultan Mahmud II violently abolished the Janissary Corps in a large massacre in Istanbul, and began establishing a European-style conscript army, which laid the foundations for the modern Turkish army as we now know it.

The Ottoman experience is relevant for the fact that both an insurgent, incipient state (such as Greece), *and* the incumbent (the Ottoman government) used irregular forces, especially in the nineteenth century. As the nascent and expanding Greek state struggled with pacifying the country and monopolizing violence in a sustained way, it attempted to bring under its control the manifold gangs that engaged in local brigandage and peasant forms of social justice. However, for decades the state was not able to carry this out even in a patchy way, and at the beginning of the twentieth century gangs still roamed the countryside. Therefore, rather than repression, it adopted a strategy of incorporation and cooptation, which proved more fruitful in establishing internal security, but reinforced the political power base of the irregular fighting

---

[6] Gábor Ágoston, "Firearms and Military Adaptation: The Ottomans and the European Military Revolution, 1450–1800," *Journal of World History* 25:1 (2014), 85–124.

[7] Baki Tezcan, *The Second Ottoman Empire: Political and Social Transformation in the Early Modern World* (New York: Cambridge University Press, 2010), 225.

groups (see Chapter 3).[8] The Ottoman case is also relevant for its portrayal in Western political and public discourse, the empire's reputation, and shifting international norms of legitimate violence. During the "Bulgarian Horrors" (the Ottomans' counterinsurgency in subduing the 1876 Bulgarian rebellion), Western media Otherized the Ottoman Empire as a rogue state using irregular militia violence (*bashibozouks*) against civilians, urging for military intervention.[9]

It was no coincidence that much violence, including property crimes, were committed in the Greek–Ottoman borderlands, an inherently unstable and porous area where Greek irredentists staged uprisings in an effort to encroach upon Ottoman land. On the other side of the Ottoman Empire, Sultan Abdulhamid II established the Hamidiye Corps, an irregular Kurdish tribal militia named after the Sultan himself. These regiments were supposedly tasked to patrol the Russo-Ottoman frontier, but they ended up as a violent counterinsurgency force against Armenians in the eastern borderlands.[10] In both cases, the use of irregular forces was formative to state-building and expanding the range and depth of state power. In both cases, the states were unable to prevail over organized violence outside its own monopoly, and therefore coopted and funneled that repository of violence into two useful channels: irredentist activity to project externally, and the formation of paramilitary units for use internally. Both were utilitarian and legitimizing moves. A similar argument, then again, can be made for the Russian Empire, in which irregular fighting forces were highly influential in the conquest of borderland regions as pro-state militias, as well as in the emergence of new states as insurgent groups. For example, "a specific feature of the Caucasus front was the extensive use of irregular troops to support the main army," such as the Terek-Mountaineer Irregular Horse Regiment's Ossetian division.[11] At the same time, it was the irregular military culture of the Cossacks within the Russian Empire that impacted Ukrainian nationalism.

[8] Giannes Koliopoulos, *Brigands with a Cause: Brigandage and Irredentism in Modern Greece, 1821–1912* (Oxford: Clarendon Press, 1987), 310–9.

[9] Davide Rodogno, *Against Massacre: Humanitarian Interventions in the Ottoman Empire, 1815–1914* (Princeton, NJ: Princeton University Press, 2012), 141–69.

[10] Janet Klein, *The Margins of Empire: Kurdish Militias in the Ottoman Tribal Zone* (Stanford, CA: Stanford University Press, 2011).

[11] Dominik Gutmeyr, *Borderlands Orientalism or How the Savage Lost his Nobility: The Russian Perception of the Caucasus between 1817 and 1878* (Münster: LIT Verlag, 2017), 193.

The Rise of Modern Paramilitaries, 1900–1945

In many ways, paramilitarism experienced its heyday in the first half of the twentieth century. From the Balkan Wars to World War I, and its immediate aftermath, paramilitary forces were active across Europe in different national settings and revolutionary convulsions. The interwar period also saw several significant moments of paramilitarism both in Europe and the colonies, whereas the rise of Nazism catapulted para-militaries, old and young, to the helm of global power. This violent epoch also saw a movement of paramilitarism from the periphery to the center, both geographically and politically: what had (wrongly) been perceived as a uniquely Balkans or Southeast European phenomenon now marched through the high streets of Vienna, and what had been brushed off as mountain brigands ascended to the corridors of power. Paramilitarism would leave an indelible mark on the politics and culture of the societies that experienced the phenomenon most intensely. Two societies have been studied particularly well for their paramilitary movements: Germany and the Southern Balkans.

The entanglement of banditry, politics, and paramilitarism has too often been reduced to a Balkan *Sonderweg*. The Orientalist image of "rough" bands committing "wild" violence without purpose or ideo-logical direction has been influential up to and including the Yugoslav wars of dissolution.[12] But paramilitarism in the former lands of the great land empires (Romanov, Habsburg, and Osman) was a product of the erosion of imperial authority and legitimacy, and the rise of modern ideologies like nationalism and communism in these multi-ethnic lands. At the same time, paramilitarism could also be a product of moderniz-ing states' attempts to assert their authority over particular populations and regions. Greece in this period is an instructive example of how these processes functioned. On the one hand, when the state weakened due to overreach during the Greco-Turkish war, paramilitaries filled the power vacuum and operated freely by taxing peasants and providing security to the countryside. On the other hand, paramilitary gangs in the northern borderlands also went through a process by which they were

---

[12] Robert William Seton-Watson, *The Rise of Nationality in the Balkans* (New York: E. P. Dutton and Company, 1918), 47.

transformed to statesmen and played an important role in the Greek nation-building process.[13]

These processes and structures were in place well before a decade of war and conflict struck the land empires. The Balkan Wars of 1912–13 were as much paramilitary wars as they were regular, state-on-state wars between standing armies. Both Serbia and Bulgaria used paramilitaries as auxiliaries who could provide local intelligence and pursue the states' nationalist agendas of homogenizing populations and territories by expelling and assaulting minority populations.[14] For example, on November 10, 1912, Bulgarian komitadjis destroyed the Muslim villages of Maden, Topuklu, and Davud, killing most inhabitants within earshot of the Bulgarian military authorities. The violence then became more participatory, as the paramilitaries forced Bulgarian civilians to participate in the killing of their neighbors. The Bulgarian authorities then announced that Muslim properties, including farmland, would be distributed among the Bulgarians.[15] But these paramilitaries were not simply buttons to push or guns for hire. They were deeply concerned with pursuing their own agendas and were in conflict with other, similar gangs, and, importantly, even with the official state authorities that provided them cover. These conflicts, not atypical for paramilitarism elsewhere, would drag on well after the Ottoman defeat in the Balkan Wars.

The Serbo-Croatian word for "gang," četa (from which the word "Chetnik" is derived) was the same word as its Turkish equivalent çete. Indeed, on the other side of the border, the Turkish-nationalist leaders of the Committee for Union and Progress (CUP) were establishing their own paramilitary infrastructure. The loss of the 1912–13 Balkan Wars and the CUP coup d'état of January 23, 1913 marked a critical shift in the nature of paramilitary violence in this period as political violence becoming commonplace. The CUP carried out assassinations of its political opponents through its paramilitary gangsters loyal to factions

---

[13] Spyros Tsoutsoumpis, "'Political Bandits': Nation-Building, Patronage and the Making of the Greek Deep State," *Balkanistica*, 30:1 (2017), 37–64.

[14] John Paul Newman, "The Origins, Attributes, and Legacies of Paramilitary Violence in the Balkans," in Robert Gerwarth and John Horne (eds), *War in Peace: Paramilitary Violence in Europe after the Great War* (Oxford: Oxford University Press, 2012), 145–63.

[15] Uğur Ümit Üngör, "Becoming and Unbecoming Refugees: The Long Ordeal of Balkan Muslims, 1912–1934," in Peter Gatrell (ed.), *Europe on the Move: The Great War and its Refugees, 1914–1918* (Cambridge: Cambridge University Press, 2017), 304–27.

around Talaat Pasha and especially Enver Pasha. His *fedayis*, assassins who were to literally "sacrifice" (*feda*) themselves for the cause, rose to state power.[16] Their experiences of paramilitary warfare in the Balkans countryside were transplanted into the offices of the Ottoman government under the auspices of the "Special Organization" (*Teşkilât-ı Mahsusa*). This was initially an intelligence service that sought to foment insurrection in enemy territory and conduct espionage, counter-espionage, and counter-insurgency tasks.[17] In 1914, it absorbed all other paramilitary groups under its wing and would be the CUP's key agency in perpetrating the Armenian Genocide of 1915. It was given clear tasks and widespread impunity to carry out massacres, arson, and plunder against the Ottoman Armenian communities, even if some individual members were reined in by the central authorities for excesses.[18]

Germany, too, saw deeply influential paramilitary movements in the immediate aftermath of the Great War. These were mostly pro-state or pro-status quo volunteer forces, in which many Germans saw the use of paramilitary force to pursue political objectives. Described as *Selbstschutz* (self-defense), *Selbsthilfe* (self-help), or *Gegengewerkschaften* (counter-unions), they were a type of state-condoned vigilantism against social change.[19] In a way, paramilitary activity was born of necessity to fill the gaps in interior security that Germany experienced in the aftermath of the war and the 1918 revolution. There were three types of volunteer forces: The *Freikorps* (Free Corps), the *Zeitfreiwilligenverbände* (Auxiliary Volunteer Forces), and the *Einwohnerwehren* (Civil Guards). The *Zeitfreiwilligenverbände* were not continually under arms and as mobile as the *Freikorps*, but only became functional in emergencies; they received monthly training and were part-time (therefore popular with adventurous students), and were attached to a *Freikorps*, which in turn was made up of former army officers. The *Einwohnerwehren* were

---

[16] Uğur Ümit Üngör, "Paramilitary Violence in the Collapsing Ottoman Empire," in Robert Gerwarth and John Horne (eds), *War in Peace: Paramilitary Violence after the Great War* (Oxford: Oxford University Press, 2012), 162–81.

[17] *Türk Silahlı Kuvvetleri Tarihi* (Ankara: Genelkurmay Basımevi, 1971), vol. III, section 6, *1908-1920*, 129–240.

[18] Raymond Kevorkian, *The Armenian Genocide: A Complete History* (London: I.B. Tauris, 2011), 180ff.

[19] Andreas Wirsching, *Vom Weltkrieg zum Bürgerkrieg? Politischer Extremismus in Deutschland und Frankreich 1918-1933/39* (Berlin: Walter de Gruyter, 1999), 234.

strictly relegated to their neighborhoods, had police rather than military functions, and included broader segments of society including non-draftable civilians and members of rifle clubs.[20] Their nature and precise operational tasks differed, but all three shared one characteristic: they were anti-Republican. By creating them, or allowing them to be created, the German government took a risk. When it failed to control them, the government lost the "monopoly of armed force and sowed the seeds for the later paramilitary activity that was to plague the Republic."[21] These groups illustrate the mutually beneficial way in which states and paramilitaries have colluded: the state thought they were useful in case of a foreign attack and provided cover, and the paramilitaries used this cover to pursue their political goals with extraparliamentary, violent means.

From west to east, World War I was indeed the major watershed that gave birth to a veritable paramilitary moment in its immediate aftermath. In Ireland, the Auxiliary Division and the Black and Tans were conducting a broad counterinsurgency operation against the IRA, killing civilians suspected of ties with the insurgents and even burning Cork city (December 11–12, 1920).[22] At the same time, Kemal Atatürk's paramilitary gangs, under the leadership of his ruthless commander Nureddin Pasha, were razing the villages of the Koçgiri Kurds in Eastern Turkey before they moved on to burn Smyrna to the ground not much later.[23] As Robert Gerwarth argues in *The Vanquished*, the violent tremors of the post-World War I period bore little resemblance to the strictly inter-state military warfare that occurred between 1914 and 1918. The aim here was not a military defeat of the enemy to force him to terms, but existential violence that was an attack on (or by) the new political establishments that attempted territorial change and nation-state building in multi-ethnic territories.[24] Regardless of their

---

[20] Arthur Brenner, "*Feme* Murder: Paramilitary 'Self-Justice' in Weimar Germany," in Bruce Campbell and Arthur Brenner (eds), *Death Squads in Global Perspective* (New York: Palgrave Macmillan, 2000), 57–83.

[21] James Diehl, *Paramilitary Politics in Weimar Germany* (Bloomington: Indiana University Press, 1977), 28.

[22] Peter Hart, *The IRA and its Enemies: Violence and Community in Cork, 1916–1923* (Oxford: Oxford University Press, 1998).

[23] Michelle Tusan, *Smyrna's Ashes: Humanitarianism, Genocide, and the Birth of the Middle East* (Berkeley: University of California Press, 2012).

[24] Robert Gerwarth, *The Vanquished: Why the First World War Failed to End, 1917–1923* (London: Allen Lane, 2016), 13.

particularities and national differences, these groups had several attributes in common. First were their nebulous identities (even if they were official): whether they were dressed in civilian or military gear (or a blend), they were often war veterans who were disillusioned or unemployed. But they were not apolitical, drunk fighting bands who were in it for the glorification of violence or the camaraderie only; on the contrary, there were clear political goals. Paramilitaries longed for "order" in what they perceived as a hostile world of democratic egalitarianism, upcoming feminism, and communist internationalism. They were also deeply authoritarian milieus that desired a definitive "cleansing" of the nation—politically, religiously, and ethnically. Their most important characteristic may well have been their commission of brutal forms of violence against civilians. Hence it was no coincidence that those tasked with carrying out orders for massacre and expulsion were paramilitary groups.[25]

The violent actors of the postwar period presided over a new cycle of violence when they seized power in the right-wing dictatorships in the 1930s. From the prominent *Freikorps* paramilitaries who first fought communists and then rose in the Nazi bureaucracy, to the Hungarian Arrow Cross leaders, who first persecuted and then helped exterminate Hungarian Jews, to the Turkish deportation bosses who expelled the Thracian Jews in 1934 and then destroyed the Dersim Kurds in 1938—wartime and interwar paramilitarism was their formative political experience.[26] This paramilitary culture shaped the intellectual and political environment from which radical right-wing movements and political parties were able to grow. In World War II, paramilitarism was elevated to a wholly different level, so much so that in Ukraine, for example, the Ukrainian Insurgent Army (UPA), strictly a non-state rebel group, bore strong resemblances to the pro-state paramilitary units that roamed elsewhere in Europe and refused to disarm and demobilize. Finally, Nazi Germany was a veritable paramilitary *state*: the SS was a crucial agency of security, surveillance, and terror, relatively autonomous from both army and police, and most importantly, it did not primarily have a military function, but the targeting of civilians for political or ethnic reasons.

[25] Robert Gerwarth and Uğur Ümit Üngör, "The Collapse of the Ottoman and Habsburg Empires and the Brutalization of the Successor States," *Journal of Modern European History*, 13:2 (2015), 226–48.
[26] Gerwarth, *The Vanquished*, 257.

Interwar paramilitarism was not a strictly European matter either. In China, weak central government control meant that provincial governors and three major warlord groups fought over the country for most of the interwar period: the Anhui, Zhili, and Fengtian cliques were successful in building up fiscal and military strength and controlling large parts of China. Each of these groups was "a confederation of warlords who were loosely brought together by their personal loyalty to the clique leader."[27] The final victory of the nationalists in 1928 only solidified the rule of the warlords and had a profound impact on Chinese state formation. A typical Chinese warlord (*junfa*) was Zang Zhiping (1869–1944), who controlled the city of Xiamen by extorting the local banks and offering security in return. In Guangdong, it was the federalist lawyer Chen Jiongming (1878–1933), who ruled the province for much of the 1910s and 1920s and was critical of centralized authoritarian government.[28] These racketeers-turned-statebuilders profoundly transformed state–society relations in China by developing the country's public infrastructure, modernizing warfare, and maintaining a fragile balance between the various regions where warlord factions ruled.[29] After 1928, it was first the nationalists, and then the communists, who inherited these developments and put them to their own use.

Latin America saw its first paramilitary structures crystallize in the interwar period, during which fascist movements emerged across the continent. In Argentina, nationalist, xenophobic, and authoritarian armed irregular groups such as the Argentine Civic Legion (LCA: Legión Civica Argentina) bore the hallmarks of paramilitarism. The LCA was initially conceived of as a reserve for the Argentine armed forces, but quickly developed into a violent militia that would foreshadow those that nestled in the state in the 1970s. It committed a plethora of violent acts against its political opponents, covered by the Argentine president and military dictator José Félix Uriburu, who had founded the movement

---

[27] Huaiyin Li, *The Making of the Modern Chinese State, 1600–1950* (New York: Routledge, 2019), 169.
[28] Arthur Waldron, "The Warlord: Twentieth-Century Chinese Understandings of Violence, Militarism, and Imperialism," *American Historical Review* 96:4 (1991), 1073–100; Mechthild Leutner and Izabella Goikhman (eds), *State, Society and Governance in Republican China* (Münster: LIT Verlag, 2014), chs 2 and 5.
[29] Philip Jowett, *The Armies of Warlord China 1911–1928* (Atglen, PA: Schiffer, 2013).

and came into power in a 1930 coup d'état.[30] General Uriburu whitewashed the Legión as "an absolutely apolitical organization that pursues the highest objective a corporation can seek, the defense of the Fatherland and of order."[31] However, it would have been more realistic to portray the LCA as a quintessentially pro-state militia. It, too, consisted of nationalist students and graduates drawn from across social classes. It, too, led noisy marches through the streets of Buenos Aires and other cities, intimidating and assaulting Jews and socialists in ways that were very similar to their German counterparts in that same decade.[32] The comparisons between interwar Latin American dictatorships and contemporaneous European fascism were just as striking as the historical continuities of militia activity within Latin American societies.

The Postwar Era

This section looks at two parallel and mirroring, but antagonistic, paramilitary constructs in the post-World War II period: the Soviet-led paramilitary groups in the new communist regimes in Central and Eastern Europe, and the paramilitary strategies that the US and NATO pursued in Western Europe, such as in Italy and Turkey.

By the end of 1948, the Soviet Union had installed communist rule in all of Central and Eastern Europe, and communism was rapidly consolidating its grip on power in Poland, Czechoslovakia, Romania, Hungary, Bulgaria, and more independently from the USSR, Yugoslavia. One of the major mechanisms of control apart from Moscow's permanent military and police threat, as well as broad censorship, was the co-opting of parts of the civilian population in these countries. Whereas the school system and the army were time-tested methods of nation-building and forging a community, the creation of paramilitary organizations was a different initiative. Communist regimes set up paramilitary organizations

---

[30] António Costa Pinto, *Latin American Dictatorships in the Era of Fascism* (New York: Routledge, 2019), 32.

[31] Robert Potash, *The Army & Politics in Argentina: 1928–1945* (Stanford, CA: Stanford University Press, 1969), 68.

[32] David Rock, *Authoritarian Argentina: The Nationalist Movement, Its History and Its Impact* (Berkeley: University of California Press, 1995), 94–7.

for teenagers and young adults in every Eastern European country, but on different scales, in different institutional contexts, and with different aims. In a way, they were all based on the Soviet DOSAAF (ДОСААФ), the Volunteer Society for Cooperation with the Army, Aviation, and Navy, a popular defense organization originally established in 1927, renamed in 1951, and abolished in 1991. The objective of DOSAAF was "active cooperation for strengthening the military capability of the country and for preparing workers for the defence of their socialist homeland."[33] The society aimed to prepare reserves for the Soviet army and its activities ranged from ordinary sports such as running and swimming to outright military training skills such as radio signaling, parachuting, and firing guns. Among Soviet youth it was a source of status and excitement, and they could earn badges and prizes by excelling in the activities.[34]

Organizations similar to DOSAAF sprung up in Eastern European states too. Close descriptions of their establishment and (early) functioning offer useful insights into how they were embedded in state structures, and how they were perceived by ordinary citizens. For example, in Czechoslovakia, workers, pupils, and students were signed up for paramilitary training in the Union for Cooperation with the Army (*Svaz pro spolupráci s armádou*, Svazarm). Svazarm was a large paramilitary organization, and even though many of its activities resembled that of the Boy Scouts rather than a proper paramilitary group, it instructed teachers to collaborate with officers in recruiting high schools kids, especially for shooting, and twice a week for throwing grenades. However, the Czechoslovakian military saw this training as insufficient and therefore Svazarm members as dilettantish.[35] Factory workers, too, due to an apparent lack of enthusiasm, were urged to enter paramilitary training. On March 26, 1952, a Major Tomek Václav gave a speech at the large Praga factory and urged workers to sacrifice more than the usual

---

[33] E. S. Williams, C. N. Donnelly, and J. E. Moore, *The Soviet Military: Political Education, Training and Morale* (Dordrecht: Springer, 1987), 35–7.

[34] Roger Reese, *The Soviet Military Experience: A History of the Soviet Army, 1917–1991* (London: Routledge, 2002), 148.

[35] Open Society Archives (Central European University, Budapest, henceforth: OSA), HU OSA 300-1-2-20405, Records of Radio Free Europe/Radio Liberty Research Institute: General Records: Information Items, "Para-Military Training Intensified at Liberec Textiliana," May 29, 1952.

three hours per week of paramilitary training, and include training in machine guns.[36] In some cases, there were problems with the skills provided to the trainees. In late November 1951, railway infrastructure near the town was vandalized near the town of Brno. A major security operation revealed that after their paramilitary training program local school kids had "gotten the idea to use their newly acquired skills on the railway platforms." The security services urged teachers to rein in the youth and admonish them not to vandalize anything.[37]

Svazarm continued to exist until the end of communism; in fact, it reached its apogee in the 1980s, with both "physical education" remaining the principal ingredient of paramilitary training, as well as profound ideological training. This trend had followed complaints from the state leadership that the army had been gradually weakened due to alcoholism and bullying, but "even worse" due to pacifism and low morale, reduced physical fitness and general disillusionment. The emphasis had therefore shifted to strengthening the paramilitary sector. To that end, special law no.73/1973 was passed, and every citizen was required to take part in paramilitary education. Within years, the ranks of Svazarm swelled, and by 1981, according to one report, "the expansion and intensification of paramilitary training have reached their high point this year...surpassing the 1950s."[38] In 1988, Czech academic Zdenek Hronek wrote an article entitled "In Support of the Development of Paramilitary Education in our Schools," in which he justified the training as crucial to the defense of "homeland" and the "victory of Communism," and listed its four elements as moral and ideological (hatred of the "class enemy"), specialized technological military preparation, physical readiness, and psychological conditioning. He also complained that the previous decade saw "liberal, pacifist, and...fatalistic opinions on war," therefore urging a stronger paramilitary concept.[39]

[36] OSA, HU OSA 300-1-2-17391, Records of Radio Free Europe/Radio Liberty Research Institute: General Records: Information Items, "Workers of Prague Car Factory Asked to Sacrifice More Time for Para-Military Training," March 26, 1952.

[37] OSA, HU OSA 300-1-2-13653, Records of Radio Free Europe/Radio Liberty Research Institute: General Records: Information Items, "Paramilitary Training Causes Damages," January 7, 1952.

[38] OSA, HU OSA 300-8-47-75-11, Records of Radio Free Europe/Radio Liberty Research Institute: Publications Department: Situation Reports, "Situation Report: Czechoslovakia, 16 June 1981," June 16, 1981.

[39] OSA, HU OSA 300-8-47-84-12, Records of Radio Free Europe/Radio Liberty Research Institute: Publications Department: Situation Reports, "Situation Report: Czechoslovakia, 11 August 1988," August 11, 1988, 27, quoting *Socialistická Škola*, no.10 (June 1988), 452–7.

In the German Democratic Republic, there were several mass organizations, some of which provided (para)military training exercises, such as the Society of Sports and Technical Training (*Gesellschaft für Sport und Technik*), which had physical fitness training and firing ranges (shooting as sports) and numbered up to 60,000 in the mid 1950s.[40] But the equivalent of DOSAAF and Svazarm were the Combat Groups of the Working Class (*Kampfgruppen der Arbeiterklasse*, KdA). Established in August 1953, not coincidentally two months after the workers' uprising, Western intelligence reports noticed their continuity with the Nazi paramilitary organizations the *Sturmabteilung* or the *Werkschutz*. The two main reasons that they were perceived as such were their recruitment from "party actives," but especially the secrecy surrounding their nature. One report notes that their secrecy was "the mark of a terror organization," since no outsider was to know their details, even their training camps being secret. Training consisted of map reading, marching, compass, shooting, "close combat" (*Nahkampf*), and political training. A key objective of the KdA was to seize the element of surprise in para-police actions like suppressing demonstrations, house clearings, and defense of factories.[41] After the uprising, they were restructured, but their links with party (district) secretaries and (district) police chiefs remained as close as ever.[42]

In Bulgaria, the Voluntary Organization for Assisting Defense (Доброволна организация за съдействие на отбраната, DOSO) was established in 1947, and was run by General Vladimir Stoitchev. There were committees at provincial, district, town, and village level, and workers at state factories were also inducted. One defector reported in 1955:

> Every Tuesday we were assembled for instruction in the use of the 'Vintovka' rifle and its spare parts. The course was followed by exercises and drill during which we practiced target shooting by using

---

[40] Paul Heider, "Die Gesellschaft für Sport und Technik (1952–1990)," in Torsten Diedrich, Hans Gotthard Ehlert, and Rüdiger Wenzke (eds), *Im Dienste der Partei: Handbuch der bewaffneten Organe der DDR* (Berlin: Ch. Links Verlag, 1998), 169–200.

[41] OSA, HU OSA 300-1-2-46444; Records of Radio Free Europe/Radio Liberty Research Institute: General Records: Information Items, "East Germany's Latest Para-Military Organization," May 14, 1954.

[42] Volker Koop, *Armee oder Freizeitclub? Die Kampfgruppen der Arbeiterklasse in der DDR* (Bonn: Bouvier, 1997).

dummy cartridges. Once we were led to a forest where we underwent training in defensive and offensive operations. The exercises held by this organization are called Pre-Military Training (*Predvoeno Obutchenie*).[43]

Shooting classes were obligatory, in both light and heavy machine guns. To become a member of DOSO, the applicant had to produce a certificate of study and behavior from DSNM (the Dimitrov Union of People's Youth), and a personal biography. Since 1951, thousands of civilians had been trained every year to be "ready both to work for and defend their country." Training was under the auspices of DOSO, which held annual congresses in Sofia. Every Bulgarian town and village had a branch, and the total membership in 1951 was about 700,000.[44] Similar to Czechoslovakia, as the ranks of DOSO swelled, its heyday was the 1980s. In 1977, DOSO was abolished, reorganized, and renamed the Organization for Cooperation in Defense (Организация за съдействие на отбраната) as it took on the role of a central umbrella organization. It upheld the same paramilitary training and "military-oriented sports," and its basic task was "to coordinate Communist education with military training, especially for the youth." The omission of the adjective "voluntary" clearly implied that membership of the organization could no longer be regarded as such, and that Bulgaria had made paramilitary training obligatory. Importantly, "neither the statutes of the OCD nor various reports on its activities have ever given any indication as of the agency in charge of it," and apparently the Ministry of Defense only had indirect control of it.[45]

From the Hungarian Voluntary Defense Association, to the Romanian Direcția Generală a Rezervelor de Muncă (DGRM), the Estonian Всегда готов к работе и обороне (BGTO), and the Service to Poland (*Slusba Polsce*) and League of Soldiers' Friends (*Liga Przyjaciół Żołnierza*) in Poland, paramilitarism blossomed in postwar communist countries.

[43] OSA, HU OSA 300-1-2-54569; Records of Radio Free Europe/Radio Liberty Research Institute: General Records: Information Items, "Para-Military Auxiliary Organizations," January 17, 1955.

[44] OSA, HU OSA 300-1-2-41198; Records of Radio Free Europe/Radio Liberty Research Institute: General Records: Information Items, "What Is D.O.S.O.?," November 21, 1953.

[45] OSA, HU OSA 300-8-47-39-6; Records of Radio Free Europe/Radio Liberty Research Institute: Publications Department: Situation Reports, "Situation Report: Bulgaria, 6 May 1983," May 6, 1983, 8–10.

The existence of these organizations is often reduced to either Soviet militarization of society or linked to their particular national prehistories of paramilitarism. But there was a specific global Cold War context to the emergence of these organizations. The impossibilities of nuclear exchanges and mutual fears of invasion drove both the Soviets and the West to establish a veritable paramilitary infrastructure culture on either side of the Iron Curtain. These groups were expected to withstand an invasion or fight as stay-behind forces. At the same time, their internal dynamic produced a certain collective identity and forged specific networks of men (and women) bonding in paramilitary training.

The Soviet Union was by no means the only global power that established covert and secretive paramilitary groups in countries on the fronts of the Cold War. The United States of America created, developed, or supported paramilitary infrastructures throughout the world: from Cuba to Turkey to Vietnam and Southern Africa, its Cold War strategy was clearly felt this way. Whether Truman, Kennedy, or Nixon, US presidents were all involved in (support for) covert operations through the country's main intelligence agency, the CIA. After all, the CIA's main objectives in the Cold War were to promote American influence and interests and combat communism globally, including in covert action operations.[46] These movements appeared simultaneously to the liberation of Europe in the 1940s and the emergence and expansion of NATO. Some of these were nebulous "stay-behind armies," while others were existing rural or urban gangs or even organized crime circles given empowerment and legitimization. As such, the post-World War II period shared similarities with the post-World War I period in terms of contractions and expansions of state power as the primary opportunity structures for paramilitary violence.

Italy is a good example of the paramilitarization of the security sector, especially in Sicily. Before the American army even landed on Sicily, it is well known that US Naval Intelligence was in prolonged contact with noted New York mobster Lucky Luciano, a liaison literally called Operation Underworld. Even though it was unclear to what extent those contacts were productive, the Allied occupation gave the Mafia more

---

[46] Sarah-Jane Corke, *US Covert Operations and Cold War Strategy: Truman, Secret Warfare and the CIA, 1945–53* (London: Routledge, 2007), 55.

freedom to operate and grow, for example by appointing several prominent Mafiosi as mayors of Sicilian towns for the Christian Democratic Party.[47] With the communists posing a formidable threat to Allied, Christian Democrat, and Mafia power in Sicily, US authorities saw the need to reinforce anti-communist, pro-American elements, and the Mafia decided to back young bandits like Salvatore Giuliano against the common enemy. Giuliano was for years profoundly violent in a series of killings, kidnappings, and robberies, and purported to defend the poor—as did the communists, ironically. During the period that this vertical nexus was functional, Giuliano's gang violence took on a specific character and dimension: it focused on communist civilians. The US pressured Sicilian politicians, who in turn either directly enabled or indirectly and tacitly condoned Giuliano in committing violence against the communist movement.[48] This entanglement was beneficial at all levels: the US fought global communism, the Christian Democrats seized control of a key constituency, the Mafia gained political protection, and Giuliano gained fame and power. As the Mafia and Christian Democrats consolidated their power bases in Sicily, this relationship in principle continued to keep men like Giuliano "on a retainer."

An equally durable and murky influence on Italian politics was the emergence of GLADIO, a NATO plan that foresaw the set-up of "stay-behind" networks operating behind enemy lines in case of a possible Soviet invasion of Western Europe. This transnational resistance movement would support national and local formations in counter-intelligence and counter-insurgency before the communist takeover, and sabotage and assassinations after the takeover. In many ways GLADIO would resemble the European resistance against Nazi occupation. As the Soviet invasion never materialized, but politically strong communist parties threatened the democracies of Europe, this covert paramilitary network purportedly fought a secret war against the political left in every

---

[47] Diego Gambetta, *The Sicilian Mafia: The Business of Private Protection* (Cambridge, MA: Harvard University Press, 1996), 92; Ezio Costanzo, *Mafia & alleati: servizi segreti americani e sbarco in Sicilia: da Lucky Luciano ai sindaci "uomini d'onore"* (Catania: Le nove muse, 2006).

[48] Timothy Newark, *The Mafia at War: Allied Collusion with the Mob* (Philadelphia, PA: Casemate Publishers, 2012), 275. In fairly typical fashion, the virtually untouchable Giuliano was found assassinated in 1950, most likely "cleaned up" by the Mafia after his services were no longer needed and he became a thorn in their side by drawing *carabinieri* to Sicily. The parallels with earlier and later bandits are noteworthy.

non-communist country in Europe, except Finland and Ireland.[49] According to one comparative study, they

> were involved in a whole series of terrorist operations and human rights violations…and ranged from bomb massacres in trains and market squares (Italy), the use of systematic torture of opponents of the regime (Turkey), the support for right-wing coup d'états (Greece and Turkey), to the smashing of opposition groups (Portugal and Spain).[50]

The extant documentation demonstrates that World War II loomed large in the imagination of the architects of GLADIO. The gloom-and-doom scenario of a Soviet takeover of Europe seems to be equated with the horrific past of the brutal Nazi occupation of the same lands. For example, the earliest reference to "Gladio" we have is a US National Security Council document dated March 15, 1954, which quite explicitly mentions the necessity "to develop underground resistance and facilitate covert and guerrilla operations" in Europe.[51]

In Italy specifically, General Giovanni De Lorenzo signed a formal agreement, kept secret from parliament and civilian oversight, the first of many secret paramilitary operations. In all cases, these paramilitary groups were trained by the British intelligence service, funded by the CIA, authorized by elements of the Italian state, and staffed by operatives who were disproportionately drawn from ex-fascists.[52] A recent source-based cross-cultural examination of GLADIO argued that "the most controversial and difficult question historians have to deal with is the possibility that the networks were involved not only in clandestine but also in illegal activities, ranging from political espionage against 'domestic'

---

[49] William Blum, *Killing Hope: US Military and CIA Interventions since World War II* (London: Zed Books, 2003), 106.

[50] Daniele Ganser, *NATO's Secret Armies: Operation GLADIO and Terrorism in Western Europe* (London: Routledge, 2005). This is the only real monograph on GLADIO, but it portrays GLADIO as a uniform, well-oiled conspiracy without glitches or contingencies, and jumps to conclusions using a too narrow source base, too much conjecture, and untenable assumptions.

[51] Franco Ferraresi, *Threats to Democracy: The Radical Right in Italy After the War* (Princeton, NJ: Princeton University Press, 1996), 77.

[52] Tom Behan, *The Italian Resistance: Fascists, Guerrillas and the Allies* (London: Pluto, 2009), 141.

enemies."[53] The burden of evidence is high for these types of events, but it suffices to say that the Italian GLADIO launched a "strategy of tension," a purposeful violent strategy intended to shift Italy's political center of gravity to the right. As such, GLADIO was responsible for at least part of a string of explosions, from the bombing of a Milan bank in 1969 (killing sixteen people) to the Bologna train station massacre of August 2, 1980 (eighty-five killed, 200 wounded).[54] GLADIO networks might not have been this violent in Norway or the Netherlands,[55] but in Italy and Turkey, where a communist takeover was entirely plausible in the 1970s, they operated through the ballot and bullet, respectively.

GLADIO did not only exist in Italy. Another important theater of operation was the Republic of Turkey. Turkey not only bordered on the Soviet Union but also had a viable communist movement throughout the Cold War. Furthermore, Turkey had a strong paramilitary prehistory that had successfully served various purposes, including resolving ethnic and political security threats. From the 1950s on, GLADIO geared into these paramilitary organizations and strengthened the violent potential of the Turkish state. The scholarship on these entanglements is shrouded in myth and conspiracy theory, but there is a clear set of established facts. Turkey joined the Western bloc after World War II and NATO in 1952, and its military began liaising intensively with US army and intelligence forces, especially through the Joint United States Military Mission for Aid to Turkey (JUSMMAT). JUSMMAT provided equipment, training, and education to the Turkish army and its officers, including sixteen officers who received training in the US, one of the areas being counter-insurgency warfare.[56] It was within this dense cooperative network that the paramilitary industry flourished.

The first organization to be formally set up was the Mobilization Research Council (*Seferberlik Tetkik Kurulu*, STK) in September 1952; it was later renamed the Special Warfare Department (*Özel Harp Dairesi*,

---

[53] See the *Journal of Strategic Studies*, 30:6 (2007), Special Section: Preparing for a Soviet Occupation: The Strategy of "Stay-Behind."

[54] Jeffrey McKenzie, *The 'Black' Terrorist International: Neo-Fascist Paramilitary Networks and the 'Strategy of Tension' in Italy, 1968–1974* (Ann Arbor, MI, UMI Dissertation Service, 1995, UMI Number: 9529217).

[55] Bob de Graaff and Cees Wiebes, *Gladio der vrije jongens: een particuliere geheime dienst in Koude Oorlogstijd* (Den Haag: SDU, 1992).

[56] Ömer Aslan, *The United States and Military Coups in Turkey and Pakistan: Between Conspiracy and Reality* (London: Palgrave Macmillan, 2017), 152–3.

ÖHD) in 1967, Special Forces Command (*Özel Kuvvetler Komutanlığı*, ÖKK) in 1991, and finally Special Forces (*Özel Kuvvetler*, ÖK) from 1994.[57] These were funded annually to the tune of US$1 million and housed in the same building as the headquarters of JUSMMAT in Ankara. Whereas the expressed objective of the Special Warfare Department was to combat communism and to protect Turkey against the Soviet communist threat, successive Turkish governments did not restrict its use to communism only. They appear to have employed the ÖHD against a range of political and social movements in Turkey, and the Kurdish, Alevi, Assyrian, and Armenian communities more broadly. One of the most prominent members of the ÖHD was Captain Alparslan Türkeş (1917–1997), later chairman of the extreme right-wing Nationalist Action Party (*Milliyetçi Hareket Partisi*, MHP) in the 1960s. Another member, Colonel Daniş Karabelen (1898–1983), served in the Korean War (1950–3) as commander of Turkish troops and returned to become the first commander of the ÖHD.[58] The commander of the ÖHD between 1967 and 1974 was Kemal Yamak (1924–2009), who argued in a voluminous and informative but apologetic memoir that the ÖHD was an operation modeled on NATO's concept of "covert operation," and that Turkey's geostrategic location necessitated such an organization.[59]

The parallel biographies of these men span irregular war experiences during the late Ottoman Empire in the Special Organization, counter-insurgency against the Kurdish uprisings in the interwar period, and the anti-communist and anti-minority repression of the 1970s and beyond. The ÖHD institution was a great opportunity for these "autocratic cliques" in the Turkish military to run their own nationalist agendas as a state within a state, a parallel state, or "deep state," as it became known in Turkish culture.[60] Whereas Turkish *elected* officials from the left, center, and right all acknowledged that the ÖHD was responsible for many unsolved murders in the post-1950s, they also claimed to have been powerless in counteracting or curbing its activities.[61] The existence of a stay-behind network was publicly disclosed by Turkish Prime Minister

---

[57] Mehtap Söyler, *The Turkish Deep State: State Consolidation, Civil–Military Relations and Democracy* (London: Routledge, 2015), 101.

[58] Ecevit Kılıç, *Özel Harp Dairesi* (Istanbul: Timaş, 2010), 22–47.

[59] Kemal Yamak, *Gölgede Kalan İzler ve Gölgeleşen Bizler* (Istanbul: Doğan, 2006), 248.

[60] Söyler, *The Turkish Deep State.*

[61] Belma Akçura, *Derin Devlet Oldu Devlet* (Istanbul: Belge, 2009), 25–34.

Bülent Ecevit in 1973—and later by Italian Prime Minister Giulio Andreotti in August 1990. In both cases, the revelations opened a veritable Pandora's Box of speculations and allegations. For example, the September 6–7, 1955 pogrom against non-Muslims in Istanbul was carried out for a large part by nationalist masses mobilized most likely by the ÖHD. In the pogrom, Turkish-nationalist mobs ransacked and destroyed Christian and Jewish businesses and houses, raped women, and murdered an Armenian priest. In the 1978 massacre of Alevis in the southeastern city Kahramanmaraş, the ÖHD was heavily implicated by contemporary activists, politicians, and journalists, although no conclusive evidence ever emerged of its involvement in the instigation of the massacre. Finally, when the guerrilla war between the Kurdistan Workers' Party (PKK) and the Turkish state radicalized in the 1990s, the ÖHD and its paramilitaries really came to the forefront: death squads, disappearances, village burnings, torture, and extrajudicial executions occurred on a massive, unprecedented scale in postwar Turkey. All in all, both in Italy and in Turkey, these groups bore important characteristics of paramilitary groups: covertness and secrecy, plausible deniability, and outsourcing of violence.

As a brainchild of NATO, GLADIO was deeply nurtured as part of US foreign policy. In hindsight, this was hardly surprising, since successive American governments were directly active in fostering paramilitary groups. The CIA organized a covert action department called the Paramilitary Staff Section (PSS) which inserted paramilitary teams into Tibet in October 1950, sponsored irregular Korean groups in the Korean War, and most unsuccessfully attempted to invade southern Cuba to topple the Castro regime in April 1961. Cuba figures as an early, and in any case a prime example, of this trend. The declassification of CIA documents about the Bay of Pigs invasion has offered an improved look into the paramilitary activities of the PSS. Its reports are all stamped "secret" and its founding policy paper heralds "the development of an adequate paramilitary force outside of Cuba, together with the mechanisms for the necessary logistic support of covert military operations on the Island." After screening, trainers will prepare cadres "at secure locations outside of the US" for six to eight months, all of it "under deep cover as a commercial operation in another country."[62] The Bay of Pigs

---

[62] CIA Online Archive, RDP85-00664R000700150001-8, Memorandum titled "Paramilitary Critique" (May 5, 1961), 5, at https://www.cia.gov/library/readingroom/docs/CIA-RDP85-00664R000700150001-8.pdf (accessed April 11, 2018).

invasion was a fiasco, and according to the report's instructive conclusions, the American people found the idea of covert paramilitary actions "repugnant," political oversight over these paramilitary affairs was impractical and, most importantly,

> Paramilitary operations of any appreciable size cannot be conducted on a completely covert basis, and *the requirement for non-attributability introduces tremendous complications in the accomplishment of what would otherwise be simple tasks.* Since paramilitary operations on an increasing scale will probably be required as we face years of cold war in the future, the United States should be prepared to operate more boldly and overtly in this field.[63]

The failure of the Bay of Pigs invasion taught the US this valuable lesson, one that it would draw on as the Cold War spread to the Global South.

The Cold War in the Global South

Paramilitarism really came to fruition in the Global South during and after the Cold War. From countries as disparate as Argentina and Uganda to Indonesia, paramilitary groups wreaked havoc and irreversibly changed political landscapes. Much of this was related to postcolonial state formation. The postcolonial state typically was unable and, in many cases, unwilling to successfully consolidate its monopoly of violence through sustained centripetal efforts, despite expanding bureaucracies and general centralization. Research on the security structures and cultures of postcolonial states demonstrates the limitations of these new states, but also the "inheritance" of security apparatuses.[64] But external involvement was as relevant. On February 17, 1970, US President Richard Nixon signed one of the most prominent documents on paramilitarism ever. He authorized covert actions to undermine communism globally: "By covert action operations I mean those activities which, although designed to further official US programs and policies abroad, are so planned and executed that the hand of the US Government is not apparent

---

[63] Ibid., 46–7, emphasis added.
[64] Roger Owen, *State, Power and Politics in the Making of the Modern Middle East* (London: Routledge, 2004), 23–38.

to unauthorized persons…Covert action operations shall include any type of activity necessary to carry out approved purposes *except that they will not include armed conflict by regular military forces*."[65] The two key elements in this document are secrecy and concealment on the one hand, and unconventional warfare on the other hand. This broad authorization would generate paramilitarism in the Americas and beyond, in Asia and Africa, among which the most destructive to human lives were the genocides in Guatemala and Indonesia. Yes, these were culturally and politically very different societies, but both saw similar anti-left campaigns of collective violence, both enjoyed direct US support, and both were carried out by paramilitaries.

Paramilitarism is a sociopolitical process that has become synonymous with Latin America, much like "organized crime" has left an indelible impression on Sicily, or "sectarianism" has become the stereotypical characterization of Lebanon. Throughout the twentieth century, paramilitary and para-police forces have been involved in a series of regional conflicts that have wrought major changes to politics, society, and culture. Therefore, any analysis of the concept should begin with a brief discussion of the main issues relating to Latin American paramilitarism. The paramilitarization of Latin America in the 1970s was a confluence of internal ideological and political polarization and external US support for authoritarianism. Decades of research now convincingly demonstrate that Latin American regimes and political elites deployed paramilitaries in similar ways, not only because of path-dependent trajectories dating back to the 1930s (e.g. Colombia and Mexico), but significantly because of American influence. The United States covertly launched "Operation Condor," a (para-)military network created in the 1970s to destroy communism in Latin America by eliminating communists collectively and individually. The anticommunist dictatorships in Chile, Argentina, Uruguay, Bolivia, Paraguay, Brazil, Peru, and Ecuador were in principle different states and societies, but strong US coordination through Operation Condor resulted in isomorph paramilitary structures and similarly violent results. Operation Condor was not simply an extension of GLADIO, but a specifically Latin

---

[65] The White House, National Security Decision Memorandum 40, "Responsibility for the Conduct, Supervision and Coordination of Covert Action Operations," February 17, 1970, signed Richard Nixon, available at https://fas.org/irp/offdocs/nsdm-nixon/nsdm-40.pdf (accessed January 19, 2018), emphasis added.

American project in which the US was much deeper involved at the levels of preparation and instigation, logistical support, and direct operational involvement.[66]

Both comparative syntheses on the whole region and detailed case studies of particular countries converge on what has driven authoritarian regimes and political elites to employ paramilitaries.[67] Four important concerns seem to stand out. First, increasing the number of armed men in a counter-insurgency for the numerical upper hand. This could be significant: for example, out of a total population of 9 million, the Guatemalan army enlisted 900,000 men in paramilitary units during the civil war.[68] Second, institutionalizing and consolidating a self-sustaining system. The pro-government Autodefensas Unidas de Colombia, for example, over time became a veritable state within a state in Colombia, controlling the economy in the regions they invigilated, and even infiltrating high politics—a process called *parapolitica* in Spanish.[69] María Ramírez's research on Colombian paramilitaries suggests that they were not interested per se in taking over the political center, but certainly had a strong interest in controlling territories that the army was unable or unwilling to control.[70]

Third, not necessarily related to the violence but certainly to winning "hearts and minds," paramilitarism in Latin America has also assisted certain development plans, services, and infrastructure. Paramilitarism is seen as an "emergency strategy" of regimes allied with the United

---

[66] Patrice McSherry, *Predatory States: Operation Condor and Covert War in Latin America* (Lanham, MD: Rowman & Littlefield, 2005); Fernando López, *The Feathers of Condor: Transnational State Terrorism, Exiles and Civilian Anticommunism in South America* (Cambridge: Cambridge Scholars, 2016); Cecilia Menjívar and Néstor Rodríguez (eds), *When States Kill: Latin America, the U.S., and Technologies of Terror* (Austin: University of Texas Press, 2005). For a set of eyewitness accounts, see Jennifer Edwards (ed.), *The Flight of the Condor: Stories of Violence and War from Colombia* (Madison: University of Wisconsin Press, 2007).

[67] The literature is too vast to review in any meaningful way. For a typology of paramilitary groups in Latin America, see Kees Koonings and Dirk Kruijt (eds), *Societies of Fear: The Legacy of Civil War, Violence and Terror in Latin America* (London: Zed Books, 1999), 14–5.

[68] Anika Oettler, "Guatemala: The State of Research" (March 28, 2008), at http://www.sciencespo.fr/mass-violence-war-massacre-resistance/en/document/guatemala-state-research (accessed May 11, 2018).

[69] León Valencia (ed.), *Parapolítica: la ruta de la expansión paramilitar y los acuerdos políticos* (Bogotá: Intermedio, 2007).

[70] María Clemencia Ramírez, "Maintaining Democracy in Colombia through Political Exclusion, States of Exception, Counterinsurgency and Dirty War," in Enrique Desmond Arias and David Goldstein (eds), *Violent Democracies in Latin America* (Durham, NC: Duke University Press, 2010), 84–107.

States government and engaged in a civil war. In a 1996 report, Human Rights Watch called it "a sophisticated mechanism, in part supported by years of advice, training, weaponry, and official silence by the United States, that allows the Colombian military to fight a dirty war and Colombian officialdom to deny it."[71] Indeed, international coverage by the United States government was pivotal in setting up and adapting this system in all aspects of its functioning.[72] The system caused a profound disruption of societies: permanent ruptures of social ties between perpetrator groups and victim groups, terror and trauma in victim communities, insecurity caused by impunity, local economic damage resulting from mass displacement, and the criminalization of societies.[73] Another important finding that appears in the literature is the notion that a state maintaining a paramilitary structure is a state that is potentially genocidal, because the type of violence that paramilitaries are tasked to carry out, is often exclusively mass violence against civilians. Comparative research on cases of massacre and genocide in Latin America has convincingly demonstrated the central role of paramilitary units in the mass killings. This may not have been the case in all instances of state repression, as in Argentina or Chile for example, but it was certainly so in ethnicity- and class-based massacres in Guatemala and Colombia.[74]

Fourth, and most importantly for our comparative purposes, is deniability. In a most lucid treatment of paramilitarism in Colombia, Winifred Tate conceptualizes it as "contemporary state practices of privatized and extrastate forms of political violence operating alongside public denial and strategies of concealment" and concludes:

> Government security officers supported brutal paramilitary counterinsurgency operations not in spite of their claims to be transparent, accountable, and professional, but because of the contradictory demands

[71] Human Rights Watch, *Colombia's Killer Networks: The Military–Paramilitary Partnership and the United States* (New York: Human Rights Watch, 1996), 96.

[72] Lesley Gill, *The School of the Americas: Military Training and Political Violence in the Americas* (Durham, NC: Duke University Press, 2004), 192.

[73] Julie Mazzei, *Death Squads or Self-Defense Forces? How Paramilitary Groups Emerge and Threaten Democracy in Latin America* (Chapel Hill: University of North Carolina Press, 2009).

[74] Marcia Esparza, Daniel Feierstein, and Henry Huttenbach (eds), *State Violence and Genocide in Latin America: The Cold War Years* (London: Routledge, 2009).

of their local military mission and other international entanglements that required transparency, and accountability, and professionalism.[75]

McSherry's comprehensive examinations of Operation Condor also emphasizes the importance of deniability, as "Military rulers could attribute the waves of torture, disappearance, and assassination throughout the region to 'out-of-control death squads' or internal disputes within the left," thereby maintaining even if partially, "an appearance of moderation and legitimacy."[76] Green, too, argues that "[p]aramilitaries provide distance and degrees of deniability, even though they inhabit legal frameworks of occasional legality and legitimacy."[77] From the incredible to the laughable, deniability has remained one of the most constitutive issues of paramilitarism, whether in the 1970s or in the 2010s.

Paramilitarism was by no means an exclusively Latin American phenomenon. In Asia, the Cold War period saw profound political changes and shake-ups due to paramilitary violence. During the Korean War, for example, the US involvement fostered collaborative relationships between the Rightists paramilitary youth squads, the Korean National Police, and the United States Army Military Government in Korea. The main right-wing youth band was the Northwest Young Men's Association, admirers of Hitlerjugend and the SS, and often led by retired or active criminals. They were continuously active in forced evictions, labor suppression, political murders, and in several cases in massacres during the Cheju Insurgency.[78] US involvement was even more influential in Vietnam. The Phoenix Program, a covert CIA campaign to eliminate the Vietcong, similar to Condor or GLADIO, included the Provincial Reconnaissance Units (PRU), heavily armed paramilitaries who were authorized to kill, torture, and detain suspected communists. Most of the PRU's members were former Vietnamese soldiers who were

---

[75] Winifred Tate, *Drugs, Thugs, and Diplomats: U.S. Policymaking in Colombia* (Stanford, CA: Stanford University Press, 2015), 85, 86.

[76] McSherry, *Predatory States*, 244.

[77] John Green, *A History of Political Murder in Latin America: Killing the Messengers of Change* (New York: SUNY Press, 2015), 69.

[78] Jonson Porteux, "Police, Paramilitaries, Nationalists and Gangsters: The Processes of State Building in Korea" (PhD dissertation, Department of Political Science, University of Michigan, 2013), 70–85.

motivated by revenge against the Vietcong.[79] In both cases, American anti-communism was the driving force behind the creation of these forces, and in both cases the paramilitaries were empowered, armed, and could act with impunity.

Indonesia had had a long history of pro-state paramilitarism, but the 1965–6 genocide must have been the zenith of paramilitary activity: the army mobilized several different paramilitary groups, from pre-existing ones like Kap-Gestapu, to those who were mobilized after the failed coup like Pemuda Pancasila, Hansip, and Hanra. Whether political party youth or petty criminal gangs, mobilizing pre-existing structures and re-purposing them for mass violence must have been more efficient than spawning them from zero amid the conflict.[80] Melvin's research on Indonesian military documents seems to have resolved debates on the relationship between the militias and the army, and a consensus has emerged that the army had superior control and outsourced massacres to the paramilitaries. Manufacturing ambiguity was often a stated objective during and after the commission of the violence, even though we can infer from the patterns of violence who the likely perpetrators must have been. The Indonesian army made the genocide *appear* spontaneous by noting in their documentation that a victim had been slain by "killer unknown."[81] This fits well in the global history of paramilitarism, as this type of framing and distancing device furthers the notion that killings and massacres are inter-ethnic rivalries, criminal score-settling, and so on, but are in any case spontaneous outbreaks of violence and certainly not of the government's making. Interestingly, two decades after the 1965 genocide, Indonesia would experience a similar wave of government-sponsored assassinations of suspected criminals. These "mysterious shootings" (*penembakan misterius*) were later convincingly argued to have been organized by the state, more specifically the army.[82]

[79] William Rosenau and Austin Long, *The Phoenix Program and Contemporary Counterinsurgency* (Santa Monica, CA: RAND Corporation, 2009), 10–15; Douglas Valentine, *The Phoenix Program* (New York: Open Road Media, 2016).

[80] Geoffrey B. Robinson, *The Killing Season: A History of the Indonesian Massacres, 1965–66* (Princeton, NJ: Princeton University Press, 2018), 166ff.

[81] Jess Melvin, *The Army and the Indonesian Genocide: Mechanics of Mass Murder* (London: Routledge, 2018).

[82] Justus van der Kroef, "'Petrus': Patterns of Prophylactic Murder in Indonesia," *Asian Survey* 25:7 (1985), 745–59.

The continuities and discontinuities between these two processes of mass violence remain poorly understood.

Right about the time of the Indonesian anti-communist genocide, in China a pro-communist mirror image developed in the Cultural Revolution. From 1966 to 1968, with the personal encouragement of Chairman Mao and his entourage, a generation of students began forming the Red Guards, a mass paramilitary mobilization which grew increasingly violent and targeted "bourgeois" culture and "revisionist" people, in order to restore "true Communism."[83] The Red Guards persecuted millions of people, who suffered a wide range of abuses from public humiliation to imprisonment and torture, to hard labor and dispossession of property, and outright execution; between 500,000 and 3 million people (and possibly more) died over a span of two years. Frequent clashes broke out between the Red Guards and police officers and the army, sowing confusion and creating chaos.[84] But Mao consistently threw his support behind the Red Guards, an organization that became a veritable state within a state, or a parallel authority. In 1968, the People's Liberation Army suppressed the Red Guard movement violently through arrests and mass executions.[85] The Red Guards fit seamlessly within the global history of paramilitarism for three reasons: they were an authoritarian creation that relied on personal ties with Chairman Mao, they committed very public violence against real and imagined enemies of the state, and were discontinued when they were no longer needed or their impunity had become a liability to the state itself.

Post-Cold War Europe

By the end of the Cold War, paramilitarism was seen as inherent to weak post-colonial states in the Global South. But in the late 1970s and especially early 1990s, paramilitary units appeared also on the European continent,

[83] Guobin Yang, *The Red Guard Generation and Political Activism in China* (New York: Columbia University Press, 2016); Yarong Jiang and David Ashley, *Mao's Children in the New China: Voices From the Red Guard Generation* (London: Routledge, 2013).

[84] Andrew Walder, *Fractured Rebellion: The Beijing Red Guard Movement* (Cambridge, MA: Harvard University Press, 2012).

[85] Xiaobing Li (ed.), *China at War: An Encyclopedia* (Oxford: ABC-CLIO, 2012), 376.

wreaking havoc in several conflicts from Northern Ireland to Yugoslavia, Kurdistan, and Chechnya. The conduct of the counter-insurgencies and organization of the violence by the (respectively British, Serbian, Turkish, and Russian) states bear relevance beyond the immediate country context and are reflective of broader theoretical as well as empirical concerns. Although Latin American paramilitarism operated in a different international, political, historical, and ideological context than the European counter-insurgencies and civil wars of the late twentieth century, there are both structural and phenomenological similarities and dissimilarities. First and foremost, external and internal pressures became more pressing. As the global human rights movement gained strength, external pressure on these states mounted and more intelligent and sophisticated diversions were required to distance paramilitary violence from the state. Internally, too, democratic pressures and curious journalists brought to the forefront the key issue of accountability and responsibility inside the societies.

Paramilitaries became the illustrious fighters identified with the Northern Irish conflict, which straddled the transition period from the Cold War to its aftermath. Both Catholic and Protestant militias were dubbed "paramilitaries," even though they were anti-state and pro-state, respectively. Paramilitarism became such a prominent part of the fabric of Northern Irish society, and with research being fairly manageable in terms of risks, a rich body of knowledge developed on especially the heavily armed, secretive loyalist paramilitary groups such as the Ulster Volunteer Force (UVF) and the Ulster Defence Association (UDA). Whereas the Irish Republican Army (IRA) targeted mostly British security personnel, the majority of UDA and UVF killings were of ordinary Catholic civilians, the vast majority having no connection with the IRA. This vast and complex literature cannot be done justice in this chapter, but three elements relevant to the broader scholarship stand out: the security dilemma between identity communities, collusion with the state, and criminal infighting after the war. First, the Northern Ireland conflict, as an ethno-religious (or "sectarian") conflict, in essence is about the coexistence of two collective identity groups. The long history of relations between Protestants and Catholics, and Unionists and Republicans, developed into a security dilemma in the 1970s when riots erupted in 1969 and the violence escalated rapidly thereafter into a low-intensity conflict in which series of sectarian tit-for-tat bloodshed occurred. As militias armed and mobilized, gaining membership in loyalist paramilitary groups and committing violence for them was admired by young Protestant boys. Having entered the paramilitary world, they rarely foresaw the consequences of their actions. Thus, loyalist paramilitaries were not secretly spawned by the British government but enjoyed significant grassroots support and a community "Umfeld."[86]

Second, collusion, the secret coordination between two groups for an illegal or deceitful purpose, is a hot topic in the historiography of the Northern Ireland conflict. Unionist public opinion was ambivalent toward the paramilitaries:

> Most Unionists remained of the opinion that if one wanted to partici-
> pate in the armed defence of the Union, the proper course of action
> was to join the security forces…The loyalist paramilitaries…were
> confronted continuously by the presence of armed men doing the
> same work which they felt called upon to perform…the only raison
> d'être for loyalist violence which made any sense to Unionists was the
> need to defend Protestant communities from republican attacks.[87]

So, too, the relationship between the British state and the loyalists was a contradictory one: on the one hand, it was distanced and conflictive, and "the front line security forces treated loyalist paramilitaries with the same disdain they felt towards the IRA."[88] Nevertheless, there is strong evidence for collusion between loyalist paramilitaries and powerful individuals in, and elements of, British state institutions in Northern Ireland.[89] Collusion comprises such actions as passing on security infor-mation, diverting law enforcement away from loyalist crimes, failing to

---

[86] Lee A. Smithey, *Unionists, Loyalists, and Conflict Transformation in Northern Ireland* (Oxford: Oxford University Press, 2011), 72ff.

[87] Alan Bairner, "Paramilitarism," in Arthur Aughey and Duncan Morrow (eds), *Northern Ireland Politics* (London: Longman, 1996), 159–72.

[88] Jonathan Tonge, *Northern Ireland* (Cambridge: Polity, 2006), 160.

[89] Anne Cadwallader, *Lethal Allies: British Collusion in Ireland* (Chester Springs, PA: Dufour Editions, 2013); Maurice Punch, *State Violence, Collusion and the Troubles: Counter Insurgency, Government Deviance and Northern Ireland* (London: Pluto Press, 2012), 117–47. For a sensa-tionalist memoir that takes a maximalist position on government–paramilitary collusion, see Simon Cursey, *MRF Shadow Troop: The Untold True Story of Top Secret British Military Intelligence Undercover Operations in Belfast, Northern Ireland, 1972–1974* (London: Thistle, 2013).

provide protection to threatened persons, failing to investigate loyalist killings, and providing firearms to loyalists.[90] All of these instances happened in the course of various assassinations in Northern Ireland. The fact that conclusive evidence of the killings was never produced is testimony to the effectiveness of collusion: it was designed not to be found out.

Finally, after the Good Friday peace accords, feuding and criminalization became a major part of postwar paramilitary life. Even though the UVF and UDA attempted to change, and set up veterans' associations, skill-building organizations, and community development, that is, nonviolent politics and civic involvement, these possibilities were limited. As the polarization of the conflict receded somewhat, the levels of consensus within loyalist paramilitary groups fragmented and conflicts simmering within them began to burst. For example, Johnny "Mad Dog" Adair, veteran criminal and the UDA's most notorious paramilitary and leader of the Shankill Road "C Company," tried to reinvent himself as a politician and peacebuilder. After serving part of a sixteen-year sentence for directing "terrorism," he was released from jail in 1999, but reincarcerated in 2002 for starting a vendetta with the rival UVF, which resulted in seven people losing their lives.[91] A police source said: "To portray any of these paramilitaries as having some deep-seated ideology is total rubbish. This is about drugs, money, territory and power."[92] If the history of Northern Irish paramilitarism teaches us anything, it is the relevance of collective identity cleavages, the difficulty of proving collusion, and the volatile afterlife of paramilitaries. Seen from this perspective, and with the benefit of hindsight, the developments in the following cases were not surprising.

The Yugoslav wars of succession saw the formation of several paramilitary units under the regime of Slobodan Milošević through the offices of the Interior Ministry, the Socialist Party of Serbia (SPS), and

[90] Human Rights Watch, *To Serve Without Favor: Policing, Human Rights, and Accountability in Northern Ireland* (New York: Human Rights Watch, 1997), ch. 6. This definition is fairly broad. A narrower definition would be that there has to be a *proven* record of *sustained* collaboration between powerful elements or individuals in formal state positions and the paramilitaries themselves.

[91] David Lister and Hugh Jordan, *Mad Dog: The Rise and Fall of Johnny Adair and 'C Company'* (London: Mainstream, 2004).

[92] Rosie Cowan, "From UDA hero to traitor in five months, the violent rise and fall of Johnny Adair," *The Guardian*, September 28, 2002.

personal ties with political and paramilitary actors in Croatia, Bosnia and Herzegovina, and Kosovo. These armed groups, often named after predatory animals like *Tigers*, *Eagles*, or *Scorpions*, appeared in Croatia and Bosnia in the 1990s and were responsible for widespread violations of human rights.[93] Preliminary investigation of these paramilitary units revealed two puzzling patterns: they maintained close links with political elites including heads of state, and they were largely drawn from the social milieu of organized crime.[94] Deeper research on the Serbian case demonstrates a close interplay between organized crime, politics, and state institutions across Serb-controlled territories (see Chapter 3). The wartime violence that the Serb paramilitaries committed against civilians is also important to examine from the perspective of (plausible) deniability.[95] It appears that the war provided a unique opportunity to these groups to accumulate economic capital, and Serb paramilitaries in Bosnia were accused of joining the war primarily for material gain rather than ideology.[96]

An important open question is to what extent Milošević controlled them and how exactly his "parallel structures" and chain of command functioned.[97] Indeed, the question of command and control bears importance beyond just the Serbian case and must take a central position in any discussion on paramilitarism. The end of the Bosnian war in 1995 saw the dissolution or legalization of the paramilitary units and in most cases the return of the paramilitaries to Serbia proper, where some became active in politics and others demobilized and disappeared back into their criminal networks, especially in Belgrade.[98] Some reappeared

---

[93] Two excellent recent studies are Kate Ferguson, *Architectures of Violence: The Command Structures of Modern Mass Atrocities, from Yugoslavia to Syria* (London: Hurst, 2018); Aleksandra Milicevic, "Joining Serbia's Wars: Volunteers and Draft-Dodgers, 1991–1995" (PhD thesis, University of California, Los Angeles, 2004).

[94] Christian Axboe Nielsen, "War Crimes and Organized Crime in the Former Yugoslavia," *Suedosteuropa-Mitteilungen* 52:3 (2012): 6–17.

[95] James Ron, "Territoriality and Plausible Deniability: Serbian Paramilitaries in the Bosnian War," in Bruce Campbell and Arthur Brenner (eds), *Death Squads in Global Perspective: Murder with Deniability* (New York: Palgrave Macmillan, 2000), 287–312.

[96] Kenneth Morrison, "The Criminal State Symbiosis and the Yugoslav Wars of Succession," in Alejandro Colás and Bryan Mabee (eds), *Mercenaries, Pirates, Bandits, and Empires: Private Violence in Historical Context* (New York: Columbia University Press, 2010), 159–86.

[97] ICTY Milošević trial transcript, December 6, 2002, at https://www.icty.org/x/cases/slobodan_milosevic/trans/en/021206IT.htm (accessed September 29, 2015).

[98] Aleksandar Knežević and Vojislav Tufegdžić, *Kriminal koji je izmenio Srbiju* (Belgrade: B-92, 1995).

in Kosovo in 1999.[99] The symbiosis between the state and organized crime nurtured by Milošević has outlasted the wars and the regime, increased crime in society (violence, black markets), and undermined public trust in the rule of law.[100] The relevance of Serbia's paramilitary history increased when on May 30, 2013, the ICTY acquitted two former heads of the State Security Service of crimes against humanity, absolving Serbia of responsibility for atrocities committed by its covert network of paramilitary units trained, paid, and supervised by the secret police.[101] What the Serbian case demonstrates most of all is how the Milošević regime spun an intricate web of politics, business, and administration, which produced a very focused and particular violence.

The picture of paramilitarism in the Turkish–Kurdish war (1984–99) appears to be somewhat similar to the Serbian case, but has its own peculiarities. "Serbian-style" paramilitary units sprouted when the regular army's strategy proved unable to combat the Kurdistan Workers' Party (PKK). In 1987, the Turkish government led by President Kenan Evren therefore set up the secret Gendarmerie Intelligence Organization (JİTEM), which became strongly affiliated with organized crime networks as well as far-right youth groups.[102] The current state of scholarship leaves no doubt about the fact that these groups collaborated in the military and paramilitary effort against the PKK. For example, the Turkish government argued consistently that the murders of prominent Kurdish individuals in the 1990s was carried out not by these death squads, but "unknown assailants" (faili meçhul).[103] But how exactly these configurations (the "deep state") interlocked and developed in terms of command and control, patronage networks, access to economic resources, and political parties is not fully clear yet. One key difference with the Serbian case was that Kurds were also involved in the paramilitary effort against the PKK. Kurdish "village guards" were involved in

---

[99] Human Rights Watch, *Under Orders: War Crimes in Kosovo* (New York: Human Rights Watch, 2001), ch. 3.

[100] Klaus Schlichte, "Na krilima patriotisma/On the Wings of Patriotism: Delegated and Spin-Off Violence in Serbia," *Armed Forces & Society* 36:2 (2010): 310–26.

[101] "Jovica Stanišić and Franko Simatović acquitted of all charges," ICTY press release, May 30, 2013, at https://www.icty.org/sid/11329 (accessed September 29, 2015).

[102] Selahattin Çelik, *Verbrecher Staat: Der "Susurluk-Zwischenfall" und die Verflechtung von Staat, Unterwelt und Kontrerguerilla in der Türkei* (Frankfurt am Main: Zambon, 1998).

[103] Ramazan Aras, *The Formation of Kurdishness in Turkey: Political Violence, Fear and Pain* (London: Routledge, 2013), 98.

counter-insurgency operations against the PKK, including targeted assassinations, massacres of civilians, and material and environmental destruction.[104] In arming and mobilizing anti-PKK Kurds, the Turkish government "Kurdified" the conflict and fomented a veritable civil war among the Kurds.

As long as they combated Kurdish nationalism, the Turkish government sanctioned the paramilitaries to engage in creative ways to fund themselves. Some smuggled drugs, others traded arms, laundered political contributions, and pursued vendettas between tribes. Indeed, paramilitarism undermined democratization and the rule of law in Turkey as it profoundly weakened the civic and judicial structures of Southeast Turkey.[105] Well-meaning officers or lawyers would find themselves first undermined, and if they went too far, threatened by shady individuals with "connections." Consequently, the Turkish government, parliament, judiciary, and police were unable to discontinue JİTEM even after the war ended. Stathis Kalyvas' discussion of how cleavage in civil wars runs through families and sets tribes against each other is best exemplified in the Chechen and Kurdish cases: when one tribe went over to the rebels for ideological or pragmatic reasons, a rival tribe often saw opportunities in or no other option than resorting to the state—or vice versa.[106] The authorities' use and deployment of paramilitarism then strengthened tribal ties and gave the civil wars much more locally diffuse dimensions.

The Azeri–Armenian war in the Nagorno-Karabakh Autonomous Oblast (NKAO) was a low-intensity conflict that broke out when influential Armenian political groups in Karabakh declared their intention to secede from Azerbaijan in 1988. As political structures such as the Karabakh Committee emerged and expanded, so did military and paramilitary ones.[107] In September 1989, so-called Armenian self-defense

---

[104] Elise Massicard, "'Gangs in Uniform' in Turkey: Politics at the Articulation between Security Institutions and the Criminal World," in Jean-Louis Briquet and Gilles Favarel-Garrigues (eds), *Organized Crime and States: The Hidden Face of Politics* (New York: Palgrave, 2010), 41–72.

[105] Hamit Bozarslan, "Kurdistan: Économie de guerre, économie dans la guerre," in François Jean and Jean-Christophe Ruffin (eds), *Economie des guerres civiles* (Paris: Hachette, 1996), 104–46.

[106] Stathis Kalyvas, *The Logic of Violence in Civil War* (Cambridge: Cambridge University Press, 2006), 374–5.

[107] Christoph Zürcher, *The Post-Soviet Wars: Rebellion, Ethnic Conflict, and Nationhood in the Caucasus* (New York: New York University Press, 2007).

groups sprung up in villages and cities in Karabakh and began battling armed Azeri groups for territorial control. The conflict went through a rapid process of mobilization, radicalization, and sustained large-scale violence including warfare, mass expulsions, executions, plunder, and destruction of villages.[108] Armenian paramilitaries fought battles against the Azerbaijani army, but also engaged in violence against civilians. Cities such as Shusha and Agdam were severely damaged and destroyed in this process, and massacres occurred in towns such as Khojali and Malibeyli.[109] Neighboring countries like Russia, Turkey, and Iran disagreed on the causes of and solutions to the conflict, and several international efforts to resolve the conflict failed. Meanwhile, one million Azeris fled to Azerbaijan and became one of the largest internally displaced person (IDP) communities in the world.[110]

The state of "frozen conflict" or "no war, no peace" between Azerbaijan and Armenia offered a window of opportunity to examine violence and its consequences in Karabakh. Much of this new research was carried out in Yerevan and Stepanakert on chronicles and diaries of the war, as well as interviews with former combatants and eyewitnesses. Papazian's research suggests that Armenian paramilitarism seemed to stand out from other cases. The units seem to have been loosely organized from the bottom up, and the Armenian state appears to have become more and more involved in supporting and controlling them.[111] Souleimanov argues that then Armenian President Levon Ter-Petrosyan, pragmatically managed "to take control of some of the more unruly paramilitary groups, . . . sprung up during the clashes in Karabakh and along the border with Azerbaijan."[112] In other words, Armenian paramilitaries gradually became centralized and unified throughout the war. To what extent Yerevan actually controlled them at various moments in the war,

---

[108] Vicken Cheterian, *War and Peace in the Caucasus: Russia's Troubled Frontier* (New York: Columbia University Press, 2011), 87–154.

[109] Caroline Cox and John Eibner, *Ethnic Cleansing in Progress: War in Nagorno Karabakh* (London: Christian Solidarity Worldwide, 1999); Françoise Ardillier-Carras, "Sud-Caucase: conflit du Karabagh et nettoyage ethnique," *Bulletin de l'Association de Géographes Français*, 83:4 (2006), 409–32.

[110] Ohannes Geukjian, *Ethnicity, Nationalism and Conflict in the South Caucasus: Nagorno-Karabakh and the Legacy of Soviet Nationalities Policy* (London: Routledge, 2016), 187ff.

[111] Taline Papazian, *L'Arménie à l'épreuve du feu: Forger l'état à travers la guerre* (Paris: Karthala, 2016).

[112] Emil Souleimanov, *Understanding Ethnopolitical Conflict: Karabakh, South Ossetia, and Abkhazia Wars Reconsidered* (London: Palgrave, 2013), 88.

remains an open question. Furthermore, the international context is an important dimension to be taken into account: inter-state conflict between Armenia and Azerbaijan, pogroms and massacres against Armenians in Azerbaijan, Armenian diaspora support for Karabakh, (post-)Soviet military and political intervention in the region, all influenced the emergence and shapes taken by paramilitarism.[113] The cessation of armed activity in Karabakh in 1994 saw the unification and legalization of the paramilitary units into the standing army of Artsakh ("Karabakh" in Armenian). In some cases, paramilitary leaders became military commanders, whereas others demobilized and became active in politics.

Chechnya saw widespread paramilitary activity during both of its post-Soviet era wars. The Second Chechen War of 1999–2009 differed from the first (1994–6) as it saw the formation of several loyalist paramilitary units under the regime of the Interior Ministry's security services.[114] These covert networks of paramilitary units were trained, paid for, and supervised by the Federal Security Services, and included Russian "contract soldiers" (*kontraktniki*) and Chechen "warriors" (*boyeviki*), both of whom committed various forms of mass violence against Chechen civilians.[115] Understanding the interplay between the Russian state and the militias requires an examination of paramilitary violence against civilians from the perspective of deniability.[116] The war provided a unique opportunity to these groups to accumulate economic capital, and pro-Russian paramilitaries in Chechnya reportedly joined the war primarily for material gain rather than ideology or even defense of the status quo. In 2009, the Russian government declared victory in the second Chechen war and established itself firmly in Chechnya through its local strongman, Ramzan Kadyrov. According to human rights reports, repression and violence against civilians continued in more furtive forms.[117]

[113] Michael Kambeck and Sargis Ghazaryan (eds), *Europe's Next Avoidable War: Nagorno-Karabakh* (London: Palgrave, 2013).

[114] Mark Galeotti, *Russian Security and Paramilitary Forces since 1991* (Oxford: Osprey, 2013); Jason Lyall, "Are Coethnics More Effective Counterinsurgents? Evidence from the Second Chechen War," *American Political Science Review* 104:1 (2010), 1–20.

[115] Valerii Tishkov, *Chechnya: Life in a War-Torn Society* (Berkeley: University of California Press, 2004), 107–50; Emma Gilligan, *Terror in Chechnya: Russia and the Tragedy of Civilians in War* (Princeton, NJ: Princeton University Press, 2009).

[116] Ilyas Akhmadov, *The Chechen Struggle: Independence Won and Lost* (London: Palgrave, 2010).

[117] Human Rights Watch, *"What Your Children Do Will Touch Upon You": Punitive House-Burning in Chechnya* (New York: Human Rights Watch, 2009).

Much of this violence was committed by the *kadyrovtsy*, the militias loyal to Chechen president Ramzan Kadyrov. Recent research on the conduct of these pro-state paramilitaries in the war strongly suggests that concerns for their physical survival, promises of family and clan protection, as well as rampant unemployment drove many young Chechens (including former insurgents) into the arms of the *kadyrovtsy*. The "Chechenization" of the conflict through the elevation of one clan (Kadyrov) over the other ones, alienated and re-tribalized Chechen society, as other pro-Russian clans such as the Baysarov and Yamadayev felt a strong sense of relative deprivation.[118] After every phase of fighting, the dissolution or legalization of the paramilitary units saw their transformation, as some leaders became active in politics and administration, whereas others demobilized and disappeared back into their prewar occupations, private security firms, or into organized crime; some reappeared in Ukraine in 2014.[119]

Beyond postcolonialism in the Global South and Europe after the Cold War, paramilitarism really came into being in the twenty-first-century Global South, with the Philippines and India as prominent and brutal examples. The populist Filipino politician Rodrigo Duterte was mayor of Davao City in the southern province of Mindanao, where he ran the Davao Death Squad, which according to human rights groups committed over 1,400 killings of mainly drug users, petty criminals, and street children between 1998 and May 2016.[120] When Duterte won the 2016 presidential elections and assumed office, it was not surprising that he expanded his local paramilitary fiefdom to the national level. He immediately launched a war on drugs with profanity-laden speeches exhorting not just the police force, but ordinary Filipinos to commit extrajudicial killings of drug users and sellers. As a result, police officers, vigilantes, and militias killed over 12,000 people within three years.

---

[118] Emil Souleimanov, "An Ethnography of Counterinsurgency: Kadyrovtsy and Russia's Policy of Chechenization," *Post-Soviet Affairs* 31:2 (2015), 91–114; Tomáš Šmída and Miroslav Mareša, "'Kadyrovtsy': Russia's Counterinsurgency Strategy and the Wars of Paramilitary Clans," *Journal of Strategic Studies* 38:5 (2015), 650–77.

[119] Anne Le Huérou, "State Violence against Civilians in Post-War Chechen Republic," in Anne Le Huérou et al. (eds), *Chechnya at War and Beyond* (London: Routledge, 2014), 152–75.

[120] Jonathan Miller, *Rodrigo Duterte: Fire and Fury in the Philippines* (Melbourne: Scribe, 2018).

As long as the victims were among those groups that the president had marked as targets, the killings were allowed and encouraged.[121]

The story of Narendra Modi is similar, as he too went from a local government position where he presided over a violent parastate to becoming head of state. In February 2002, Modi, Chief Minister of Gujarat at the time, was responsible for initiating and condoning a large-scale massacre against Gujarati Muslims in which Hindu-nationalist militias of the Bajrang Dal, Rashtriya Swayamsevak Sangh, and Vishva Hindu Parishad organizations killed approximately 2,000 people.[122] The massacre emanated from a classical parastate construction: armed militias connected to Modi's Hindu-nationalist Bharatiya Janata Party were secretly provided with addresses of Muslims civilians and businesses, massacred the victims in broad daylight while police were watching, and were either provided with immunity through Gujarat's corrupt legal system, or portrayed as low-level, spontaneous actors who were unconnected to Modi.[123] When Modi became prime minister of India in May 2014, similar to Duterte, many feared that he would carry his nationalist paramilitarism to the much bigger platform of national politics. Under his presidency, Hindu vigilantes have attacked and killed cattle traders, and the police often "stalled investigations, ignored procedures, or even played a complicit role in the killings and cover-up of crimes."[124]

Both countries have long prehistories of paramilitarism: the Philippines has a history of vigilantism and "bossism," and India's militias have wreaked havoc during ethnic riots in inner cities ever since independence. Duterte and Modi inherited these legacies of paramilitarism, which offered them real advantages to accumulate leverage, polarize ethnic and religious relations, and entrench their formerly provincial parastate into the highest office.[125]

---

[121] *Duterte Killings Continue: State Terror & Human Rights in the Philippines* (Quezon City: IBON International, 2018), 11–14.

[122] Human Rights Watch, *We Have No Orders To Save You: State Participation and Complicity in Communal Violence in Gujarat* (New York: Human Rights Watch, 2002).

[123] Ward Berenschot, *Riot Politics: Hindu–Muslim Violence and the Indian State* (London: Hurst, 2011).

[124] Human Rights Watch, *Violent Cow Protection in India: Vigilante Groups Attack Minorities* (New York: Human Rights Watch, 2019), 38–53.

[125] For similar examples from the Middle East and Central Africa, see Geraint Hughes, "Militias in Internal Warfare: From the Colonial Era to the Contemporary Middle East," *Small*

Conclusions

With the onset of the twenty-first century, paramilitarism seemed a relic from the past. But in February 2003, the conflict between the Sudanese government and the Darfur insurgency escalated and paramilitaries reappeared with a vengeance. That simmering conflict flared up as the Sudanese army suffered a sensitive military defeat in the provincial capital, prompting the government to adopt a new counter-insurgency strategy.[126] Instead of merely fighting rebel groups in Darfur, the government deployed a special paramilitary organization, the Janjaweed, to attack civilians and thereby undermine the support base of the rebels. The Janjaweed perpetrated massive human rights violations including massacres, destruction of villages, expulsions, sexual violence, torture, and property crimes. According to reliable estimates, at least 200,000 civilians were killed in the following three years.[127] How exactly these networks were embedded in the Sudanese state during the conflict, and how exactly and why they were recruited are questions exceptionally difficult to research due to the levels of repression and censorship in Sudan (prior to the 2019 revolution), but close ethnographic research leaves no doubt about it that the state was prime in mobilizing, organizing, composing, structuring, and covering the Janjaweed.[128] Their patterns of violence and motives of involvement are strikingly similar to the cases preceding the Darfur genocide, described in this chapter. Indeed, as the first twenty-first-century case, Sudan demonstrates that twentieth-century paramilitarism was not a spent force, and every single element of modern pro-state paramilitarism was present in the Darfur genocide.

The Janjaweed appeared on the scene in Darfur in 2003, but in fact had a clear prehistory as the pan-Arabist paramilitary legions set up by

Wars & Insurgencies 27:2 (2016), 196–225; Comfort Ero, "Vigilantes, Civil Defence Forces and Militia Groups: The Other Side of the Privatisation of Security in Africa," *Conflict Trends* 1 (June 2000), 25–9.

[126] Julie Flint and Alex de Waal, *Darfur: A New History of a Long War* (London: Zed Books, 2008).
[127] Gérard Prunier, *Darfur: A 21st Century Genocide* (Ithaca, NY: Cornell University Press, 2008); Samuel Totten, *An Oral and Documentary History of the Darfur Genocide* (Santa Barbara, CA: Greenwood, 2011).
[128] Usman A. Tar, "The Perverse Manifestations of Civil Militias in Africa: Evidence from Western Sudan," *Peace, Conflict and Development* 7 (2005), 135–73.

Muammar Gaddafi in 1987. Throughout the 1990s, these groups were mostly militants who pursued local and criminal agendas such as smuggling contraband and controlling access to grazing territory.[129] The main leaders of the Janjaweed, such as Mohammed Hamdan Dagalo (a.k.a. Hemedti), Musa Hilal, and Ali Kushayb, maintained close personal ties with the Sudanese Interior Minister and middleman Ahmed Haroun, who reported directly to President Omar al-Bashir.[130] The paramilitaries were mostly drawn from loyalist Arab tribes who competed with other tribes for control of arable land. Their involvement in the militias seemed to be informed by a mix of ideological, Arab-nationalist/racist convictions and pragmatic concerns for economic and criminal interests.[131] The years 2004 and 2005 saw much international attention on Darfur as the International Criminal Court (ICC) opened an investigation and indicted the president and six senior Janjaweed members for crimes against humanity. For example, the ICC indicted Ahmad Haroun and Ali Kushayb formally for a long list of well-documented crimes, including massacre, torture, sexual violence, plunder, and expulsion.[132] But the increased attention affected the Sudanese government's conduct of the paramilitary groups in profound ways. There are strong suggestions that the Sudanese government became ever more surreptitious, duplicitous, and denialist in the face of overwhelming evidence of the Janjaweed's crimes. In Musa Hilal's own words: "I don't have a relation or link by which they can talk to me personally."[133] But leaked and stolen Sudanese government documents, as well as eyewitness testimony, places Hilal at the helm of scorched-earth campaigns against the

[129] Ali Haggar, "The Origins and Organization of the Janjawiid in Darfur," in Alex de Waal (ed.), *War in Darfur and the Search for Peace* (Cambridge, MA: Harvard University Press, 2007), 113–39.

[130] Øystein H. Rolandsen, "Sudan: The Janjawiid and Government Militias," in Morten Bøås (ed.), *African Guerrillas: Raging against the Machine* (Boulder, CO: Lynne Rienner, 2007), 151–70; Hamza Hendawi, "Out of the Darfur Desert: The Rise of Sudanese General Mohammed Hamdan Dagalo," *The National*, April 29, 2019, at https://www.thenational.ae/world/africa/out-of-the-darfur-desert-the-rise-of-sudanese-general-mohammed-hamdan-dagalo-1.855219 (accessed May 1, 2019).

[131] Scott Straus, *Making and Unmaking Nations: War, Leadership, and Genocide in Modern Africa* (Ithaca, NY: Cornell University Press, 2015), 232–72.

[132] International Criminal Court, "Warrant of Arrest for Ali Kushayb" (April 27, 2007), at https://www.icc-cpi.int/CourtRecords/CR2007_02907.PDF (accessed May 10, 2018).

[133] Human Rights Watch, "Video Transcript: Exclusive Video Interview with Alleged Janjaweed Leader" (March 2, 2005), at https://www.hrw.org/news/2005/03/02/video-transcript-exclusive-video-interview-alleged-janjaweed-leader (accessed May 10, 2018).

Fur population. And so Darfur became a textbook case of a typical paramilitary infrastructure, hidden in plain sight, plausibly denied, and institutionalized in the state apparatus of violence through personal connections.

A diachronic comparison across these cases demonstrates that the two key issues in understanding paramilitarism are the state, and violence. First and foremost, paramilitarism was a phase of state building, both in the broader European area and in the postwar and postcolonial contexts. As it was a phase of state formation, it could always be reversed and take a different shape and direction. Certainly not all states were the same, from Florence to the Ottomans, from Mao to Milosevic, but generally monopolization was beneficial to the state in times of peace, but during internal conflicts, challenges, and contestation, a certain "decoupling" of the monopoly of violence and hybrid forms of security could substitute or supplement the state's apparatus of violence. Changing relationships between the state and its paramilitary groups resemble the attraction between a planet and satellites, respectively. Sometimes paramilitary groups "fly ahead" of the state and develop as an organic, bottom-up, community-driven phenomenon, and sometimes they are created by the state and have to be continuously propelled forward. Some paramilitary groups are more ideological than others, but they all share the characteristic of politics in the demi-monde. Alfred McCoy has argued that the Cold War was a "historic high tide for covert action," with secret services wielding unprecedented power and projecting a "netherworld" onto Third World states, thereby "fraying their borders, compromising capacities, and enmeshing them in international economic circuits of corruption and illegality."[134]

The second central issue in paramilitarism is violence. The long-term view of paramilitary violence demonstrates that paramilitaries emerged as states' autonomous tactic of outsourcing illegal and illegitimate violence. At the same time, the comparative global perspective shows the relevance of transnational transfers. Transnational transfer can occur between neighboring countries in continental contexts, but transfers can also occur across time and space, without direct cultural or

---

[134] Alfred W. McCoy, "Covert Netherworld: An Invisible Interstice in the Modern World System," *Comparative Studies in Society and History* 58:4 (2016), 847–79, at 878–9.

territorial contact. It remains to be seen whether political elites really learned from each other (e.g. whether Milošević was actively drawing lessons from the Indonesian example), but one thing is certain: it was the superpower interventions that subverted democracies (e.g. through GLADIO), brutalized political culture in those countries, deepened existing left–right polarizations, empowered bandits and thugs to operate with widespread impunity, and produced victims who could never hope for any form of justice and therefore turned to more radical measures. Hannah Arendt's critically appraised argument that World War II was the violent homecoming of colonialism could perhaps be extended: was the European paramilitary experience after 1990 a similar process, as paramilitary violence boomeranged back to Europe from the Global South? In any case, the forms of violence in comparable settings of political contestation were strikingly similar. In this way, the Global South was ahead of Europe: Suharto had understood very well the benefits of outsourcing mass violence against civilians. They included making use of local knowledge, implicating broader sections of society in the killings, and generating plausible deniability. In very, very few of these cases were there profound, official investigations, nor did there appear incontrovertible evidence and crystal-clear primary sources on the phenomenon. The paramilitary secret is so dirty and incriminating that it is dangerous to probe into it *during* the violence, or even *after* the violence, and it is deeply demoralizing for a society to realize how their leaders have conspired for the purpose of such transgressive forms of brutality.

3

Organized Crime, the State, and Paramilitarism

Introduction: From Ancient to Modern Banditry

On Sunday November 3, 1996 around 7:15 pm, near the somniferous western Turkish town of Susurluk, a black Mercedes 600 SEL with tinted windows crashed into a truck at high speed. Of the four passengers in the Mercedes, three died and one survived. What seemed to be just another routine traffic accident on Turkey's unsafe, bloody roads, turned out to be a veritable political, social, and cultural earthquake in Turkey and beyond. The Mercedes was registered in the name of the sole survivor, Sedat Bucak, MP for the True Path Party in the southeastern province Şanlıurfa, chief of the Kurdish Bucak tribe, and head of its paramilitary counter-insurgency militia, the village guards (*korucu*). Those who perished were just as illustrious: Abdullah Çatlı (1956–1996), former right-wing militant leader of the Grey Wolves, contract killer, and mob boss wanted by Turkish police and Interpol for multiple murders and drug trafficking; Huseyin Kocadağ (1944–1996), deputy chief of the Istanbul police department; and Gonca Us (1970–1996), former beauty queen and Çatlı's girlfriend. In the trunk of the car, the police found bizarre pieces of evidence: Çatlı had been carrying diplomatic credentials and a fake passport, a weapons permit, numerous Beretta pistols and submachine guns (some with silencers), listening devices, a suitcase of narcotics, and thousands of US dollars. As soon as the news broke, the Turkish public asked the one and the same question: what were these people doing in the same car together? The Susurluk denouement was a remarkable example that demonstrated in a nutshell the nexus between the state, organized crime, and paramilitarism. Journalistic, legal, and academic investigations into that nexus played an important role in unraveling these configurations, which were termed the "deep state" (*derin devlet* in Turkish)—a set of interlocking networks of patronage, legal and illegal economic interests, security services, and political parties at the heart of the Turkish Republic.[1]

But "Susurluk" was by no means unique, neither as an example of the relationships that states can foster with Mafia figures, nor an illustration of the symbiosis between paramilitarism and organized crime. Indeed, no discussion of paramilitarism is even minimally complete without an examination of how it is related to organized crime. Therefore, this chapter examines the complex and multi-dimensional relationships between states, organized crime, and paramilitarism. How are paramilitarism and crime related? Empirical analyses of paramilitarism in different countries make abundantly clear that (organized) crime plays an important role in paramilitarism: the trade in illicit commodities and services and the fact that criminal gangs operate in secrecy are two phenomena that are closely related to paramilitary activity. The influences seem to run both ways: criminals benefit from paramilitarism, and paramilitarism often engenders crime. Furthermore, in certain countries and contexts, entire organized crime structures have collided with states and paramilitary units. This chapter offers a deeper look at the relationships between paramilitarism and crime. It briefly discusses histories of banditry, before it examines three central problems: the relationships between states, politics, and crime; the ways that (civil) wars and crime are related; and finally, how crime functions as a resource in (civil) wars. As such, the chapter is limited in its discussions to two distinct historical dynamics: the long-term relationships between crime and state, from state consolidation to the post-Weberian world, and the short-term relationships between crime and state within the contingencies of war and civil war. It concludes with a comparative discussion of several paramilitary-criminal profiles.

Crime is as old as humankind, and there are countless forms and modalities of crime across the centuries and continents. As diverse a phenomenon as it is, crime has two essential features: it is covert, and it

---

[1] Mehtap Söyler, *The Turkish Deep State: State Consolidation, Civil–Military Relations and Democracy* (London: Routledge, 2015).

relies on private violence.[2] Modernity, and its major global-historical processes such as capitalism and globalization, has profoundly affected the ways that crime is conducted and perceived. Indeed, the neoliberal changes that took place after 1990 brought structural changes to global crime, in particular pragmatic collusion with politics. The influence of neoliberal market reforms also encouraged the outsourcing of public works, and facilitated corruption in procurement and services. One of the many different forms of crime is organized crime, a fairly new phenomenon that affects economics, politics, security, and ultimately societies at large. According to one global survey, "people in Latin America, Africa, Asia and the Middle East all see crime and corruption as the greatest problems in their countries."[3] The 2010 Ukrainian and Arab revolutions erupted because of indignation and public disgust at the corruption and links between organized crime and government authorities. Perceptions of criminalized governance not only provoke outrage, but also opportunities for would-be criminals. Schneider and Schneider argue that organized crime, or "mafia," forms "when a group of people, by common accord, engages in a continuing, reproducible, conspiracy to monopolize illegal enterprises and use illegal means to control legal enterprises." In their definition, these groups operate *without* the benefit of state-enforced contracts and they are in continuous conflict with the state.[4] Yet Robert Merton found that many of its constitutive features are identical with that of legitimate businesses.[5]

In each and every country-specific case, organized crime has precursors. Bandits and social bandits are one of them. First and foremost, the term "bandit" is a deeply contested concept, much like the term "war" or "terrorism." Stathis Kalyvas points out that during wars, the term "war" is usually "sought out by insurgents in search of legitimacy, and denied by incumbents who label their opponents 'bad guys', bandits, criminals, subversives, or terrorists—and describe the war as banditry,

---

    [2] Mark Findlay, *The Globalisation of Crime: Understanding Transitional Relationships in Context* (Cambridge: Cambridge University Press, 1999).
    [3] Pew Research Center, "Crime and Corruption: Top Problems in Emerging and Developing Countries," November 2014, at https://www.pewresearch.org/global/2014/11/06/crime-and-corruption-top-problems-in-emerging-and-developing-countries/.
    [4] Jane Schneider and Peter Schneider, "The Anthropology of Crime and Criminalization," *Annual Review of Anthropology* 37 (2008), 351–73, at 362.
    [5] Robert Merton, *Social Theory and Social Structure* (New York: Free Press, 1968), 134–6.

terrorism, delinquent subversion, and other cognate terms."[6] During their occupation of the Soviet Union, the Nazis used similar language: the term "partisan" was to be replaced by "bandit," they argued, "for psychological reasons." Accordingly, anti-partisan operations were to be called "anti-bandit warfare" and areas of suspected partisan presence were referred to as areas "contaminated with bandit groups."[7]

In his classic study *Bandits*, Hobsbawm defined social bandits as "peasant outlaws whom the lord and state regard as criminals, but who remain within peasant society, and are considered by their people as heroes, as champions, avengers, fighters for justice, perhaps even leaders of liberation." He further observed: "Banditry tended to become epidemic in times of pauperization and economic crisis."[8] Hobsbawm distinguished bandits from two other phenomena: gangs drawn from the professional underworld, and communities who raided as a way of life. He saw bandits as symptoms of major transformations in society, yet not transformative themselves. He also profiled the membership of these gangs as young bachelors, poor laborers, migrants, shepherds, veterans, and deserters. These men would escape into the mountains for personal reasons and live the lives of desperados, supported by local communities but ultimately often betrayed by them. The assumption of conflict with the state persisted for many decades. For example, Curott and Fink more recently argued that banditry conflicted with the state through at least three separate mechanisms: bandits break laws that are enforced by the ruling elites for whom the populace have no sympathy (e.g., prohibition), banditry provides a system of checks and balances on privileges of the ruling classes and state power, and banditry provides a system of rules and accompanying enforcement where the government fails to do so.[9]

Hobsbawm's thesis has been criticized by Anton Blok and other scholars, who have argued that class conflict should not be overemphasized as a causal mechanism, and bandits not romanticized as popular

---

[6] Stathis N. Kalyvas, *The Logic of Violence in Civil War* (Cambridge: Cambridge University Press, 2006), 17.
[7] Hannes Heer, "The Logic of the War of Extermination: The Wehrmacht and the Anti-Partisan War," in Hannes Heer and Klaus Naumann (eds), *War of Extermination: The German Military in World War II, 1941–1944* (New York: Berghahn Books, 2000), 92–126, at 113.
[8] Eric Hobsbawm, *Bandits* (London: Weidenfeld and Nicolson, 2000 [1969]), 20, 26.
[9] Nicholas Curott and Alexander Fink, "Bandit Heroes: Social, Mythical or Rational?," *American Journal of Economics and Sociology* 71:2 (2012), 470–97.

heroes who champion the poor, but rather as predatory, acquisitive, and violent groups who oppress poor peasants. Blok also argued that bandits suppressed collective peasant action through terror and weakened collective peasant action by foregrounding individual achievements.[10] These new lines of research underline, importantly, that bandits required protection for survival, which mostly came from local politicians and state officials. The key issue was that collusion, not conflict with the state, characterized the vicissitudes of banditry. Indeed, bandits and criminals were effective in state-making from Mexico to China. A corollary following from this argument is that state formation could indirectly generate banditry as policies of pacification and disarmament marginalized outlaws. Even if we are aware of these constraints and critiques, and despite the existence of many case studies on banditry, there are no synchronic comparative studies, nor are there diachronic understandings of why (social) banditry persisted in one society, or morphed into organized crime. A comprehensive examination like that is beyond the scope of this study, but it is worth taking a closer look at cultures of banditry before the age of organized crime, starting with the Ottoman Empire.

The Ottoman Empire never pacified all of its territory to the same degree. In the cities and towns, the monopoly of violence was often sufficient for most inhabitants to feel safe walking the streets unarmed. But in the highland areas of Albania, Yemen, or Kurdistan the "negotiated empire" lacked a combination of the technology, manpower, political will, and popular support required to successfully establish and maintain a functioning state monopoly of violence.[11] In these peripheral areas, the state faced a number of tribes and gangs able to mobilize both quantitatively and qualitatively superior resources and means of violence. Many tribes were well armed, some of them could mobilize thousands of mounted men, and they knew the territory well. Karen Barkey, in concluding her study of Ottoman state formation in the seventeenth century, observes that "the Ottoman state centralized mostly through

---

[10] Anton Blok, "The Peasant and the Brigand: Social Banditry Reconsidered," *Comparative Studies in Society and History* 14 (1972), 494–503; Eric Hobsbawm, "Social Bandits: A Reply," *Comparative Studies in Society and History* 14 (1972), 503–5; Richard W. Slatta, "Eric J. Hobsbawm's Social Bandit: A Critique and Revision," *A Contracorriente* 2 (2004), 1–30.
[11] Karen Barkey, *Empire of Difference: The Ottomans in Comparative Perspective* (Cambridge: Cambridge University Press, 2008), 67–97.

negotiation and incorporation of bandit armies that were largely the product of state consolidation in the first place."[12] Reşat Kasaba has argued similarly that the Ottoman authorities sought not only to pacify or eliminate tribal groups, but also to enlist and accommodate them in the region. Especially in frontier regions, these groups were an important source of state power, and at times they were the state.[13] The famous folk heroes Karacaoğlan and Köroğlu were social bandits (eşkiya), whose tales have become an inextricable part of the oral tradition of Anatolia.

Banditry was deeply ingrained in Ottoman culture, from Albania to Yemen.[14] The seventeenth-century wartime Sultan Ahmed I regularly made deals with bandits, by using subterfuge to ensure control through elimination or incorporation of local rivals, as Barkey argued: "Both the elimination of rivals and the incorporation of potential rivals were important political activities of the Ottoman state...as a way to incorporate the claims of bandit chiefs at the helm of large bands of mercenary troops." For example, the infamous bandit Canboladoğlu Ali went from rural bandit to socialite at the Ottoman palace. Ottoman state formation in this period represents archetypal consolidation of state power by deal-making with bandits, who "were co-opted to be sent away from battle when perceived to be a liability to the Ottoman armies or co-opted when their manpower became necessary for prolonged military campaigns."[15] Bandit rebellions were therefore veiled demands for appointments to state positions, incorporation, and mobility in the system. Importantly, the tradition of patrimonial rule with a brokerage style of centralization continued across various different Sultans' rule. For example, in the late eighteenth century, the infamous Rumelian bandit Kara Feyzi became a bone of contention between two competing influential Pashas, each of whom appealed to Sultan Selim III to grant them the exclusive right to combat the local bandit gangs. Tolga Esmer explains the motives of each Pasha as "to combat the bandit problem

[12] Karen Barkey, *Bandits and Bureaucrats: The Ottoman Route of State Centralization* (Ithaca, NY: Cornell University Press, 1994), 230–1.
[13] Reşat Kasaba, *A Moveable Empire: Ottoman Nomads, Migrants, and Refugees* (Seattle: University of Washington Press, 2009).
[14] Frederick Anscombe, "Albanian and 'Mountain Bandits,'" in Frederick Anscombe (ed.), *Ottoman Balkans, 1750–1830* (Princeton, NJ: Markus Wiener Publishers, 2005), 87–114.
[15] Barkey, *Bandits and Bureaucrats*, 191–5.

[as it] would guarantee years of resources, promotion, and opportunities to distinguish himself."[16]

Social banditry persisted throughout the nineteenth and early twentieth centuries. Yaşar Kemal, one of Turkey's most prominent novelists, wrote his masterpiece *Memed, my Hawk* on a bandit who was treated unjustly, then wreaked havoc in the countryside, finally to be taken out by the state. The legendary bandit Memed fights the police in his village and subverts the state, as his violent campaign is a constant reminder of the state's inability to monopolize violence.[17] The transition from classical late Ottoman bandits to modern organized crime straddles the period of Ottoman collapse, from the Balkan Wars (1912–13), World War I, and the Greco–Turkish War (1919–21). Ryan Gingeras has explained how the modern underworld of Black Sea mafias is rooted in that period's banditry. He argues that the development of modern criminal syndicates among ethnic Laz migrants in Istanbul during the first half of the twentieth century emerged from a background of Black Sea banditry, which was active in that region around World War I.[18]

Yaşar Kemal did, however, disregard collusion between the state and the bandits, which truly came to the surface in the modern wars of imperial dissolution. During the Great War, the Ottoman government began drawing up paramilitary formations by releasing ordinary criminal convicts from prisons. The highest offices oversaw the operation, which released convicts from prisons and enlisted them into paramilitary units under the command of regular army officers. Particular preference would be given to prisoners "who have a reputation leading outlaw gangs."[19] To facilitate the formation of these units, the Ottoman Justice Ministry issued a special amnesty through a temporary law that became permanent in 1916.[20] As a result of these measures, thousands of criminals were released from Ottoman prisons and drafted into paramilitary units. The convicts, named "savages and criminals" even by government

---

[16] Tolga U. Esmer, "Notes on a Scandal: Transregional Networks of Violence, Gossip, and Imperial Sovereignty in the Late Eighteenth-Century Ottoman Empire," *Comparative Studies in Society and History* 58:1 (2016), 99–128.

[17] Yaşar Kemal, *İnce Memed* (Istanbul: Remzi, 1960).

[18] Ryan Gingeras, "Beyond Istanbul's 'Laz Underworld': Ottoman Paramilitarism and the Rise of Turkish Organised Crime, 1908–1950," *Contemporary European History* 19 (2010), 215–30.

[19] A. Mil, "Umumi Harpte Teşkilâtı Mahsusa," *Vakit*, November 5 and 29, 1933.

[20] Tarık Zafer Tunaya, *Türkiye'de Siyasal Partiler* (Istanbul: İletişim, 1997), vol. 3, *İttihat ve Terakki*, 285–6.

officials, were very often local outlaws and bandits who had committed crimes such as theft, racketeering, or murder. According to one source, they were drilled in Istanbul for one week before being deployed to various regions: "These gangs were composed of murderers and thieves who had been released from incarceration. They received a week of instruction in the courtyard of the War Ministry and were then sent to the Caucasus border through the agency of the Special Organization."[21]

The life and death of Kurdish bandit Ömerê Perîxanê illustrates this particular problem of banditry poignantly. The Kurdish Raman tribe, located roughly east of Diyarbekir city, had a tense relationship with the state in the late nineteenth century. When a major tribal chieftain passed away, among the two favorite contenders for succession were the oldest sons Ömer and Emîn, of whom Ömer was best known for his ferocity and acumen, and therefore slated for succession of leadership.[22] Before the war, this archetypal bandit had waged a campaign of plunder, bravado, and provocation of government forces. In the summer of 1914, the government declared him *persona non grata* and ordered his arrest and incarceration, but Ömer escaped prosecution and retreated far into the mountains as an outlaw. By contrast, his brother Emîn organized a paramilitary unit and in the winter of 1914 successfully fought with the Ottoman army on the Caucasus front.[23] In the spring of 1915, the Ottoman Empire was profoundly at war on three fronts, and the Armenian Genocide was about to be launched after the April 24, 1915 mass arrests and executions of Armenian elites. Right at that time, the governor of Diyarbekir, the fanatical Turkish nationalist Dr. Mehmed Reshid (1873–1919), summoned Ömer and asked him to undertake a secret mission. When the roughneck traveled to the governor's office in Diyarbekir, terrified and confused urbanites saw the outlaw and his intimidating entourage enter the city, vividly described by an Armenian witness:

Ömer was of a short stature, darkish, with smallpox scars on his face. He wore a big turban around which hung many colored silk insignias

[21] Uğur Ümit Üngör, "Paramilitary Violence in the Collapsing Ottoman Empire," in Robert Gerwarth and John Horne (eds), *War in Peace: Paramilitary Violence after the Great War* (Oxford: Oxford University Press, 2012), 162–81.
[22] Salihê Kevirbirî, *Filîtê Qûto: Serpêhatî, Dîrok, Sosyolojî* (Istanbul: Pêrî, 2001), 49–58.
[23] Hüseyin Demirer, *Ha Wer Delal: Emînê Perîxanê'nin Hayatı* (Istanbul: Avesta, 2008).

to show that he was a Kurdish chieftain. He also wore a black short tunic (locally made), long breeches, and red shoes...being armed with a Mauser rifle, two revolvers, a sword, a dagger, a *yataghan* [a short sabre], and carrying with him an enormous quantity of bullets and cartridges.[24]

When Dr. Reshid received him, he explained that the Armenians were betraying the country by helping the Russian army. The governor suggested that he would deliver to Ömer convoys of Armenians that they would escort down the Tigris on rafts, ultimately to kill them all. If Ömer agreed, he could take half of the booty seized. Absolute secrecy would be vital. Seduced by the prospect of riches and amnesty, Ömer agreed and the plan was set in motion. On May 30, 1915, Ömer's militiamen handcuffed more than 600 notables, including the Armenian bishop, sailed them downstream, moored at a bank, stripped the victims of their clothes and valuables, and massacred them, dumping their corpses in the river.[25] After the massacre, Ömer was invited to the governor's house, where they celebrated their accomplishment and sold the expensive clothing they had taken from the victims in the bazaar. Reshid also congratulated them for their "bravery, patriotism, and services to the state," and appealed to the Interior Ministry to have Ömer and his gang rewarded and awarded medals for their outstanding performances. His wish was granted by the Directorate for General Security, and the militia members received financial benefits and were decorated with medals.[26] Three other convoys followed and were destroyed in a similar way. But Ömer did not end up well: as soon as the massacring was finished, Dr. Reshid ordered his assassination, and Ömer was set upon by Reshid's agents and killed in his sleep in the late summer of 1915.[27] (His brother Emîn continued to provide similar services for the Turkish government, and would not fare well either: he was eliminated by the Kemalist government in 1933.)

---

[24] Thomas Muggerditchian, *Dikranagerdee Nahankin Tcharteru yev Kurderou Kazanioutounneru* (Cairo: Djihanian, 1919), 57–8.
[25] Uğur Ümit Üngör, "Rethinking the Violence of Pacification: State Formation and Bandits in the Young Turk Era, 1914–1937," *Comparative Studies in Society and History* 54:4 (2012), 746–69.
[26] Ibid., 755.   [27] Demirer, *Ha Wer Delal*, 87.

As this example demonstrates, cooperation between the state and bandits provided the former with an effective way of carrying out dirty jobs, while allowing the chieftains to perpetuate their own authority. From this picture of violence and counter-violence emerges an axis of tension between peripheral marginalization and state empowerment. How was it possible that in this period of crisis, bandits were among the executioners in the most secret operations but were also seen as the most insidious insurgents? In other words, the state did not necessarily clash with social bandits, but recruited them when necessary. Remarkably similar processes were underway in Greece. John Koliopoulos has demonstrated not only the collusion between classical bandits and the Greek state, but the formative nature of the bandits for state-building.[28] His conclusions on border patrolling and segmented monopolization of violence can be extended to other borderlands as well. Bandits reached the peak of their power in 1922–3, when the Greek state was struggling to hold its territories in Asia Minor against Kemalist forces. In 1925, General Pagalos consolidated his dictatorship and enlisted Ottoman-era bandits in Northern Greece as private armed forces for combating his political enemies. Spyros Tsoutsoumpis' profound research into these links reveals a fatal convergence between gangs, security services, and the political class, giving rise to new forms of criminality, no longer in remote rural backwaters but in the urban centers of Greece. Tsoutsoumpis quotes a local newspaper, which reported that "the bandits have finally left the mountains and are now comfortably situated in the towns where they hatch their plans at their own leisure—they have been transformed to a true mafia that dominates every kind of activity."[29]

The Iranian tradition of *Luti* or *Chomaqdar* consisted of rural and urban bandits. The *Luti* were groups of men organized in neighborhood associations and operating according to a clear social code of manliness (*javanmardi*). This included upholding an ethic of hard work, supporting the needy, and of course defending their neighborhood and town. *Luti*s derived their identity from their style, consumption, relationships, and most of all their potential for mobilizing violence. They would

---

[28] John S. Koliopoulos, *Brigands with a Cause: Brigandage and Irredentism in Modern Greece 1821–1912* (Oxford: Oxford University Press, 1987).
[29] Spyros Tsoutsoumpis, "'Political Bandits': Nation-Building, Patronage and the Making of the Greek Deep State," *Balkanistica* 30:1 (2017), 1–27, at 13.

wear distinctive, stylish clothing, with special objects such as chains, handkerchiefs, knives, and so on, and entertain themselves with pigeon flying, cock fighting, gambling, drinking, and speaking in a secret jargon known only to themselves. *Luti*s would invariably be found in the traditional gyms called *zurkhana* ("house of strength") to develop muscles and learn wrestling and fighting. (As this colorful lifestyle sparks the imagination, the *Luti* have indeed been immortalized in many Iranian tough-guy movies.[30]) With *Luti*s of other neighborhoods they coexisted but also fought at times, mostly due to their diverging associations with local politicians. *Luti*s were neither strictly secular nor religious; some drank, womanized, and gambled, whereas others were pious Shi'ites who prayed, chanted Shia religious lamentations, and led the Shia mourning processions in the holy month Muharram. They did not adhere to any particular ideology, left or right, except for self-aggrandizement and secur-ing their own narrow interests. Most importantly, due to their fighting skills and strong local community ties, both secular and religious political leaders utilized *Luti*s as proxies and enforcers. As Cronin argued, "banditry had possessed a symbiotic relationship with such rudimentary forces of law and order as existed on a local level... and governors might be in league with bandits, whose plunder they would share."[31] The longer these relationships persisted, the more difficult it became to control the *Luti*s, who could easily take control of an entire town. In the twentieth century, *Luti* banditry underwent a mutation from traditional banditry into modern organized crime, including smuggling and trafficking. The Iranian Revolution of 1979 split them into two, as some went to fight for the Shah, and others joined revolutionaries of various plumages.

The Caucasus is also no stranger to banditry and brigandage. The Chechen *abrek* is the Caucasian equivalent of the fearless warrior, or "brave man," abandoning worldly pleasures and making a personal commitment to banditry that could last for years, with no contact even with relatives. *Abrek*s would often be fugitives escaping vendettas and hiding in forests and mountains. Whereas the Russian political culture attached a negative meaning to the term, locals often viewed them as great

---

[30] Hamid Naficy, *A Social History of Iranian Cinema, Volume 2: The Industrializing Years, 1941–1978* (Durham, NC: Duke University Press, 2011), 267.

[31] Stephanie Cronin, *Tribal Politics in Iran: Rural Conflict and the New State, 1921–1941* (New York: Routledge, 2007), 106.

heroes standing up against foreign oppressors to restore justice, bringing in food, gold, and weapons to help poor people. *Abrek*s emerged under the impact of Russian conquest of the Caucasus and were "bound by a system of honor to refrain from killing women and children."[32] One famous *abrek* was Zelimkhan Gushmazukayev (1872–1913), who fought off Russian troops and Cossack settlers in the Chechen highlands through robbery and cattle rustling.[33] In her study of the vernacular literatures of the Caucasus in the nineteenth and twentieth centuries, Rebecca Gould asserts that the *abrek* was central to contemporary Chechen identity as it was to that of the nineteenth century. She launches the concept of transgressive sanctity: a process through which sanctity is made transgressive and transgression is made sacred through violence against the state. Violence is aestheticized and aesthetics is endowed with the capacity to generate violence, against legal norms that, because they have been illegitimately imposed, can be legitimately violated.[34] Although *abrek* culture was mostly anti-state, as it morphed into modern organized crime in the 1990s, it would be co-opted by the fledgling Chechen state under its first president Dzhokhar Dudayev (1944–1996).[35]

Mexico has perhaps one of the longest and most complex histories of social banditry, from the nineteenth-century *bandidos* to the twenty-first-century *narcos*. Mexican bandits emerged from the peasantry, mostly targeting *haciendas* and trains (which were halted and robbed), and continued their banditry activities during the Mexican Revolution, which gave it its social and political characteristics. Indeed, Mexican banditry was neither mere constant criminality nor a rudimentary form of peasant political consciousness, but a complex interplay between local politics, criminal opportunities, and civil unrest or insurgency.[36]

---

[32] Ali Askerov, *Historical Dictionary of the Chechen Conflict* (New York: Rowman & Littlefield, 2015), 32–3.

[33] Vladimir Bobrovnikov, "Bandits and the State: Designing a 'Traditional' Culture of Violence in the Russian Caucasus," in Jane Burbank, Mark Von Hagen, and A. V. Remnev (eds), *Russian Empire: Space, People, Power, 1700–1930* (Blooomington: Indiana University Press, 2007), 239–67.

[34] Rebecca Gould, "Transgressive Sanctity: The Abrek in Chechen Culture," *Kritika: Explorations in Russian and Eurasian History* 8:2 (2007), 271–306.

[35] For a thorough study of traditional banditry and modern organized crime in Chechnya, see Jeff Meyers, *The Criminal–Terror Nexus in Chechnya: A Historical, Social, and Religious Analysis* (New York: Lexington Books, 2017).

[36] Alan Knight, *The Mexican Revolution: Counter-Revolution and Reconstruction* (Omaha: University of Nebraska Press, 1990), vol. 2, 354–7.

Banditry and its domestic and international discourse stood at the center of elite and popular class attempts to imagine and construct the emerging Mexican nation state.[37] The most famous and popular heroes Pancho Villa, Chucho el Roto, and Heraclio Bernal all hail from the period of the Meixcan Revolution and new forms of state-building. Although most bandits may have been anti-establishment, many others colluded with state authorities, such as Francisco "Pancho" Villa, who was first vilified as a *bandido*, but later came to enter the pantheon of officially sanctioned heroes of the Revolution. Villa is now interred, along with other revolutionary contemporaries, in the *Monumento de la Revolución*.[38] The capacity of the Mexican state to root out all banditry was limited, and banditry modernized and adapted well to the twentieth century. The contemporary *narco* bosses can be seen as modern bandits in terms of their functions, cultures, and relationships with the state.[39] In his wide-ranging study of Latin American and especially Mexican banditry, Pascale Baker notes with irony that the traditional bandits had all been insurgents and rebels, but their contemporary counterparts have all been co-opted by local and national authorities, firmly established in the same system they had so vehemently opposed.[40]

In Turkey's *eşkiya*s, Mexico's *bandido*s, Serbia's *vojvoda*s, Ukraine's *ataman*s, banditry had existed in similar ways for centuries, and once the modern era arrived it was confronted with a modern problem: how to relate to the modern state.

The State and Crime

Dutch children of my age regularly sang this song in primary schools in the 1980s, often without a full awareness of its ramifications:

[37] Chris Frazer, *Bandit Nation: A History of Outlaws and Cultural Struggle in Mexico, 1810–1920* (Lincoln: University of Nebraska Press, 2006).

[38] Richard Slatta, "Banditry as Political Participation in Latin America," *Criminal Justice History: An International Annual* 11 (1990), 171–87.

[39] Mónica Serrano, "States of Violence: State–Crime Relations in Mexico," in Wil Pansters (ed.), *Violence, Coercion, and State-Making in Twentieth-Century Mexico* (Stanford, CA: Stanford University Press, 2012), 135–58.

[40] Pascale Baker, *Revolutionaries, Rebels and Robbers: The Golden Age of Banditry in Mexico, Latin America and the Chicano American Southwest, 1850–1950* (Cardiff: University of Wales Press, 2015), ch. 2.

Did you hear about the treasure fleet,
the silver fleet from Spain?
The ships were loaded with silver coins,
and oranges, pearls, and spices!

Piet Hein! Piet Hein! Piet Hein, his name is short,
His deeds however great, his deeds however great,
He conquered the Spanish silver fleet,
He conquered the silver, the silver fleet![41]

The folk song extols the exploits of Admiral Piet Hein (1577–1629), the privateer for the Republic during the Eighty Years' War. Hein robbed the Spanish fleet of the Silver Fleet, over 11 million guilders of booty in gold, silver, and other expensive trade goods. This early modern form of state-sponsored organized crime generated good funds for the Dutch army for a while.[42] Although this was quite common in the early modern age, toward the modern age perhaps only the historical context changed, not necessarily the structures of cooperation between crime and state.

Classical banditry and modern organized crime are varied, multidimensional phenomena, including non-state actors and outer-state actors, but as this book focuses on paramilitarism, it will look at the complex relationships between states and organized crime. The literature on organized crime has only recently begun to delve empirically and comparatively into these relations, and create a sub-literature around that theme. The dearth of literature is surprising considering the prevalence of the phenomenon in so many societies. For example, the massive *SAGE Handbook of Criminological Research Methods* does not even include a chapter on state crime, and most other discussions of the state–crime nexus by criminologists working on traditional cases of organized crime examine Italy, the United States, and Russia, bypassing many other important cases from the Global South, and even Europe

---

[41] Heb je van de zilveren vloot wel gehoord, De zilveren vloot van Spanje? Die had er veel Spaanse matten aan boord en appeltjes van Oranje! Piet Hein! Piet Hein! Piet Hein, zijn naam is klein, zijn daden bennen groot, zijn daden bennen groot. Hij heeft gewonnen de zilveren vloot. Die heeft gewonnen, gewonnen de Zilvervloot!

[42] Ronald Prud'homme van Reine, *Admiraal Zilvervloot: Biografie van Piet Hein* (Amsterdam: De Arbeiderspers, 2003).

(such as Serbia or Georgia). This section looks at two issues germane to the nature of those relations: vital distinctions between and within states, and the mutual interests and trade-offs between states and organized crime groups.

The first studies that took seriously the relationships between states and organized crime were by American sociologists who came of age in the roaring '20s and the dirty '30s. In his classic study *Organized Crime in Chicago* (1929), John Landesco wrote that "the relationship of the gangster and the politician becomes most obvious to the public on election day" and went on to examine all the types of electoral fraud that gangsters—Irish and Italians alike—commit on behalf of the politicians they support. "Post-election contests and recounts expose the election frauds committed by the gangster in [*sic*] behalf of the politicians."[43] Two years later, Walter Lippmann argued in "The Underworld as Servant" for a distinction between crime and underworld, as activities that were illegal but merely predatory versus those that were illegal but offered services to "conventionally respectable members of society," because "from among them it draws its revenues; among them it finds many of its patrons; by them it is in various ways protected." Lippmann examined the fairly extensive personal relations between certain politicians and the lords of the underworld such as Al Capone, Arnold Rothstein, and Jack Diamond, who exercised enough political influence to stay out of jail. Lippmann agreed with Landesco about reciprocal relations between gangsters and politicians finding especially fertile ground in democratic elections, as criminal gangs played a considerable part in primary elections: colonizing districts, repeating or stuffing ballot boxes, or terrorizing voters.[44]

Later generations developed these ideas. Giorgio Del Vecchio rejected the idea that the state is always the protector of law and order, and argued that it facilitated or committed a host of acts illegal by its own laws or international law, including organized crime and war crimes.[45]

---

[43] John Landesco, *Organized Crime in Chicago* (Chicago: Illinois Association for Criminal Justice, 1929), 1001.

[44] Walter Lippmann, "Underworld: Our Secret Servant," *Forum* 85 (January 1931), 1–4. Lippmann also believed that the goal pursued by gangsters, wealth and power, was shared by most Americans, including politicians, and formed the engine of Western capitalism in general. Therefore, he was not surprised by the collusion between gangsters and politicians.

[45] Giorgio Del Vecchio, "Der Staat als Verbrecher," *Archiv für Rechts- und Sozialphilosophie* 51:2 (1965), 161–5.

Throughout his career William Chambliss argued that organized crime was not at all a monopoly of the Mafia, but was rather "a political phenomenon which takes its character from the economic institutions that exist at a particular point in time." He saw organized crime as central to politics and states responsible for piracy, smuggling arms and narcotics, money laundering, and assassinations.[46] Finally, Charles Tilly famously wrote that state-making was a form of organized crime itself, and states were little more than successful crime syndicates that had monopolized violence and taxation, since much like them, states based their power on coercion, rent extraction, "protection," and extortion analogous to the dynamics of organized crime.[47] This effective metaphor can be unpacked as the relationship between states and crime is much more complex than the political buzzwords of "mafia states" in obscure areas such as Transnistria or Michoacan, which are portrayed in the media as irredeemably criminal.

The classic theory of state formation is that when a state retreats, organized crime fills the gaps. In other words, state and crime were seen as mutually exclusive in the economic and political spaces they aspire to control. But organized crime is often more complementary than exclusive, and the commonalities between the two are striking. They both claim control of a territory and impose governance and order with clear rules on its inhabitants. Beyond commonalities, there is a wide scope of forms of collusion and amalgamation between the two. Renate Bridenthal provides some examples:

> When corruption appears to stabilize states, when smuggling builds national economies, when the criminalization of cultural traditions serves imperial exploitation, when the illegal activities of diasporas support their states of origin, when states resort to breaches of their own laws in order to maintain or transform themselves, then we see how ambiguous the relationship between the state and criminal enterprises can be and how they mutually constitute each other.[48]

---

[46] William Chambliss, "State-Organized Crime," *Criminology* 27:2 (1989), 183–208.

[47] Charles Tilly, "War Making and State Making as Organized Crime," in Peter Evans et al. (eds), *Bringing the State Back In* (Cambridge: Cambridge University Press, 1985), 169–86.

[48] Renate Bridenthal, *The Hidden History of Crime, Corruption, and States* (New York: Berghahn Books, 2017), 2.

Beyond ambiguity, Achilles Batalas argued that the ideology of political elites bore importance as they could co-opt bandits, as in nineteenth-century Greece, where they were used for "irredentist adventures."[49] Taking this argument further, Alfred McCoy examined empirically how during the Cold War and its aftermath, "covert netherworlds" emerged worldwide from various political sources through a confluence of two main elements, "reliance of modern states on *covert methods for power projection* at home and abroad" and "the consequent emergence of a clandestine social milieu populated by secret services and criminal syndicates."[50] It is these social milieus that we need to understand better if we are to make sense of much pro-state paramilitarism. Much of this research also forces us to think about the state each and every time we make an attempt to study organized crime.

When we think of how crime and the state interrelate, two distinctions need to be made: regime type and institutions. There seems to be no correlation between regime type and cooperation with organized crime. Authoritarian regimes do not all necessarily co-opt criminals, and neither is democratization a panacea for transparency and distancing from organized crime. Indeed, scholars of organized crime concur that processes of democratization have unsettled low-violence equilibria that had been developed between states and criminal groups, which allowed organized crime to emerge. In particular, democratization dismantled criminal–political patronage networks, allowed mass defections of police and army to mafias, rendered politics much more competitive among increasing numbers of political elites, and finally took down state protection of organized crime.[51] "Mafias thrive in democracies," writes Federico Varese even more emphatically.[52] This might have been true for the Italian case, since Mussolini used the authoritarian Italian state that was at his disposal to fight the Sicilian Mafia, but the American

---

[49] Achilles Batalas, "Send a Thief to Catch a Thief: State-Building and the Employment of Irregular Military Formations in Mid-Nineteenth-Century Greece," in Diane Davis and Anthony Pereira (eds), *Irregular Armed Forces and their Role in Politics and State Formation* (New York: Cambridge University Press, 2002), 149–77.

[50] Alfred McCoy, "Covert Netherworld: An Invisible Interstice in the Modern World System," *Comparative Studies in Society and History* 58:4 (2016), 847–79.

[51] Stathis Kalyvas, "How Civil Wars Help Explain Organized Crime—and How They Do Not," *Journal of Conflict Resolution* 59:8 (2015), 1517–40, at 1524.

[52] Federico Varese, *Mafia Life: Love, Death and Money at the Heart of Organized Crime* (Oxford: Oxford University Press, 2018), 158–88.

authorities (notably under a Democratic government) revived the Mafia from 1944 onward. According to a popular account that arose after the end of World War II, as prime minister of the Kingdom of Italy, Mussolini had visited Sicily in May 1924 and passed through Piana dei Greci, where he was received by the mayor and Mafia boss Don Francesco Cuccia. At some point Cuccia expressed surprise at Mussolini's police escort and is said to have whispered in his ear: "You are with me, you are under my protection. What do you need all these cops for?"[53] But Don Cuccia had missed the point: not only did authoritarian Fascist Italy aim to clamp down on the Mafia, but also, alliances between states and criminals were fleeting and could change at any given moment in favor of one or another mob boss.

If we look at authoritarian regimes, they are by no means "clean." Mexico, for example, went through a process in which "the war on banditry reinforced an authoritarian and coercive reflex in Mexican statecraft."[54] Even though levels of crime inside the Socialist Federal Republic of Yugoslavia were very low, Tito's socialist authoritarian regime forged a significant number of alliances with known criminals, such as Arkan, Giška, and Karate Bob. The Yugoslav secret service, UDBA, co-opted these men and tasked them to assassinate certain influential exiles in Western Europe.[55] Argentina under General Videla, too, worked closely with pre-existing crime groups, large and small. There was deep collusion between the general's regime and individual convicted criminals, as well as the kidnapping ring of the Puccio family, which helped the secret service abduct, disappear, and murder opposi-tionists in the 1970s. These events were vividly portrayed in the movies *El Secreto de sus Ojos* and *El Clan*, respectively.[56] So, too, in El Salvador in the 1980s, extreme-right military officer and death-squad leader

---

[53] John Dickie, *Cosa Nostra: A History of the Sicilian Mafia* (New York: St. Martin's Press, 2015), 152.
[54] Frazer, *Bandit Nation*, 21.
[55] See e.g. Slobodan Mitrić, *Tito's moordmachine* (St. Willebrord: Karate Europa, 1982).
[56] Rodolfo Palacios, *El clan Puccio* (Buenos Aires: Planeta, 2015). In one gripping scene in *El secreto de sus ojos*, a scarred veteran police chief (Ricardo Darín) and a young idealistic prosecutor (Soledad Villamil) walk into the office of the Minister of Justice, complaining that they are being obstructed in their pursuit of justice for the victim of a rape, whose perpetrator is working for the government's death squads. The minister curtly explains to them that Argentina is under a "new order" and that the more important struggle is against the "subversives" and Communists. When the demoralized duo leaves, they are confronted in the elevator with that very rapist, who casually steps in, pulls out his gun, loads it, and places it back into his holster.

Roberto D'Aubuisson ran a kidnapping-for-profit ring with a motley crew of criminals.[57] All in all, authoritarian regimes do not seem to be immune to criminal ties. In fact, because these regimes uphold a "tough-on-crime" image, long periods of imprisonment expose criminals to prolonged intensive contact with law enforcement. This facilitates recruitment networks as contacts predate ethno-political conflicts.

When analyzing the phenomenon of organized crime, most studies tend to employ two diverging perspectives: either one revolving around security, or one based on a problem of weakness in public institutions. Institutions are a second problem in understanding these relations, especially distinctions *within* governments *between* the agencies of the state: the ministries, secretariats, departments, commissariats, and other physical organs and staffing of the state. We should not conceptualize the modern state as the monolithic Leviathan, but as an ensemble and set of institutions, "the humanly devised constraints that structure political, economic, and social interaction. They consist of both informal constraints (sanctions, taboos, customs, traditions, and codes of conduct), and formal rules (constitutions, laws, property rights)."[58] Institutions are thought to have been devised by human societies to create order and reduce uncertainty. They govern the relationships between state agencies, and they are vulnerable to influence by organized crime. Organized crime is keen to occupy the interstices of states that have suffered institutional fragmentation, in very diverse countries.[59] Kauzlarich, Mullins, and Matthews follow this line of thought and argue that "criminality will not spring from a lack of access to social resources, but from having excessive control over social resources—specifically full access to and control of key social institutions."[60] Paoli's most central conclusion on the Italian case was that "the most durable and powerful Italian mafia associations—the Sicilian Cosa Nostra and the Calabrian 'Ndrangheta, upon which our attention will be largely focused—are those that have

[57] Bruce Campbell and Arthur Brenner (eds), *Death Squads in Global Perspective* (New York: Palgrave Macmillan, 2000), 99.

[58] Douglass North, "Institutions," *Journal of Economic Perspectives* 5:1 (1991), 97–112, at 97.

[59] Ivan Briscoe and Pamela Kalkman, *The New Criminal Powers: The Spread of Illicit Links to Politics across the World and How it can be Tackled* (The Hague: Clingendael Institute, 2016), 23.

[60] David Kauzlarich, Christopher Mullins, and Rick Matthews, "A Complicity Continuum of State Crime," *Contemporary Justice Review* 6:3 (2003), 241–54, at 242.

been able to infiltrate state institutions most deeply."[61] Green and Ward represent an approach that builds on the notion that organized crime is most prevalent in societies characterized by clientelism and patrimonialism.[62] In patrimonial regimes, strong personal relations between heads of agencies often weaken mechanisms of oversight and create opportunities for powerful men in security forces to forge relationships with criminals.

Much corruption is found in complex, opaque business arrangements and contracts, where the apparatus of law and state power both disguises and facilitates a joint criminal enterprise. Among these opportunity structures emerges a nebulous gray zone which facilitates crimes of omission *and* commission, such as lack of bureaucratic oversight, tacit encouragement, and active neglect. But how does party politics influence the interplay between organized crime and the state? Castells wrote in *The Information Age*:

> Besides the ability of criminals to bribe and/or intimidate police, judges, and government officials, there is a more insidious and devastating penetration: the corruption of democratic politics. *The increasingly important financial needs of political candidates and parties create a golden opportunity for organized crime to offer support in critical moments of political campaigns...* Furthermore, the domination of the democratic process by scandal politics, character assassination, and image-making also offers organized crime a privileged terrain of political influence.[63]

The fragmentation of political parties, opaque rules of financing, and democratic competition in general creates incentives for politicians to see the state as a resource and to distribute key bureaucratic posts among their networks and relationships. Since all support is welcome in this grab for power, this leads to an "exchange of services" between criminals and politicians, and the politicization of the state's bureaucracies once in

---

[61] Letizia Paoli, "The Political–Criminal Nexus in Italy," *Trends in Organized Crime* 5:2 (1999), 15–58, at 15.

[62] Penny Green and Tony Ward, *State Crime: Governments, Violence and Corruption* (London: Pluto Press, 2004).

[63] Manuel Castells, *The Rise of the Network Society: The Information Age* (Oxford: Blackwell, 1996), 211, emphasis added.

power. Indeed, "mafia leaders deploy money bribes, they are more likely to ingratiate themselves with political, economic, and religious elites by mediating local elections."[64] Bulgaria is a very good example of the state–crime nexus, because the country has close connections between state institutions (at all levels) and organized crime (in all formats), but did not experience war, like Yugoslavia. Researchers on the symbiosis between organized crime and the Bulgarian state concluded that it is a "result from the unfinished transition to democracy and the delayed reforms in former secret services," especially the lack of democratic-institutional oversight and accountability of security services.[65] Italy is another excellent example: the influence of the 'Ndrangheta can be mostly explained by its skillful capacity to form and maintain lasting collusion with locally dominant political parties, through a combination of veiled threats or economic connivance. The social capital that Mafia families accumulate through years of relationships facilitates access to public contracts, footholds in power in Rome, and control over their territories.[66]

Shared Interests and Trade-Offs

What do states and organized crime stand to gain from one another? Marcus Felson's notion that "the Underworld depends on the Upperworld" is historically accurate.[67] As Thomas Gallant pointed out in his broad overview of brigandage, piracy, capitalism, and state formation, "out-laws...were deeply implicated in the processes of state formation and state consolidation. They became embroiled in peasant mass movements, rebellions, and even revolutions against governments and the authorities, or they participated in power struggles between big men."[68] In other words, Felson's proposition also works the other way around: the

---

[64] Schneider and Schneider, "The Anthropology of Crime and Criminalization," 363.

[65] Center for the Study of Democracy, *Partners in Crime: The Risks of Symbiosis between the Security Sector and Organized Crime in Southeast Europe* (Sofia: CSD, 2004), 95.

[66] Rocco Sciarrone, "Mafia and Civil Society: Economico-Criminal Collusion and Territorial Control in Calabria," in Jean-Louis Briquet and Gilles Favarel-Garrigues (eds), *Organized Crime and States: The Hidden Face of Politics* (New York: Palgrave, 2010), 173–96.

[67] Marcus Felson, *The Ecosystem for Organized Crime*, HEUNI Paper 26 (Helsinki: The European Institute for Crime Prevention and Control, 2006), 15.

[68] Thomas Gallant, "Brigandage, Piracy, Capitalism, and State-Formation: Transnational Crime from a Historical World-Systems Perspective," in Josiah Heyman (ed.), *States and Illegal Practices* (New York: Berg, 1999), 25–61.

Upperworld also depends on the Underworld. Let us look at the state first, and then turn to the criminals.

What do states get out of relations with crime? Or to be more precise: how and why do politicians benefit from criminals, and vice versa? An early example is the collusion, in the United States of the 1930s, between the Office of Naval Intelligence and waterfront racketeers to undermine the influence of labor unions and communist sympathizers. It demonstrates that it is relevant to examine the links between intelligence agencies and organized crime "when such an alliance serves the interests of each party."[69] Politicians co-opting criminals and criminal networks is often reduced to financial explanations.[70] Fair enough, the magnitude of the phenomenon cannot be underestimated. In the mid-1990s, organized crime was controlling around 40 percent of Russia's GDP,[71] and the post-Soviet "thieves-in-law" (*vory v zakonè*) controlled innumerable legal businesses and had direct access to federal, regional, and local budgetary resources.[72] Around the same time, almost half of all Colombian elected officials were estimated to be in the pockets of one or another cartel, with untold millions of dollars flowing between them. The leaders of the Medellín and Calí cartels would negotiate from a position of strength with Colombian state officials rather than be criminalized by them.[73] However, it seems rather obvious that the nexus of politics and crime is about more than money in politics, and includes power balances (both in politics and crime), territorial control, and evolutions in criminal practice. US policies in Cuba encapsulate these three elements well. In February 1961, William Harvey (CIA head in Cuba) and Richard Bissell (CIA deputy director of operations) met to plan the assassination of Fidel Castro by outsourcing it to Mafia hitmen. The (failed) assassination

[69] Alan A. Block, "A Modern Marriage of Convenience: A Collaboration between Organized Crime and U.S. Intelligence," in Robert J. Kelly (ed.), *Organized Crime: A Global Perspective* (Totowa, NJ: Rowman & Littlefield, 1986), 58–77.

[70] See e.g. Joseph Serio, *Investigating the Russian Mafia: An Introduction for Students, Law Enforcement, and International Business* (Durham, NC: Carolina Academic Press, 2008), 175–203.

[71] Yuriy A. Voronin, "The Emerging Criminal State: Economic and Political Aspects of Organized Crime in Russia," in Phil Williams (ed.), *Russian Organized Crime: The New Threat?* (London: Frank Cass, 1997), 53–62.

[72] Gilles Favarel-Garrigues, "Mafia Violence and Political Power in Russia," in Jean-Louis Briquet and Gilles Favarel-Garrigues (eds), *Organized Crime and States: The Hidden Face of Politics* (London: Palgrave, 2010), 147–71.

[73] Aldo Civico, *The Para-State: An Ethnography of Colombia's Death Squads* (Berkeley: University of California Press, 2015), 31.

plot would eliminate Castro, open up Cuba for US infiltration, and offer the Mafia new markets.[74]

The days when banditry and state-building developed through ceremonial gift-giving and patronage, traditional forms of political intercourse that did not necessarily amount to forms of mass bribery and organized nepotism, are over. It is undeniable that global criminal revenue has increased significantly, both in gross terms and as a share of the world economy, thereby increasing the risks of criminal influence over politics and eroding traditional institutions of legitimate authority. States build political authority and develop their legal economies by periodically allying with organized crime. As Reno has shown, drug and diamond smuggling has become central to state-building in many post-colonial African countries.[75] Criminal organizations are also coveted by states if there are particularly sensitive tasks that need to be undertaken, which necessitate the trust that characterizes interpersonal relationships within criminal groups. States then select criminals for their skills and know-how, including of course various forms of violence, easy access to money, building patronage networks, and so on.[76] Prisons are readily available repositories of criminals with highly useful skill sets, including kidnapping, smuggling, command of international money flows, environmental and wildlife crime, robbery, homicide, hostage taking for ransom, theft, identity theft, prostitution, drugs, corruption, counter-feiting, human trafficking, street racketeering, and much more. It is the conjoining of interests and alignment of objectives that produces tem-porary but destructive forms of violence as a trade-off between the state and organized crime. These relationships are mutually beneficial, because they allow criminal groups to pursue and achieve a range of objectives.

So what do criminals aspire to gain from relationships with the state? There is a lot to profit from, but the two main ways that criminals intend to benefit from the state are power as an end, and power as a means for other ends (mostly financial).

---

[74] Timothy Melley, *The Covert Sphere: Secrecy, Fiction, and the National Security State* (Ithaca, NY: Cornell University Press, 2012), 18.

[75] William Reno, "Clandestine Economies, Violence and States in Africa," *Journal of International Affairs* 53 (2000), 433–59.

[76] For a discussion of patronage networks, called *krysha* in Russian, see Vadim Volkov, *Violent Entrepreneurs: The Use of Force in the Making of Russian Capitalism* (Ithaca, NY: Cornell University Press, 2002), 167ff.

Criminals and criminal networks, including a range of "interface actors," such as lawyers, accountants, shadow intermediaries, brokers, financiers, and front companies, attempt to embrace politicians mostly for the acquisition of power.[77] Consolidation and perpetuation of a power base is their primary concern. For example, the Italian 'Ndrangheta is famous for its highly intelligent capacity to form and maintain lasting collusion with local political and economic actors.[78] Another major concern for them is impunity. Criminals in Yugoslavia (and later in Serbia) wanted nothing more than to be released from prison in the 1970s to expunge their criminal records and curry favor with the state. Therefore, as Naim rightly argues, "police departments, secret services, courts, local and provincial governments, passport-issuing agencies, and customs offices have all become coveted targets for criminal takeovers."[79] Criminals covet having law enforcement officers on their payroll for counter-intelligence on their criminal competitors and prosecutors' offices designs and actions. Criminals can also make themselves available for states to legitimize their current activities or future career moves. Building social capital with state actors gives them immense advantages over their competitors. For example, the powerful Chinese warlord Feng Yu-Hsiang, who was active in the 1920s, regulated his relationship with the state so that he gradually acquired a monopoly of force and eliminated competition.[80] Another famous example is the role of the Shanghai "Green Gang" in supporting Chiang Kai-shek and the Kuomintang dictatorship in 1927:

In return for their help in eliminating the Communist Party and union organizations in Shanghai, Chiang not only gave the Green Gang and its most prominent leader, Du Yue-Sheng, free reign in Shanghai's

[77] Phil Williams, "Organizing Transnational Crime: Networks, Markets and Hierarchies," in Dimitri Vlassis and Phil Williams (eds), *Combating Transnational Crime: Concepts, Activities and Responses* (London: Frank Cass, 2001), 57–87.

[78] Rocco Sciarrone, "'Ndrangheta: A Reticular Organization," in Nicoletta Serenata (ed.), *The 'Ndrangheta and Sacra Corona Unita: The History, Organization and Operations of Two Unknown Mafia Groups* (New York: Springer, 2014), 81–99.

[79] Moisés Naím, "Mafia States: Organized Crime Takes Office," *Foreign Affairs* (May/June 2012), at https://www.foreignaffairs.com/articles/2012-04-20/mafia-states (accessed July 17, 2018).

[80] Phil Billingsley, *Bandits in Republican China* (Stanford, CA: Stanford University Press, 1988); James E. Sheridan, *Chinese Warlord: The Career of Feng Yu-Hsiang* (Stanford, CA: Stanford University Press, 1966).

underworld and the narcotics trade, gang members also became officers and members of the Nationalist army and police.[81]

State–crime relations operate differently at different levels: leading politicians will be in contact with top crime bosses, one rung lower one can find mid-level bureaucrats liaising with wholesale dealers and organizers, and at the bottom of the hierarchy there are ordinary police officers in daily contact with street gangs and thugs, in or out prison.

To understand the second way that criminals benefit from the state one has to follow the money. Karstedt emphatically argued that "corruption has become the main portal through which organized criminal groups have associated with an array of state and security officials in the construction of illicit networks."[82] The collapse of the Soviet Union is an excellent example of the rise of mafia networks that had immense influence over the state. Russian mafias especially penetrated the KGB to gain access to sophisticated communication equipment, including computers and the latest military and intelligence technology. The concepts of "security market" and "violent entrepreneurs" have been used in analyses of Russia in the 1990s,[83] where entire ammunition dumps were disappearing and blanket privatization was also affecting the security sector.[84] In Colombia, the two main cartels (Medellín and Cali) each developed ties with the army, paramilitary groups, and the police, to compete against each other: protect their investments, channel their funds, and develop intelligence capacities.[85] Extortion, trade in illegal goods and services—these can function as a re-ordering of the market. Criminal actors organize the type of crime that a particular historical moment in state formation offers, such as municipal elections, labor union regulations, or economic competition of companies. In a way, organized crime groups are much like any other political lobby groups,

---

[81] Alfredo Schulte-Bockholt, *The Politics of Organized Crime and the Organized Crime of Politics: A Study in Criminal Power* (New York: Lexington Books, 2006), 90.

[82] Susanne Karstedt, "Organizing Crime: The State as Agent," in Letizia Paoli (ed.), *The Oxford Handbook of Organized Crime* (Oxford: Oxford University Press, 2014), 303–20, at 313.

[83] See also Molly Dunigan and Ulrich Petersohn (eds), *The Markets for Force: Privatization of Security across World Regions* (Philadelphia: University of Pennsylvania Press, 2015); Volkov, *Violent Entrepreneurs*.

[84] Martin McCauley, *Bandits, Gangsters and the Mafia: Russia, the Baltic States and the CIS since 1991* (London: Routledge, 2014), 223.

[85] Patrick Clawson and Rensselaer Lee, *The Andean Cocaine Industry* (London: Palgrave, 1996), 176.

as they try to influence legislation and state policies to their own benefit, especially those that relate to the drug trade. Farer even argued that "narcos" are frequently the principal source of election funding in some Latin American countries.[86] In other words, organized crime is a fundamentally historical process with peaks and troughs, as are ties between crime and states. Two common examples at different historical moments and places demonstrate this well: Pablo Escobar and El Chapo Guzman.

The most (in)famous drug baron in the twentieth century is arguably Pablo Escobar (1949–1993), subject of a large number of fictional and non-fictional books, films, and series. Whereas the charm of these forms of popular representation comes from the danger of violence and risk of drug smuggling, what set Escobar apart from many other drug lords was that he made considerable efforts to seek political office. Not only did he set up his own political movement Civismo en Marcha (Citizenship on the March), he also successfully ran for membership of the Colombian congress. According to his brother's memoirs, Escobar was obsessed with gaining political immunity against extradition in order to protect and expand his empire.[87] A similar process has been ongoing in Mexico, where drug cartels influence the state at all levels of government: municipal, state, and federal. Cartels buy this influence in order for state officials to engage in crimes of commission and omission, for example by bribing local police officials to carry out, prevent, or disregard a murder. The painstaking, dangerous research by Mexican investigative journalists has exposed a spectrum of collusion of larger-than-life cartel kingpins such as El Chapo with various levels of government. Joaquín Guzmán, also known as El Chapo ("Shorty"), has bribed every level of the Mexican government to safeguard his interests: the Drug Enforcement Administration by offering them the revenue of the drug trade through his tunnels, the local officials of Guaymas city's Department of Planning to set up a secret airstrip in the south of Sonora state, and prison guards to escape from federal maximum-security prisons.[88] Before his arrest and extradition, El Chapo's elusiveness from law enforcement made him

---

[86] Tom J. Farer (ed), *Transnational Organized Crime in the Americas* (New York: Routledge, 1999), 289.

[87] Roberto Escobar Gaviria, *The Accountant's Story: Inside the Violent World of the Medellín Cartel* (New York: Grand Central Publishing, 2009), 185.

[88] Anabel Hernandez, *Narcoland: The Mexican Drug Lords and their Godfathers* (London: Verso, 2014), 6, 171, 194–7.

a legendary figure in Mexico's narcotics folklore, a modern social bandit like few others. For example, he would stroll into a restaurant, his body-guards confiscating people's mobile phones, the boss would eat his meal and leave after paying everyone's tab.[89] For all of his collusion with politicians and government officials, El Chapo was not interested in gaining political power, but maintaining respectability, preserving his assets, and developing his activities. Escobar and El Chapo may well have been crime bosses, but they had different ties to the state, different political ambitions, and different ends to their careers.

In a focused report on criminalization of states, Briscoe and Kalkman characterized their relationships as "mercurial" and "opportunistic."[90] But these relationships are also structural and long-lasting. Schulte-Bockholt conceptualized the development of criminal organizations in terms of their politicization: the more criminals seek to inject themselves into existing structures of political power, the more entrenched they become, up to the point of symbiosis.[91] Von Lampe uses three ideal-type forms to think through the relationships between organized crime and government: evasion, corruption, and confrontation.[92] Roy Godson posited the state and crime as fundamental opposites that compete for a zero-sum political and economic space which stretches out in between them, in which "[s]ometimes the politicians will dominate, sometimes the criminals." The more influence of the one, the less of the other, and vice versa.[93] Kupatadze used a similar, binary spectrum in which on the one end of the continuum, there is elite dominance, and on the other lies underworld dominance. In between there is a range of activities on a dotted line, with the notion of "state capture" representing the co-optation of state institutions by organized crime groups.[94] In a wide-ranging study of the relationships between states and crime, Cockayne identified six

---

[89]   Patrick Radden Keefe, "The Hunt for El Chapo," *The New Yorker*, May 5, 2014.
[90]   Briscoe and Kalkman, *The New Criminal Powers*, 15.
[91]   Schulte-Bockholt, *The Politics of Organized Crime and the Organized Crime of Politics*, 22.
[92]   Klaus von Lampe, *Organized Crime: Analyzing Illegal Activities, Criminal Structures, and Extra-legal Governance* (London: SAGE, 2015), 265.
[93]   Roy Godson (ed.), *Menace to Society: Political–Criminal Collaboration around the World* (London: Transaction, 2003), 5.
[94]   Alexander Kupatadze, *Organized Crime, Political Transitions and State Formation in Post-Soviet Eurasia* (London: Palgrave, 2012). So whereas under Boris Yeltsin, the criminals were influencing the state (left pole), under Vladimir Putin the uncompromising reassertion of state authority meant that no challenges to the government were to be accepted (right pole). See Mark Galeotti, *Vory: Russia's Super Mafia* (New Haven, CT: Yale University Press, 2018), 117–18.

distinct positioning strategies that criminal organizations adopt when competing with states in a "market for government": (1) intermediation (used by mafias); (2) autonomy (used by warlords and gang rulers); (3) mergers (joint ventures with states); (4) strategic alliances in competitions against other political and/or criminal actors; (5) terrorism as a criminal strategy; and (6) relocation or blue ocean strategy.[95] Finally, Lupsha developed a highly useful three-stage evolutionary paradigm to explain crime–state relations: a predatory stage when crime uses violence to gain power, a parasitical stage in which prohibitions, sanctions, and war offer conditions conducive for criminality, and a symbiotic stage in which "organised crime has become a part of the state; a state within a state."[96]

These studies all demystify and enlighten aspects of the map. However, they do not necessarily answer the question which forces propel a move to the left or a push to the right. Furthermore, can we argue that the deeper the symbiosis, the more painful it will become to excise the criminals' hold over the state? Most importantly, things change in war. What the above approaches have in common is their neglect of the fact that in state–crime relations, both actors work toward a limited win-win situation (a trade-off). We are not dealing with a weakening of the state when organized crime is strong, or vice versa, a weakening of the mafia when the state is strong. Rather, we often see their simultaneous strengthening: these ties expand the power of the state into the illegal and illegitimate domain, and they accord a legitimacy to and normalization of organized crime structures that would have been unthinkable and impossible otherwise. In other words, it is a true win-win situation, especially during wars and civil wars.

War and Crime

Crime occurs both in peacetime and wartime. However, it has different functions, forms, and public perceptions. In peacetime, the law is seen

[95] James Cockayne, *Hidden Power: The Strategic Logic of Organized Crime* (Oxford: Oxford University Press, 2016).
[96] Peter A. Lupsha, "Transnational Organized Crime versus the Nation-State," in *Transnational Organized Crime* 2 (1996), 21–48.

as legitimate and most violations therefore as immoral and illegitimate and therefore subject to punishment. When it comes to war, it depends very much on the legitimacy or justness of that war for certain crimes to be perceived similarly or differently. If wartime circumstances such as scarcity of goods or persecution of population sectors change existing notions of right and wrong, public expectations of justice can be affected. Thus, the same crimes of smuggling, theft, or murder will be assessed as "rightful resistance" depending on the subjective moral positions of perpetrators and victims, because categories of crime are social constructs after all. Wartime circumstances can stretch, contract, or distort views on right and wrong in relation to crime, as a result of which notions of morality and criminality can be divorced or merged in new ways. In a penetrating study of the ties between organized crime and the state in the Balkans, Mappes-Niediek writes about peace criminals (*Friedensverbrecher*) and war criminals (*Kriegsverbrecher*) as inhabiting the same criminal microcosm, but in a different universe. A privately or politically motivated murder can be seen as an abhorrent crime in peacetime, but as an obligatory killing of an enemy in conditions of war.[97] Most of all, criminal activities need violence: provision of security around drug labs or brothels, the vehicles transporting illegal drugs and money, the collection of unpaid debt, the elimination of rivals, and confrontations or negotiations with the police. In any case, all require the service of armed individuals, which is hugely facilitated by civil war, as countless heavily armed young men are roaming the country.

In at least three relevant ways, crime and war are related, often under the broad rubric of "criminalization." First, criminals can use war or an overarching violent political conflict as an opportunity to pursue new objectives or the usual economic benefits of illegal markets. Second, states use (civil) wars to pursue illegitimate objectives that are lost in the "fog" or "organized chaos" of war. Third, criminals can flee *from* or *to* a country to escape or hide from punishment, thereby unsettling existing forms of law enforcement; they are then rarely chased down by an overwhelmed state involved in running a counter-insurgency, or are shielded by an indifferent or proactively protective state.

---

[97] Norbert Mappes-Niediek, *Balkan-Mafia: Staaten in der Hand des Verbrechens—Eine Gefahr für Europa* (Berlin: Ch. Links Verlag, 2011).

So far, this chapter has focused on organized crime in peacetime and its relations to state-building. But how do these processes shift in a context of war or civil war? First and foremost, it is clear that insurgencies and organized crime share some important characteristics:

> They are 1) involved in illegal activities and frequently need the same supplies; 2) exploit excessive violence and the threat of violence; 3) commit kidnappings, assassinations and extortion; 4) act in secrecy; 5) challenge the state and the laws (unless they are state funded); 6) have back up leaders and foot soldiers; 7) are exceedingly adaptable, open to innovations, and are flexible; 8) threaten global security; 9) quitting the group can result in deadly consequences for former members.[98]

Both rebel groups and organized crime groups are involved in illegal markets in order to extract economic benefits to finance their activities. Both effectively challenge the state's monopoly of violence. Furthermore, Jasmin Hristov argues that conceptualizations of paramilitarism need to avoid two fallacies: one is to equate paramilitarism with drug trafficking, the other is to conceptualize the two as mutually exclusive categories of violence. She argues that political violence and criminal violence are closely related, especially embodied by a variety of "illegal armed actors, such as private justice groups, self-defence forces, death squads, and paramilitary groups, none of whom aim to take over state power."[99] Indeed, there are many cases in which there is no relationship between organized crime and armed conflict, such as in Bolivia and Morocco. However, whereas their means might be similar, their goals are definitely not. Kalyvas disputes the notion that civil war and organized crime are interchangeable, synonymous, or even congruous phenomena, arguing that neither "civil war as organized crime," nor "organized crime as civil war" works in meaningful ways, adding: "Unlike an effective rebel group, which is either a group that succeeds in overthrowing a government or keep[s] surviving and fighting, an effective criminal group is

---

[98] Mitchel Roth and Murat Sever, "The Kurdish Workers Party (PKK) as Criminal Syndicate: Funding Terrorism through Organized Crime, a Case Study," *Studies in Conflict and Terrorism* 30:10 (2007), 903.

[99] Jasmin Hristov, *Paramilitarism and Neoliberalism: Violent Systems of Capital Accumulation in Colombia and Beyond* (London: Pluto, 2014), 31.

one that manages to transform itself while maintaining the capacity to profit from its core business."[100] Instead, he identifies four areas of cross-fertilization between organized crime studies and civil war studies: onset and termination, organization, combat and violence, and governance and territory. Both organized crime conflicts and civil wars consist of explicitly *organized* forms of violence, with significant levels of potential upscaling (from the local to the national). This applies also to paramilitary groups. Much like how these groups emerge in civil wars, they also do so during organized crime wars, as in the Mexican state of Michoacán.[101] These comparisons of organized crime and civil war from a phenomenological perspective lead us to the question of how organized crime changes due to violent conflict.

The key shift in wartime is, according to Varese: "In a time of war, security trumps legality."[102] Security is about predictability, and organized crime figures or paramilitaries are capricious rather than predictable. Nevertheless, both are used by states in (civil) wars. How? First and foremost, we must depart from the notion that civil wars are historical processes, with relatively clear, distinguishable phases, even if they differ from conflict to conflict. Following Kalyvas, let us start with the onset of the cooperation between crime and state during civil wars. In areas rife with organized crime, it is to be expected that the dynamics of a civil war would incorporate and integrate those criminal activities. For example, the Segovias region in Nicaragua, well before any violent conflict, was infamous for being "a haven for smugglers, outlaws, and bandits, as a crucible for rebellions against the national state, and as a conduit for revolutionary armies and movements..." It was no surprise then that criminalized paramilitarism became rampant during the civil war of the 1980s: pro-government paramilitaries such as Juan Butón, a notorious rapist and murderer allied with the conservative elite in the Segovias region, was released from prison and resumed his criminal career, this time under the cloak of "counterinsurgency." Butón enlisted local criminals and brigands who robbed, raped, and murdered opponents

---

[100] Kalyvas, "How Civil Wars Help Explain Organized Crime," 1527.
[101] Romain Le Cour Grandmaison, "Armed Militias: For a State Strategy in Michoacan, Mexico" (July 9, 2014), at https://www.noria-research.com/armed-militias-for-a-state-strategy-in-michoacan/ (accessed November 30, 2018).
[102] Varese, *Mafia Life*, 186.

of the government.[103] A similar argument can be made about Yugoslavia in the 1990s: the leaders of paramilitary groups

> were often ex-emigré gangsters who had been sent abroad during the 1970s and 1980s by the federal intelligence services to infiltrate and harass political opposition groups. They returned in the late 1980s and early 1990s, pushed by law enforcement crackdowns in Western Europe and pulled by the opportunities for business created by the collapse of the Yugoslav federal state. Back home they had two functions. One was carrying out sensitive jobs for the Serbian secret police…the second was organizing paramilitary forces to fight in Croatia and Bosnia.[104]

Wars are also often accompanied by international embargos and sanctions. The international community, in good faith, imposed comprehensive sanctions on Yugoslavia, thereby unintentionally facilitating collusion between criminals and the rump Yugoslav state under Slobodan Milošević. His regime even organized a special evasion apparatus for sanction busting through Cypriot banks. The objective of the collusion in this phase was to generate revenue, for example through importing precious metals, and secure supplies through smuggling; its consequences were a flourishing black market, and a nouveau riche elite consisting of war profiteers.[105] Roughly around the same time, the Nagorno-Karabakh war saw similar conditions, when the blockade of Armenia by Azerbaijan and Turkey disrupted "trade and transport routes, cut key energy links, and…culminated in severe shortages of food, electricity, fuel, and other critical products and consumer goods." As a result, the struggling Armenian state was unable to mitigate the overall scarcity, and therefore resorted to the support of organized crime bosses. These "oligarchs" then also began supplying the Armenian army and paramilitary groups.[106]

---

[103] Campbell and Brenner, *Death Squads in Global Perspective*, 31.
[104] Tom Naylor, *Patriots and Profiteers: Economic Warfare, Embargo Busting, and State-Sponsored Crime* (Montreal: MQUP, 2008), 351.
[105] Ibid., XIV, 352. Naylor rightly points out the paradox that after the war, "that same international community blames organised crime and corruption for blocking much needed reforms."
[106] Richard Giragosian, "The Armenian Imperative: Confronting and Containing Oligarchs," in Mehran Kamrava (ed.), *The Great Game in West Asia: Iran, Turkey and the South Caucasus* (London: Hurst, 2017), 205–28.

The oligarchs controlled the Armenian economy, and even left an imprint on the capital's architecture. Standing on any high point, looking over the city, one can see two high towers dominating Yerevan's skyline: an impressive, limestone clock tower that is the city municipality, and right across the street, an even higher sandstone tower of a brandy wine fac tory that doubles as the unofficial headquarters of Gagik Tsarukyan (a.k.a. Dodi Gago), a major oligarch and member of parliament who is arguably more influential in Armenian politics and government than the municipality.[107]

Collusion between states and criminals also occurs when states release criminals from prisons to fight at the front, or commit violence against civilians. Various governments have used agents provocateurs from the criminal underworld, habitual criminals, but also professional ones with nationwide tentacles. These groups were promiscuous in reaching out to political patrons, and vice versa: many political patrons used more than one group.[108] Anti-communist vigilantes in the Philippines, for example, were often ex-convicts or convicts still offi-cially in prison.[109] Small-time criminals are often released by the state, whereas big fish work for themselves or are not roped in fully. The emer-gence of state-sponsored paramilitary groups during the Yugoslav wars of dissolution in the 1990s can be traced back to the Yugoslav security services' co-optation of over one hundred criminals for political assas-sinations abroad. The regime of Slobodan Milošević, particularly its Interior Ministry and party, were key in facilitating personal ties between major criminals and security officials.[110] These collaborations are very profitable from an economic perspective as well: criminals do not necessarily need salaries, because they have experience of being "self-funded" through looting and rent-seeking. One could even argue that the outsourcing of violence to paramilitaries is criminogenic in itself: no longer receiving a state salary or pension, paramilitaries can draw upon the illegal economy as a resource, thereby blurring the boundaries

---

[107] Armine Ishkanian, *Democracy Building and Civil Society in Post-Soviet Armenia* (London: Routledge, 2008), 43.

[108] Campbell and Brenner, *Death Squads in Global Perspective*, 185.

[109] Ronald James May, *Vigilantes in the Philippines: From Fanatical Cults to Citizens' Organizations* (Mānoa: University of Hawai'i at Mānoa, 1992).

[110] Christian Axboe Nielsen, "War Crimes and Organized Crime in the Former Yugoslavia," *Suedosteuropa-Mitteilungen* 52:3 (2012), 6–17.

between criminals and paramilitaries. In the South Sudan conflicts, this has resulted in a veritable social class formation, as state–crime collusion and mobilization has enriched the groups involved in unprecedented ways.[111] Collaboration of states with criminals during wars can also be a response to rebels' collusion with organized crime as they desperately try to fund their insurgency. For example, the Kurdish PKK, the Revolutionary Armed Forces of Colombia (FARC), the Albanian Kosovo Liberation Army (UÇK), the Afghan Taliban, and the Irish IRA were all involved in various ways with organized crime to raise money, for example through trafficking or racketeering.[112] Consequently, the Turkish, Colombian, Serbian, Afghan, and Irish governments too became entangled in organized crime during the counter-insurgencies. Police and criminals are in close contact and exchange over decades, but when an external political group appears to threaten that order, the dyadic relationship changes into a triadic relationship as the insurgency drives the state and organized crime together. Furthermore, there is an inter-state aspect to it as well: cooperating with organized crime can also be part of competition *between* states. Since organized crime figures operate transnationally, they can be used as a source of leverage between states. If one state decides not to employ criminals for particular tasks, but a rival neighboring state does, the latter stands to benefit from its criminal ties and expands its capacity. For example, Chechen criminals who move between the Caucasus and Anatolia are a potential asset to both Russia and Turkey, and can be used as a covert tool for the darker aspects of their respective foreign policies.[113]

The onset of war can empower criminals and criminalize a conflict, but so can the course of a war. Criminals make smart use of war zones, sieges, and new boundaries to eke out new legal and illegal markets.

---

[111] Clémence Pinaud, "South Sudan: Civil War, Predation and the Making of a Military Aristocracy," *African Affairs* 113:451 (2014), 192–211.

[112] Schneider and Schneider, "The Anthropology of Crime and Criminalization," 360. See also Varese, *Mafia Life*, 186.

[113] Mark Galeotti, "Gangster Geopolitics: The Kremlin's Use of Criminals as Assets Abroad," *Moscow Times*, January 18, 2019, at https://themoscowtimes.com/articles/gangster-geopolitics-the-kremlins-use-of-criminals-as-assets-abroad-64204 (accessed April 16, 2019). Galeotti adds: "Some elements of Russian state cooperation with criminal networks can, like the American examples above, be seen in military conflicts, declared or not: In Ukraine, for example, local gangsters in Crimea allegedly provided muscle as so-called "self-defense volunteers" alongside the infamous "little green men," and some of the forces fighting on the side of Russian-backed separatists in Donbas include organized crime figures."

Processes of radicalization and brutalization mean that the state runs into legal, societal, and ethical boundaries. Whereas rebels are not necessarily bound to these constraints, states are, and therefore can take recourse to illegitimate means and networks in order to achieve their goals, including violence against civilians. To that end, both "blue collar" and "white-collar" crime is at the disposal of the state—with different effects on the conflicts' courses. The state can employ its bureaucratic apparatuses to allow criminal violence such as extortion or kidnapping directed against particular groups or individuals, thereby using criminality instead of resolving it. Republican and Loyalist paramilitary organizations in Northern Ireland from the 1970s to the 1990s increasingly came to inhabit a gray zone between ordinary criminal violence and selective political violence. Paramilitaries *became* criminals and criminals *became* paramilitaries due to the escalation of violence. For many of these men, violence itself became a way of life, and "the money which could be made through criminal rackets planned and organized by the paramilitary groups was welcomed by those for whom unemployment and life on the poverty line were often the likeliest alternatives."[114] In Mexico, the blurring of paramilitary and criminal lines was most obvious in the Zetas Cartel, who "were not thinking like gangsters, but like a paramilitary group controlling territory."[115] In Colombia, organized crime bosses began to employ paramilitary groups, not only to attack civilians perceived as a (potential) support base for FARC's indoctrination, but also "to displace peasants from their land, making possible the transfer of land into their hands or those of agribusinesses or other companies."[116]

The proliferation of organized crime in the post-Soviet period and subsequent criminalization of post-Soviet civil wars, such as in Tajikistan, Abkhazia, Nagorno-Karabakh, and especially Chechnya, are prime examples of how the dynamic of violence can align state officials and criminals. According to Anatol Lieven, this was particularly due to the criminal gangs' skillful exploitation of the escalation of violent conflict

---

[114] Alan Bairner, "Paramilitarism," in Arthur Aughey and Duncan Morrow (eds), *Northern Ireland Politics* (London: Routledge, 2014), 159–72, at 167.

[115] Ioan Grillo, *El Narco: The Bloody Rise of Mexican Drug Cartels* (London: Bloomsbury, 2012), 106.

[116] Hristov, *Paramilitarism and Neoliberalism*, 145.

by posing as nationalist militias, in order to get access to weapons and ammunition. Lieven continues to argue that organized crime

> has increased the hostility of the Chechens' neighbours—mainly the Russians, but also fellow Caucasians, who resent the Chechens' dominance over their own mafias; it has crippled still further any chance of creating an effective modern Chechen state; it greatly strengthens tendencies to 'bastard feudalism' and rule by armed followings of particular chieftains at the expense both of democracy and of lineage rules; it has thrown up some evil individuals, like the late Ruslan Labazanov and Bislan Gantemirov, to play a quasi-feudal role; and in the period 1991–4, clashes between criminal groups contributed to a major return of the blood-feud, which Soviet rule had suppressed.[117]

The vendetta is a form of civil war violence par excellence. Much like pre-modern vendettas, in civil wars an impartial state is largely absent, and revenge and counter-revenge can be exacted at will. The patterns of violence in civil wars are highly complex and manifold, but successive and simultaneous series of revenge-taking and counter-revenge propel much of the sustained violence in a civil war. Chechen criminals' pre-existing norms of honor and revenge reinforced the civil war dynamic.[118] Handelman argued that the links between the Chechen crime syndicates and the government in Grozny might have been obscure, but there was very strong circumstantial evidence of their mutual dependence. It was no coincidence that the expansion of the Chechen gangs' scale of activities, "from small bands involved in petty extortion and stolen-car rackets into sophisticated crime conglomerates

---

[117] Anatol Lieven, *Chechnya: Tombstone of Russian Power* (New Haven, CT: Yale University Press, 1999), 219, 351. Abkhazia was no different. Lieven describes the "Mkhedrioni, a paramilitary force loyal to Djaba Yosseliani, a former bank robber and criminal boss who had played a leading part in the December 1991 coup against Gamsakhurdia...The Mkhedrioni looked like what they were—unemployed youths from the grim industrial slums of Tbilisi and Rustavi, hard-faced but soft-bodied, and in many cases clearly addicted to alcohol or something stronger. They had already gained an odious reputation for looting, rape, vandalism and general mayhem, not just against the Abkhaz, but also in Georgian areas which supported Zviad Gamsakhurdia": ibid., 34.

[118] Roger Gould, "Revenge as Sanction and Solidarity Display: An Analysis of Vendettas in Nineteenth-Century Corsica," *American Sociological Review* 65:5 (2000), 682–705.

trading in guns and drugs" coincided with the emergence of Chechnya as a fledgling independent political entity.[119]

The criminalization of violent conflict and entanglement between crime and state is best illuminated from the perspective of state officials who witnessed the process from the sidelines. A biographical vignette from Turkey exemplifies this aspect to some extent. Mustafa Ü. was born in 1945 to a working-class family from a small village south of the eastern provincial capital Erzincan. His life spans over three decades of police work, from humble beginnings in 1970 as a police officer in Ankara and rising up the ranks in various towns and departments, to retire as an Istanbul police captain in 2000. I interviewed him on three separate occasions in his house in Istanbul about his life story and career, which offered important insights into the workings of the Turkish "deep state" and the relationships between the state and organized crime. He was well-placed to observe the vicissitudes within the Turkish law enforcement community throughout the critical 1990s. Mustafa experienced a fairly successful and steady career for about two decades, the only rupture being the 1980 military coup d'état. However, he noted that at some point in the early 1990s, something impalpable changed and he was confronted with a serious shift in his work flows. For example, he remembered, "all of a sudden, the man I arrested and put in the police cell for fighting in a casino would have been released the next day without me even being informed about it." On two separate occasions, he met Hüseyin Kocadağ, "a tall, good-looking and charismatic man in his long trench coat, honorable and professional." Kocadağ apparently had heard of Mustafa, a *paisano* who also enjoyed Turkish folk music, and in October 1996 invited him for drinks at a famous bar in the upscale Bostancı district in Istanbul. Two weeks later, Kocadağ died in the fatal Susurluk accident. But Mustafa's real baptism of fire occurred in 1999, when the Interior Ministry reassigned him to an eastern province (where the civil war with the PKK was raging), as part of the routine circulatory appointment of civil servants inside Turkey. Pulling all of the strings he could to prevent his re-appointment, none of Mustafa's formal attempts worked out, until he called on mafia boss Sedat Peker to cancel the

---

[119] Stephen Handelman, *Comrade Criminal: Russia's New Mafiya* (New Haven, CT: Yale University Press, 1995), 221.

procedure. Peker made the necessary calls, and Mustafa's reassignment was canceled.[120] Due to the civil war, the same type of criminal whom he had jailed in the 1980s as a police chief was now able to influence bureaucratic procedures at the highest levels of the Interior Ministry.

Finally, criminalization is often also a consequence of violent conflict, especially when criminals pursue political power and venture to exercise state capture. There are often new institutions that extract resources and promote capital accumulation, reconstruction efforts, construction contracts, and much more to benefit from. Again, Northern Ireland is a prime example: the spread of alcohol and drug abuse in the depressing aftermath of war led to drug markets needing regulation, and former paramilitaries happily indulged, kneecapping and meting out rough justice to transgressors. The same violence that was committed during the war as a form of political violence is now categorized as "organized crime." Ricardo Vargas Meza points out how routes and strategic zones for drug trafficking and other forms of organized crime were kept intact after the Colombian conflict, so paramilitaries forced to demobilize and disarm simply morphed into other organizations (businesses and politics), and continued controlling that illegal economy.[121] Indonesia saw a crime wave in the early 1980s, because gangs empowered in the years before had grown in response to employment opportunities offered by the government and were now short of work and income, much as in Belgrade in the late 1990s. The South African Truth and Reconciliation Report summed up this dilemma as follows:

A further factor in understanding the violence of the 1990s is the extent to which covert action, the existence of large amounts of secret funds and a climate of unaccountability led to an increasingly crimi- nalised set of networks between members and ex-members of the security forces. In such cases, considerable financial interests were clearly

---

[120] Interviews with Mustafa Ü. in Turkish in Istanbul, November 3, 2017, April 18, 2018.
[121] Ricardo Vargas Meza, "Drogas, guerra y criminalidad en Colombia: una simbiosis que alimenta la prolongación del conflict," in Alvaro Camacho Guizado (ed.), *Narcotráfico: Europa, Estados Unidos, América Latina* (Bogotá: Universidad de los Andes, CESO, 2006), 225–53, at 252: "...el paramilitarismo, cuyo ingreso a la zona se efectuó alrededor de 1998, ha venido controlando el comercio de drogas en todas las cabeceras municipales del bajo Putumayo, sin importar el Plan Colombia—implementado a partir del año 2000—o el proceso de negociación con esos grupos, iniciado en 2005."

furthered by a destabilized political situation. There is considerable evidence of ex- and serving security force members engaged in, for example, gun-running, as well as a range of other criminal activities.[122]

In exceptional cases, paramilitary forces move in the opposite direction: research on post-conflict lives of militias show that they could also turn into "powerful enforcers of vigilante justice in the postwar period, effectively shielding communities from narcotrafficking cartels."[123]
In this way, criminalization can mean that state supporters too suffer from the fallout of the conflict. The shifting of moral norms can even reach across national borders. Alfred McCoy's sophisticated examination of covert actions by the American and French governments in the Global South demonstrates that "these Cold War covert operations also produced political synergies, not only facilitating intervention at the imperial periphery, whether West Africa or Central America, but also fostering political control in the metropole, whether by mass incarceration, extra-legal force, or black campaign funds."[124] The way in which the Chechen war has also criminalized the Russian metropolis is a telling example of this phenomenon, let alone the formatively criminalizing impact of the conflict on Chechnya itself:

> Organised crime and the profits it generates (together with other aspects of social and economic change) may well destroy the essential unity of Chechen society by creating, for the first time in Chechnya, glaring differences between the very rich and the mass of the popula-tion, thereby ending the egalitarianism which has been at the core of the special Chechen identity; and it is beginning, especially among youth and the Chechen diaspora, to undermine those Chechen rules of conduct which have done so much to keep Chechnya an 'ordered anarchy' and not a Hobbesian chaos—as well as forming the backbone of Chechen fighting resistance. On the other hand, to put it bluntly, the 'mafia' has brought in an awful lot of money, without which Chechnya's

---

[122] *Truth and Reconciliation Commission of South Africa Report* (Cape Town: Truth and Reconciliation Commission, 1999), vol. 2, 695.
[123] Corinna Jentzsch, Stathis Kalyvas, and Livia Schubiger, "Militias in Civil War," *Journal of Conflict Resolution* 59:5 (2015), 755–69, at 764.
[124] McCoy, "Covert Netherworld," 878.

position even before the war would have been desperate, and which may provide the only real chance of postwar reconstruction.[125]

All in all, criminalization comes in many shapes and forms. It involves a shifting of moral norms in society, almost up to the point of anomie, a significant lowering of thresholds for violence, and a gradually but inexorably broadening acceptance of private crime to solve problems and conflicts. Both as a cause (rent-seeking), and throughout the course (rent-keeping), as well as a consequence (rent-maintaining), organized crime stands a lot to gain from a violent conflict, especially when it is indulged by the state.

Paramilitary-Criminal Profiles

Now let us examine some typical criminal-paramilitary profiles. The large body of criminological case studies, adopting profiles and biographies, based on court and police records, prosecution files, and trial transcripts offer rich insights into the lives of criminal men that were involved in state violence at some point. Four vignettes are particularly instructive, in chronological order: Anwar Kongo (Indonesia), George McMullan (Northern Ireland), Arkan (Serbia), and Musa Hilal (Sudan).

In the 1965–6 genocide in Indonesia, the Suharto regime killed an estimated 500,000 communists, suspected communists, Chinese-Indonesians, and others, in one of the worst cases of mass murder during the Cold War. The documentary *The Act of Killing* examines three dimensions of this mass murder: the personalities of the men who perpetrated the 1965 Indonesian genocide, their social relationships, and the fate of Indonesian society in general. One of the killers depicted is Anwar Kongo, a slim, streetwise, and jolly 70-year-old man who at that time lived in his hometown Medan on the Indonesian island of Sumatra. The sympathetic Anwar takes great care of his personal hygiene and looks after himself: he spends a lot of time in front of the mirror, combing (and dying) his curly gray hair with precision, frequently inspecting his teeth, wearing flashy sunglasses, and dressing up in bright *batik*

---

[125] Lieven, *Chechnya*, 352.

shirts. Coming across him in the streets, one might think of him as a model grandfather who enjoys the good life, and loves to dance, drink, and sing. But this façade conceals a deep and dark history of genocide. In 1965–6, Anwar Kongo murdered approximately one thousand suspected communists and other oppositionists of the Suharto regime. *The Act of Killing* follows him and provides a disturbing image of a mass murderer who got away with genocide and is enjoying a worry-free and comfortable life.

In 1965, Anwar was a small-time gangster loitering around cinemas, drinking alcohol, selling contraband, and smoking marihuana, until the moment when the criminal fraternity was vastly empowered by the Suharto regime for the special purpose of mass murder. Standing on the very rooftop where he murdered hundreds of people, Anwar explains that the method caused too much spilled blood that had to be cleaned up, so he moved on to strangle his victims with a metal wire instead. After this initial scene, the producers ask Anwar to re-enact the killings for the camera, and he eagerly sets up dramatic scenes, including costumes and makeup, bringing to life his memories and feelings about the killings. Anwar and his consorts enjoyed gangster films, westerns, and musicals. They mimicked the heroes, replayed the scenes, and adored the pathos of righteous killing in those genres. The genocide thus emerged as a fatal cocktail of thuggish masculinity with a sentimental edge. Anwar's social environment consists mostly of right-wing Indonesian vigilantes, steeped in nationalism and sexism. Ever since the 1965 genocide, the likes of Anwar have been revered as founding fathers of the right-wing paramilitary organization Pemuda Pancasila that grew out of the death squads.[126] The documentary is an excellent study of the self-perception of a retired paramilitary gangster. His collective fantasies about his fellow perpetrators as well as his victims are the cognitive and emotional foundations of mass violence. Besides the ubiquitous

---

[126] Pancasila is so powerful that its tentacles extend to government administration, mass corruption, election rigging, racketeering, and extortion. It holds mass rallies in sports stadiums, where its martial style and hateful discourse, combined with hundreds of young unmarried men on retainer, waiting to be mobilized, demonstrates that the infrastructure for genocide is still ever so present in Indonesia. Pancasila members are uniformed and organized, though not openly armed, but nevertheless undermine the state monopoly of violence. See Loren Ryter, "Pemuda Pancasila: The Last Loyalist Free Men of Suharto's Order," *Indonesia* 66 (1998), 45–73.

impunity in Indonesia, many viewers were dumbfounded by Anwar's aesthetic style, which many characterized as bizarre, surreal, even grotesque—but it should be taken seriously. Understanding paramilitaries' self-image is vitally important, because their fantastical construction of the Self also contains the projection of the imagined Other.[127]

Fairly similar figures and processes can be discerned in the rather different national context of Northern Ireland. Scholars have long pointed out the symbiosis between organized crime and political violence in Northern Ireland.[128] A good number of memoirs have been published, some sensational (such as that of Johnny "Mad Dog" Adair), others with retrospective airbrushing or justification. One very useful memoir is that of criminal-turned-paramilitary George McMullan, whose self-published autobiography *Life's a Bowl of Cherries* offers an introspective look into the world of an adolescent growing up on the mean streets of Belfast in the 1970s. McMullan begins his story by arguing that violence was already prevalent in his early teens, as youth gangs would stone buses and petty crime was rife. He started drinking heavily from a young age, exhibited uncontrollable behavior, and failed a training school. McMullan ended up in a juvenile detention facility and then a young offenders' center, where the brutality of prison life was a major shock to him, partly because of the threats and violence from Catholic prisoners, but also from the "screws" (wardens). Released from prison, he experienced major adaptation problems and began stealing cars for joyriding and engaging in street fighting, all while mostly drunk and high on glue. Interestingly, sectarianism hardly played a central role for him: his mother was Catholic, and he writes: "I would have been under a lot of pressure if asked about the specific history and events behind the violence [except] that us Protestants were fighting to keep Northern Ireland part of Great Britain [while] Catholics wanted [the] country to be part of the rest of Ireland. This short and biased history was all I knew

---

[127] Scholars of organized crime have criticized the idea that crime influences visual culture in a linear way. Rather, they have highlighted that members of the Mafia model themselves after fictional gangsters, such as in *The Godfather* and *The Sopranos*. So, too, Anwar Kongo and his buddies imitated the characters played by Elvis Presley, Gary Cooper, or Clint Eastwood in their movies.

[128] Andrew Silke, "Drink, Drugs, and Rock'n'Roll: Financing Loyalist Terrorism in Northern Ireland," *Studies in Conflict and Terrorism* 23:2 (2000), 107–27.

about Protestantism in Ireland."[129] So far, the memoir reads like a gangster bio from a disadvantaged inner-city milieu, but the key difference was the political conflict in Northern Ireland.

Before imprisonment, loyalist paramilitaries had already captured the imagination of Protestant youth like McMullan as omnipresent role models:

> I was mesmerised by these saints of the paramilitary who were our heroes. They were willing to sacrifice their own freedom and happiness, even their lives, so that we could continue to live with our political and religious freedom . . . One of the most vivid impressions in my life over this couple of years was continuing to see the leaders of the paramilitaries living in prosperity. They still wore nice expensive suits, drove big expensive cars, and owned houses that seemed better furnished than that of the average businessman. Yet they never had to work for a living and nearly everyone in our communities still respected them.[130]

Paramilitaries provided services to their communities, such as distributing food and milk. McMullan observes that there was no need for paramilitaries to be masked within the community, because no one was able or willing to bring them to justice for their actions. If the paramilitaries indeed committed any injustices, fear of punishment, betrayal, and ostracism kept him from criticizing them. But now, running amok in the streets of Belfast got McMullan into serious trouble with the Protestant paramilitaries, who wanted to kneecap him as punishment for his havoc. Then, McMullan made a fateful decision: he joined another paramilitary group for protection. By bringing his fellow teenage gang members in, he supplied manpower to the paramilitary group, which helped him "to move up the ladder and fill one of the now vacant places," which brought perks such as free alcohol and access to "groupies."[131] A young man with criminal experience, ambition, and connections was now absorbed by a Loyalist paramilitary group. From then on, he is in and out of prison, experiencing severe bouts of depression, hunger

---

[129] George McMullan, *Life's a Bowl of Cherries* (Belfast: Arrgh Books, 2000), 80.
[130] Ibid., 12, 23.   [131] Ibid., 79.

strikes, solitary confinement, and "madness," finally hearing Jesus' voice in solitary confinement and leaving prison a born-again Christian.

The rambunctious and deeply violent life of Željko "Arkan" Ražnatović (1952–2000) is the quintessential criminal-paramilitary story. Murder, robbery, spying, business, politics, sex, drugs, football, and war crimes are all part of his biography, and Arkan has been featured in documentaries, movies, dramas, literature, and a few attempts at solid biographies.[132] Historians agree that Arkan lived through a rowdy and harsh youth, gradually sliding into ever more frequent and large-scale criminal enterprises, including bank robberies in Europe. They also converge upon the important conclusion that Tito's secret service UDBA outsourced to Arkan (and others) several important contract murders of mostly Croatian-nationalist émigrés.[133] Collusion between the state and criminal leaders was not unique to Yugoslavia, and until the civil war, Arkan's biography could even be viewed as that of an "ordinary" mafia boss. The watershed happened in the 1990s, when the Milošević regime most likely coaxed him into setting up a paramilitary group for various objectives. The Yugoslav wars brought him unprecedented empowerment and his war crimes outmatched any of his prior offenses. His men consisted of hardcore football hooligans and criminals. On one occasion, he was showing another paramilitary leader around in his base in Erdut, when he pointed into a room and remarked: "There is 250 years of prison sentence in this room."[134] Arkan's paramilitary "Tigers" were active in at least six different sites of mass violence. They instigated the ethnic cleansing of Bijeljina and massacres in Zvornik, and raped and looted their way through Bosnia-Herzegovina.[135] Even though Arkan was in the presence of top Bosnian Serb politicians such as Radovan Karadzić and Biljana Plavšić on multiple occasions, his case demonstrates the

---

[132] One decent but incomplete attempt is Christopher Stewart, *Hunting the Tiger: The Fast Life and Violent Death of the Balkans' Most Dangerous Man* (New York: Thomas Dunne Books, 2008).

[133] Kenneth Morrison, "The Criminal State Symbiosis and the Yugoslav Wars of Succession," in Alejandro Colas and Bryan Mabee (eds), *Mercenaries, Pirates, Bandits and Empires* (London: Hurst, 2010), 159–86.

[134] Filip Švarm, *Jedinica* (Documentary, 2006), Episode 1, at 28:07.

[135] See the excellent report "Arkan's Paramilitaries: Tigers Who Escaped Justice," *Balkan Insight* (December 8, 2014), at http://www.balkaninsight.com/en/article/arkan-s-paramilitaries-tigers-who-escaped-justice; "Dosije Arkan," *Vreme* 472 (January 22, 2000), at https://www.vreme.com/arhiva_html/472/05.html (both accessed December 19, 2018).

central importance of plausible deniability (see Chapter 4). The American diplomat Richard Holbrooke met Slobodan Milošević several times and wrote in his assessment of the war:

> Whenever I mentioned Arkan's name to Milošević, he seemed annoyed; he frowned and his eyes narrowed. He did not mind criticism of Karadzić or Mladić, but Arkan—who lived in Belgrade, ran a popular restaurant, and was married to a rock star—was a different matter. Milošević dismissed Arkan as a "peanut issue," and claimed he had no influence over him. But Arkan's activities in western Bosnia decreased immediately after my complaints.[136]

The Tigers were officially disbanded in April 1996, and Arkan returned to his peacetime interests in business and sports. In the second half of the 1990s, he dominated the Belgrade underworld and was unchallenged due to his manpower, firepower, and most of all, political protection.

Arkan fathered nine children with five women. One of his sons, Vojin Ražnatović, wrote a memoir of anecdotes and recollections, which offers details one otherwise does not get from Arkan's many public appearances or the many war crimes investigations. Vojin paints a picture of a petty and authoritarian father who commanded fear in the house and was prone to bursts of rage. Regarding Arkan's social identity, Vojin claims that he was an implacable Serbian nationalist and devout Orthodox Christian. Moreover, Arkan seems to have instilled in his children a myth of the Ražnatović family as one of fighters: ostensibly, Arkan's great-grandfather Jokelja returned from battle with "17 Turkish heads he had personally severed," his grandfather Mihajlo had fought in the Serbian army in World War I, and his father Veljko had fought in Kosovo during World War II. His uncle Vojin had been executed by the "fascists" in Montenegro, Arkan told his son, and burdened the young man with the memory of a dead uncle and a tradition of violent masculinity. Throughout the book, the boy claims to have been privy to events and conversations both of organized crime and of the war—indeed, he dedicates the book to his father's notorious bodyguard Rade Rakonjac. For example, he writes about the onset of war in November 1990:

---

[136] Richard Holbrooke, *To End a War* (New York: Random House, 1998), 190.

Things have drastically changed one day when my brother and I were forbidden to leave the house. Two men began escorting us to school on a daily basis. One carried a red duffle bag with a semi-automatic rifle inside and another a long silver revolver, wrapped in a black plastic bag. They waited all day for us outside of our classroom to safely escort us back home. We were told 10 years later that the new Croatian authorities had published names of all hardline Croatian Ustasha emigres who my dad had supposedly assassinated when he was employed by Tito's notorious secret service. Following the events, vengeful threats began arriving at his jail cell, some threatening to kidnap and kill his twin boys.[137]

The young man also stumbles across the ubiquitous (but to him largely invisible) organized crime and politics. One day, he happens upon a closet where he finds rifles with silencers, and crossbows. When Arkan finds out, he beats his son severely. Then, Arkan's attempt to enter Serbian politics was apparently to grab votes from the right wing, or to quench his insurmountable thirst for glory and fame. (Arkan was a poor orator and public speaker, so his rallies, advertisements, and celebrity endorsements were not sufficient to succeed in Serbian politics.) After the war, Vojin claims that Arkan "retained a decent number of hardened fighters" from the Tigers to work as enforcers for him. One of these trusted Tigers was a certain Misha, who befriended his sons and told them that after his father's assassination they should stay away from Serbia for a while, because "they know that when you mature, you will be seeking vengeance for your father's death."[138] Much of this intimate memoir demonstrates that even a seasoned criminal like Arkan could not keep his family from knowing about the deadly triangle between the state, organized crime, and war.

Finally, the example of Musa Hilal demonstrates best how persistent impunity has a long-lasting influence on societies, and how plausible deniability (see Chapter 4) can be unveiled. Hilal (1961–) hails from the Mahamid clan in Darfur, has thirteen children from three wives and was

---

[137] Vojin Ražnatović, *Stories about My Father: An Intimate Portrayal Of Europe's Most Controversial Paramilitary Commander* (Los Angeles, CA: CreateSpace Independent Publishing Platform, 2014), 187.

[138] Ibid., 62, 166.

the lynchpin of the Janjaweed in the mass violence in Darfur. The term "Janjaweed" was familiar in Sudanese society, referring to bandits and brigands from western tribes, who roamed the vast plains of Darfur, robbing and extorting people. In the Darfur genocide, the term has regained currency, as the Bashir regime's pro-government militias are often called Janjaweed. Hilal's criminal career predated the conflict: in 1997 he was arrested for killing seventeen people from African tribes, but was let off the hook due to influential connections. The year after, he led an armed robbery against the Central Bank of Nyala in which one policeman was killed; he was arrested, convicted, and transferred to high-security prisons in various regions of Sudan.[139] His key life moment was in 2003, when the Sudanese government freed him from prison for counter-insurgency purposes against the armed rebellion in Darfur. This move catapulted Hilal into power: he began recruiting "Arab" tribesmen to fight the rebels and commit violence against civilians in rebel areas. From 2006 on, the United Nations and the International Criminal Court began focusing on high-level perpetrators of the Darfur genocide, including Hilal. The Security Council imposed financial and travel bans against him, and the ICC prosecutor's office named him in many files on war crimes; he was not indicted himself, perhaps because his cooperation would have been beneficial to the prosecution of more important perpetrators. On January 18, 2008, the Sudanese president Omar Al-Bashir appointed Hilal as a special advisor to the Ministry of Federal Affairs.[140]

Musa Hilal's involvement in violence is long and bloody: he personally led attacks against Zaghawa and Fur civilians and there is credible testimony that he kidnapped women prisoners and took them to the Jabal Jur area for sexual slavery—the women were never heard of again. Eye witnesses observed that on several occasions, Musa Hilal (uniformed and armed) held rallies at the central market of Kebkabiya (North Darfur), addressed the crowds, and boasted of having led the Janjaweed to glorious victories. During those forays, the Janjaweed massacred civilians, burnt down villages, plundered property, and raped women

---

[139] Anders Hastrup, *The War in Darfur: Reclaiming Sudanese History* (London: Routledge, 2013), 95.
[140] Julie Flint and Alex de Waal, *Darfur: A New History of a Long War* (London: Zed Books, 2008), 35ff.

and girls.[141] Two important sources lift the veil of secrecy and deniability surrounding the Janjaweed: first, a leaked memo of February 13, 2004 from a government office in North Darfur ordered "security units in the locality" to "allow the activities of the mujahedeen and the volunteers under the command of Sheikh Musa Hilal to proceed in the areas of [North Darfur] and to secure their vital needs." This remarkable order specifically admonished state security officials not to interfere in Musa Hilal's work.[142] Second, Musa Hilal openly (and incredibly) contradicted the Sudanese government's claim that the state and the militias were unconnected. Human Rights Watch researchers conducted a candid video interview with him on September 27, 2004 in Khartoum. In the interview, Hilal squarely rejected the government's claim that his Janjaweed were unconnected to the state, retorting that the government armed, recruited, paid the militias, and gave them official IDs, adding that "the government has told us to mobilize people."[143] In a later interview, he stated: "Janjaweed is a thief. A criminal. I am a tribal leader, with men and women and children who follow me. How can they all be thieves and bandits? It is not possible."[144]

These four vignettes illustrate well-known cases, but there are other, much less famous yet equally relevant ones: from the Argentine criminal and death squad killer Aníbal Gordon to Khun Sa, the narcotics drug lord who transformed the heroin markets of both Europe and North America and launched a furtive attempt at a secessionist state in the northeastern Burmese–Chinese borderlands.[145] Criminals' involvement in paramilitary units can account for their conduct, group dynamics, and recruitment, including masculinity and mobility. Masculinity mattered to all of these men. Even semantically, the Calabrian word

[141] Human Rights Watch, *Entrenching Impunity: Government Responsibility for International Crimes in Darfur* (New York: Human Rights Watch, 2005), 10–21.

[142] "Video Transcript: Exclusive Video Interview with Alleged Janjaweed Leader" (March 2, 2005), at https://www.hrw.org/news/2005/03/02/video-transcript-exclusive-video-interview-alleged-janjaweed-leader (accessed December 18, 2018).

[143] "Darfur: Militia Leader Implicates Khartoum" (March 2, 2005), at https://www.hrw.org/news/2005/03/02/darfur-militia-leader-implicates-khartoum and https://www.hrw.org/news/2005/03/02/video-transcript-exclusive-video-interview-alleged-janjaweed-leader (accessed December 18, 2018).

[144] Lydia Polgreen, "Over tea, sheik denies stirring Darfur's torment," *New York Times*, June 12, 2006, A1.

[145] Alfred McCoy, "Requiem for a Drug Lord: State and Commodity in the Career of Khun Sa," in Josiah Heyman (ed.), *States and Illegal Practices* (New York: Berg, 1999), 129–69.

'Ndrangheta is derived from the Greek *andragathía* for "heroism" and "virtue," or *andragathos*, a blend of "andròs" (man) and "agathòs" (good), meaning "a courageous man." The Indonesian mobsters were called *preman* in Bahasa Indonesia, meaning "free man." These bosses (in their young years) and their recruits were mostly young men who had few opportunities to reach success through conventional manners. Mobility was only possible through illegal means, leading to the formation of new social and economic classes of modern bandits. But only under conditions of political crisis and civil war was their violent potential truly unlocked, enabling mass violence to become possible on the scale seen in Indonesia, Northern Ireland, Yugoslavia, and Sudan.

Conclusions

In 2015, Giovanni Gambino, son of Sicilian-American mobster John Gambino, gave several boastful interviews to various media outlets, in which he pontificated that the New York Mafia was better capable of protecting New Yorkers from ISIS than the FBI or Homeland Security.[146] What seemed like an unreal and dilettantish proposal from an attention seeker, was not so outlandish at it seemed. Governments have worked closely with organized crime when facing serious threats to their authority. In the revised 2000 edition of *Bandits*, Hobsbawm recognized that "banditry can thrive in late capitalism, such as the contemporary banditry associated with the demise of nation-states, Afghanistan, countries that comprised the former Yugoslavia, and Chechnya all being examples."[147] Hobsbawm rightly observed that state–crime relations are not a relic of the past, but that modern banditry is very much alive. This chapter has examined how states can collude with crime and produce opportunities for criminals to enlist in paramilitary formations. It has also looked at how the political economy of paramilitarism can undermine the rule of law by increasing crime in wartime and postwar society.

---

[146] "Mafia heir warns ISIS to stay away from New York," *Daily Mail*, November 24, 2015, at https://www.dailymail.co.uk/news/article-3331137/Son-New-York-Mafia-boss-says-protect-parts-city-ISIS-calling-Hollywood-gangsters-stand-terrorist-organization.html (accessed December 20, 2018).

[147] Eric Hobsbawm, *Bandits* (New York: The New Press, 2000), 9.

Comparative examinations of this phenomenon demonstrate that whereas there are significant differences between case studies, many of the conclusions converge—on several issues.[148] First and foremost, when civil and security institutions are weakened during major crises, governments cornered in (civil) wars may contact criminals and strongmen for various purposes, but generally for the most sensitive tasks. During crises these people are contacted, empowered, covered, and afterwards often disposed of. However, several historical cases demonstrate that even much later on, when the crisis is averted and the state's position is consolidated, the state can still keep these people on retainer throughout a patronage network, in case of new potential crises. The thugs are a permanent guarantee of emergency security.

Two main conclusions that can be drawn from this chapter are about the management of violence, and the problem of intertwinement.

First of all, paramilitarism is about the mobilization of men for the commission of (often particular forms of) violence. Criminals have skill sets that predate wars and therefore can fit into war in particular, highly useful ways; vice versa, war veterans can also slide into peacetime illegality as their experiences with weapons and killing are useful for organized crime. Volkov conceptualized these types of men as "violent entrepreneurs" who prosper by wielding "violence-managing agency" and know-how.[149] Kalyvas notes that organized crime "must deploy a paramilitary apparatus staffed by *specialists of violence.*"[150] These violence experts exist in most societies, where hardened criminals may have underground power but take a back seat, comment vacuously on the Internet, and suffer derision from good Western citizens—they just they don't have the power/visibility/frontstage (yet). The types of violence these men are tasked to commit during counter-insurgencies and genocides bear similarities with that of organized crime violence, including signaling through massacring by weak groups eager to show the state they are incapable of protecting civilians, or massive coercion intended to minimize civilian defections. Paramilitary methods of killing are

---

[148] For a different approach that focuses on criminalized rebels *and* states, see Michael Dziedzic (ed.), *Criminalized Power Structures: The Overlooked Enemies of Peace* (New York: Rowman & Littlefield, 2016).

[149] Volkov, *Violent Entrepreneurs.*

[150] Kalyvas, "How Civil Wars Help Explain Organized Crime," 1526.

often entirely mafia-style: convening at night, kidnapping a victim, shooting him in the head, weighing him down with weights, and dumping the body in a river or lake. Hiding the bodies then is an implicit acknowledgment of the criminality of the act, and an awareness of the integrity of the respective criminal justice system. Finally, paramilitary violence is often cruel and deliberately atrocious, which echoes the violence of the underworld, in which acquiring and maintaining a reputation of fearsomeness and terror is vital for successfully competing. Violent specialists and entrepreneurs are widely available in most societies, but it requires the decisions of politicians and law enforcement agencies such as the police, the army, and intelligence services, to enter that fatal state of mutually beneficial trade-offs.

Second, the relationship between organized crime and the state is subject to a variety of depictions: intertwinement, collusion, penetration, infiltration, or symbiosis, not to mention metaphors of cancers and parasites feeding off the body politic. The latter can be dismissed, for criminals using state cover and networks are not an external cancer or virus. Rather, they are an internal problem of governance and a continuous resource available to politicians and officials. In a riveting analysis of the Colombian paramilitaries and the Colombian "para-state," Aldo Civico draws comparisons with the Sicilian Mafia and its ties to the Italian state. He distinguishes the Italian term *intreccio* from intertwinement and argues that "[r]ather than an erosion, absence, or even failure of the state, the intertwinement between illegal actors and the state is an extension of the state's sovereignty into spaces that are produced as an exteriority that still lives in a natural condition...in other words, it represents an extension of the state's power not its diminution."[151] This is a convincing conclusion, with the caveat that paramilitarism is often unthinkable without crime, but only because particular networks *within* the state enlist formerly outlawed brigands and deploy them both visibly and in covert operations. Therefore, any understanding of the organization of paramilitarism requires a closer examination of the state from different perspectives.

---

[151] Civico, *The Para-State*, 23.

4

The Organization of Paramilitarism

Introduction: Between *siloviki* and *parapolítica*

How is paramilitary violence organized? Many studies of violent conflicts have demonstrated the central role of paramilitaries in the perpetration of violence against civilians. The organization of paramilitarism, from the top liaisons at the helm of the state, down to the killers who commit the violence is a crucial nexus to be examined. Mass violence is often carried out according to clear divisions of labor: between the civil and military wings of the state, but also crucially between military and paramilitary groups. This chapter examines how states organize paramilitary units. It will focus on a range of issues germane to paramilitarism, including a discussion of the place and influence of the state, the commission of violence against civilians including several horrific massacres, and the problem of plausible deniability. This examination will use various similar cases, but will not neglect variation and counter-examples. As such, it will also examine the ostensibly blurred distinctions between state violence and non-state violations of human rights.

The title of this section refers to two approaches to paramilitarism that have emerged in culturally, historically, and politically very different societies: the *siloviki* in Russia and the *parapolítica* phenomenon in Colombia. Although they refer to differing processes, they share important features, including the themes of this chapter: the state's agencies, infrastructures of violence, and deniability. The term *silovik* (literally: "person of force" from the Russian word сила) emanated in the post-Soviet 1990s as a catch-all term to encompass the men who had been employed by and were steeped in the traditions of the security services (army, police, FSB), but had now entered the world of Russian politics. One expert has defined the term as "employees of all the agencies that use any significant degree of armed force...those close associates of Putin who made their careers in the KGB."[1] The networks, work ethic, and backgrounds they brought to civilian politics opened up autonomous and unsurveilled spaces for paramilitary initiatives and collusion. Hence, in the twin Chechen wars, the *siloviki* were involved in paramilitary mobilization through liaisons with various Russian and Chechen organized crime groups. The *siloviki* tradition has had an indelible impact on Russian politics in and beyond Russia, and much paramilitary violence has been pivotal in the relationships between security agencies, politics, and crime.[2]

On the other hand, *parapolítica*, a contraction of the Spanish words *paramilitar* and *política*, refers to the diffuse forms of collaboration between individuals and (sub-)agencies inside and outside the state, who together form a network of paramilitarism. The term emerged in 2005 as the so-called *parapolítica* scandal, which exposed the creeping and ultimately profound infiltration of the right-wing paramilitary Autodefensas Unidas de Colombia (AUC) into Colombian politics and government.[3] Reportedly, this interpenetration was so intimate that, in 2001, over thirty members of congress, politicians, paramilitary leaders and top lawyers had met in a secret conference in order to formally consolidate significant paramilitary control over the Colombian state, from the local, village administrative level up to the Colombian Supreme Court, and most importantly and nefariously, the main intelligence agency DAS (Departamento Administrativo de Seguridad).[4] This was a departure from the usual informal arrangements that had governed the paramilitary–political complex, and which had defined the course of the Colombian counter-insurgency war against left-wing militant groups like the FARC or National Liberation Army (ELN). But its relevance went beyond the immediate armed conflict and extended into the world of trade, borders, immigration, governance, the rule of law, and the

---

[1] Peter Reddaway, *Russia's Domestic Security Wars: Putin's Use of Divide and Rule against His Hardline Allies* (London: Palgrave, 2018), 1–2.
[2] James Hughes, *Chechnya: From Nationalism to Jihad* (Philadelphia: University of Pennsylvania Press, 2013), 202.
[3] Jasmin Hristov, *Blood and Capital: The Paramilitarization of Colombia* (Toronto: Between the Lines, 2009).
[4] Mauricio Romero (ed.), *Parapolítica: la ruta de la expansión paramilitar y los acuerdos políticos* (Bogotá: Intermedio, 2007).

education sector. The nebulous and sometimes impersonal nature of this maze often gave it an intangible and conspiratorial air, prompting investigative journalists and academics to continuously expose and criticize it in their research and publications.

Whereas the focus on *siloviki* attributes too much influence to individuals in powerful positions, the *parapolitica* model often ventures into the rather abstract, impersonal sphere of networks and cultures of paramilitarism. This chapter will explore the middle space between the concrete behaviorist approaches and abstract structuralist understandings of paramilitarism. To do so, the chapter looks at three separately relevant but interrelated topics applicable to the organization of paramilitarism (see below). These have been chosen for three reasons: first of all, they have not been studied much before, either separately, or in connection with the other themes. For example, despite the relevance of the subject, it is remarkable that there exists no serious separate or comparative analysis of plausible deniability as a common feature of paramilitary formations. Second, these separate lines of research need to be pursued more deeply in order to explain how they influence paramilitarism. In order to understand the rise and violence of paramilitarism, it is crucial to thoroughly examine the state (including its tentacle-like reach and vicissitudes). Third, even at face value, these facets are common to all cases of paramilitary organizations. Many other aspects could also have been selected, such as their representations on national media platforms, aspects of gender and culture, or the public perception and support for paramilitarism, or the structural similarities between the actual paramilitary groups. However, by limiting the chapter to these three themes, it is possible to explain their influence in an elaborate way, and set new research agendas that must be pursued to develop potential sources of variance in their explanation.

From the Colombian province of Chocó on the Pacific Coast to the east coast of Mindanao on the Philippine Sea, paramilitarism has always revolved around the state. Therefore, the chapter will begin with two sections on how the state is involved in paramilitarism, and vice versa. In order to break a potentially huge discussion up into digestible parts, it will focus on three major topics: the state's institutions of coercion, political parties, and communities. It will then discuss the core activity of paramilitaries: violence, and particularly violence against civilians. This section will examine three major massacres in different contexts to compare how paramilitary violence is quite similar, despite different cultural and political contexts and prehistories. The fourth section focuses on a crucial but under-examined topic: the phenomenon and problem of plausible deniability that vexes *and regulates* the public face of paramilitarism and the relationship between the state and paramilitary violence. The chapter will discuss this seemingly peripheral topic, because attempting to understand paramilitarism without it runs the risk of missing out on crucial aspects of the violence, and since almost all paramilitary violence (certainly in this book) has been surrounded by deniability, it cannot be neglected.

Dual State, Deep State, Hybrid State, Parastate?

Paramilitarism is fundamentally a matter of the state, and the starting point for any examination of their relationships must be the assumption that the state is neither a monolithic nor an organic entity. It is reductive to think of the state as a Moloch, for it is a hodgepodge of bureaucracies and actors with competing and often contradictory goals, interests, and beliefs. States consist of a complex set of institutions that operate alongside, above, under, and beyond each other, and therefore must be disaggregated so their influence and dynamics can be properly examined. These institutions are both formally existing physical agencies, encapsulated in buildings and ministries, but also intangible social institutions that comprise networks, cells, cultures, and norms that differ substantially in scope, purpose, and resources.[5] Considering the complexity of modern and contemporary states, how can we theorize the state's relationships to paramilitarism? In various national and historical settings, paramilitaries have been seen as self-sustaining *non-state* armed groups that operate on their own behalf and for their own motives; *pro-state* actors that are fully accountable to the state's official structures; agents of

---

[5] Joel S. Migdal, "The State in Society: An Approach to Struggles for Domination," in Joel S. Migdal, Atul Kohli, and Vivienne Shue (eds), *State Power and Social Forces: Domination and Transformation in the Third World* (Cambridge: Cambridge University Press, 1994), 7–34.

the *dual state* as formulated by Ernst Fraenkel;[6] shadowy figures and groups who operate on behalf of an autonomous *deep state*; or *parastate* characters that were formed beyond regular state institutions. Although these characterizations all bear a modicum of truth, they are also incomplete and do not sufficiently cover the variation within global paramilitarism.

These notions of vague power centers and disfigurations of the state loom large in the popular imagination.[7] In American political jargon, a "smoke-filled room" is used to describe secret political gatherings of an inner circle of powerful, well-connected, cigar-smoking regents that make the "real" decisions against the democratic will of the population. The similar notion of "shadow government" or "cryptocracy" veers toward conspiracy theories based on the idea that actual political power resides not with publicly elected representatives, but with shadowy power brokers who operate behind the scenes. These (often paranoid) theories do attempt to explain the phenomena of paramilitarism and paramilitary violence, but blame it on the Freemasons, "international Jewry," intelligence agencies, or other secret societies. Ostensibly, these omniscient and omnipotent groups manipulate state policy in their own interests, and therefore paramilitary violence cannot be attributed to the state. The problem with all these interpretations, both the serious and absurd ones, is that they are too monolithic and static. The relationships between the state and paramilitarism must be seen as a dynamic process. The deep state in Turkey, para-institutional state-building in Mexico, the dual state dynamic in Myanmar, or the weak state accusations of the Central African Republic all forego the conclusion that these are fundamentally processes, not snapshots, and that the secretive nature of

---

[6] Fraenkel defined Nazi Germany as a dual state, in which a *normative* state was the closest to a rule-of-law state (a *Rechtsstaat*), and a *prerogative* state, a "governmental system which exercises unlimited arbitrariness and violence unchecked by any legal guarantees." The Nazis' paramilitary and secret service structures then were part and parcel of the prerogative state. See Ernst Fraenkel, *The Dual State: A Contribution to the Theory of Dictatorship* (New York: Oxford University Press, 1941), xiii.

[7] The murky world of paramilitarism has even figured in video games. The immensely popular action game *Grand Theft Auto V* includes chapters in which a "Federal Investigation Bureau" (FIB) and an "International Affairs Agency" (IAA) outsource political murders to heavy criminals. In the immersive stealth game *Hitman*, the main figure carries out assassinations for the "Sigma deniable operations paramilitary unit."

paramilitary networks does not automatically mean that the separate actors and groups involved are secret.

Furthermore, the fact that paramilitarism can be deeply rooted and paramilitary violence spectacular and influential, should not lead us to the facile conclusion that the state therefore must be weak. Indeed, discussions of paramilitarism have often departed from weak state theory or variations thereof, and whereas weak state theory is helpful in understanding (aspects of) the dynamics of the onset of civil war, it sets limits to our knowledge.[8] Even paramilitary leaders themselves often mention state weakness and foreground their roles as strongmen. Aldo Civico's ethnographic fieldwork on Colombian paramilitaries painted a piercing portrait of murderous AUC commander Fabio Acevedo, who legitimized the existence of strongmen:

> We were illegal, but honestly, it was because of the inefficiency of the state, its inability to protect the maximum well-being of every citizen and its lack of presence in these communes…In our speeches, we always talked about supporting institutions, about the respect that there should be towards the state. Even if the state was weak and imperfect, it deserved respect.[9]

Acevedo's comments are telling, because he alleges state weakness and acknowledges the illegality of paramilitaries, but at the same time recognizes the legitimacy of the state. Jenny Pearce wrote that across Latin America, the state's lack of monopoly over the means of violence is not a case of state weakness, but of legitimacy, as criminal disorder or civil unrest provides justification for the state to violently impose order.[10] In several cases of paramilitary violence, in which entire regions are razed and countless lives destroyed, we can hardly call those states "weak." A "weak paramilitary state" sounds much like the often-used term "weak dictator," whereas clearly a state can be weak in some areas, but strong in

---

[8] James Fearon and David Laitin, "Ethnicity, Insurgency, and Civil War," *American Political Science Review* 97:1 (2003), 75–90.

[9] Aldo Civico, *The Para-State: An Ethnography of Colombia's Death Squads* (Berkeley: University of California Press, 2016), 168–70.

[10] Jenny Pearce, "Perverse State Formation and Securitized Democracy in Latin America," *Democratization* 17:2 (2010), 286–306.

others, not just territorially and temporally, but institutionally. A state like Syria might perhaps appear weak in some areas, for example in its capacity to insure state employees or manage higher education, but it is astoundingly strong in other areas; for example, it commands over a dozen intelligence agencies and prisons, not to mention a host of paramilitary organizations.

Indeed, the term itself must be criticized, for what is state "weakness"? Charles Tilly defined strength and weakness of states as government capacity, "the extent to which governmental agents control resources, activities, and populations within the government's territory."[11] Michael Mann famously distinguished government strength as divided between infrastructural power and despotic power, in which weakness in either would constitute weakness in general.[12] Neither can weakness be conceptualized only from the state's own weakness. Resistance from societal power centers affects state capacity just as much. Joel Migdal theorized that states' capacities to mobilize the public and implement social policies depends on and relates to the structure of society. According to him, state ineffectiveness "has stemmed from the nature of the societies they have confronted—from the resistance posed by chiefs, landlords, bosses, rich peasants, clan leaders, *za'im*, *effendi*s, *agha*s, *cacique*s, *kulak*s."[13] The state has to contend with these "strongmen," some of whom are social bandits or mob bosses (see Chapter 3) who command fully illegal structures; others are chieftains of tribes in informal power hierarchies; and others still are heads of the state's own agencies, who oppose certain policies. The strongman is a holder of local authority in the framework of a traditional social organization, attempts to survive against the grain of state power, and is in control of a clientelistic patronage network. Indeed, some scholars have argued that secret patron–client relations are the main plausibly deniable instruments of illicit government power that permit/encourage paramilitarism.[14] Of course, the

[11] Charles Tilly, *The Politics of Collective Violence* (Cambridge: Cambridge University Press, 2003), 41.

[12] Michael Mann, *The Sources of Social Power: Volume 1, A History of Power from the Beginning to AD 1760* (Cambridge: Cambridge University Press, 1986), 170ff.

[13] Joel S. Migdal, *Strong Societies and Weak States: State–Society Relations and State Capabilities in the Third World* (Princeton, NJ: Princeton University Press, 1988), 33.

[14] Max G. Manwaring, *Gangs, Pseudo-Militaries, and Other Modern Mercenaries: New Dynamics in Uncomfortable Wars* (Norman: University of Oklahoma Press, 2012), 41.

state itself actively allows or produces strongmen, and it is in the "perverse state formation" of these social figurations where paramilitarism thrives. Hence it makes sense to look closely into the coercive capacities of states in which paramilitarism has been prevalent.

The two following sections will examine the state from at least three analytical perspectives and institutions: security agencies, political parties, and communities. It is the complex interaction between these three elements that constitute the infrastructure behind paramilitary violence.

Paramilitarization is often propelled according to divisions of labor: between the civil and military wings of the state, but also crucially between the security services and political parties. This section examines how otherwise neutral and technocratic institutions, organizations, and agencies have collaborated in paramilitary violence. Since violence is the currency paramilitaries deal in, we start with the monopoly of violence—or oligopoly of violence, since coercive power is shared between three main institutions: armies, police, and intelligence services. Any analysis of paramilitarism anywhere must start with the army, or broader, the Ministry of Defense. In many ways, everything starts there, from weapons and training, to funding and permissions to enter securitized zones. Military laws, rules, and institutions are the grid through which paramilitarism must meander in order to be effective. This "grid" includes tangible things such as allocation of resources, from the level of a Minister of Defense's discretionary funds down to localized arrangements under provincial army detachments. A comparative examination of armies demonstrates that they are essential to dispense money, arms, and impunity to paramilitaries, but also that it is difficult to paint armies with a single brush. In some cases, as in the Indonesian genocide, evidence from military documents demonstrates that the Indonesian army empowered and armed paramilitaries in a fairly straightforward way (see Chapter 2).[15] Also, if one pro-government armed group uses coercion, violence, or threats as a means of reducing or eliminating a similar group's relative power

---

[15] Jess Melvin, *The Army and the Indonesian Genocide: Mechanics of Mass Murder* (London: Routledge, 2018).

position, this might alter the internal power distribution within that state, but it does not necessarily change the status quo or the direction of the violence.[16] In any case, armies' involvement with paramilitarism is often deeply ambivalent.

Colombian paramilitarism is a prime example of these relations, and its army was both complicit in and resistant to the rise of paramilitarism: whereas some generals and brigades were deeply involved in the groups, others were highly critical of them.[17] For example, in the Uraba region, Alejo Rojas, commander of the 17th Brigade of the Colombian army, stated that the paramilitaries were a greater threat to the country than were the guerrillas: "The military's influence and control over paramilitaries may be tenuous at best and non-existent in some cases."[18] Among the ranks of the Colombian army, reportedly, paramilitaries were seen as allies against a common enemy: communist rebels (FARC and ELN). Another reason the army colluded was that it had been pressured by the United States and international human rights monitors to clean up its human rights record. Therefore, it began to shift much illegitimate violence to paramilitary groups, including torture, disappearances, and summary executions. The Colombian military tacitly condoned these abuses by the paramilitaries because of its "body count mentality": the higher the number of dead rebels, the more impressed superiors would be. Indeed, many higher officers simply shrugged off any responsibility for the violence.[19] American officials were aware of the collusion between the army and paramilitaries—which was no wonder, since the US had trained the Colombian army, intelligence service, and even the paramilitaries. In 1998, Ambassador David Passage wrote

[16] Jon Rosenbaum and Peter Sederberg, "Vigilantism: An Analysis of Establishment Violence," *Comparative Politics* 6:4 (1974), 541–70.

[17] Michael Evans has edited a broad range of US National Security Archive files on Colombia that clarify the role of Colombian army and intelligence as major colluders with paramilitary forces. See https://nsarchive.gwu.edu/project/colombia-project (accessed February 13, 2019).

[18] National Security Archive, Electronic Briefing Book No. 217, Document 5: "Colombian Prosecutor Comments on Paramilitaries in Uraba," December 7, 1996, at https://nsarchive2.gwu.edu/NSAEBB/NSAEBB217/doc05.pdf (accessed November 1, 2018).

[19] National Security Archive, Electronic Briefing Book No. 166, Document 1, "Cashiered Colonel Talks Freely About the Army He Left Behind," December 24, 1997, at https://nsarchive2.gwu.edu//NSAEBB/NSAEBB166/19971224.pdf (accessed November 2, 2018).

an unusually passionate memo criticizing the Colombian army's collusion with the paramilitaries:

> We know the Colombian military doesn't control all the paramilitary organizations—but we also know there are enough ties between many of them and Colombian military officers that it becomes impossible for us to turn a blind eye. NO, we're not going to identify them; you know who they are. Heal yourselves before you ask for help!...Stop protecting incompetent officers! Clean up internal corruption![20]

One man who embodies this attitude was General Mario Montoya Uribe, who according to intelligence reports liked "to drink Scotch whisky, but not to excess." Montoya was heavily involved with a Medellin-based paramilitary group, both directly in joint operations, and indirectly in allowing paramilitaries to pass through army checkpoints.[21]

Turkey has a long history of paramilitary mobilization (see Chapter 2) that emanated from political parties as well as the gendarmerie. During the Republic, it was the army that initially played a leading role in establishing and coordinating paramilitary structures, such as the formally existing Special Warfare Department, but much of this changed during the war with the PKK.[22] In the early 1990s, then Chief of Staff General Doğan Güreş transformed that department into the Special Forces Command.[23] This trend of increasing paramilitarization continued, for example with the expansion of the village guards system, and reached an apex with the establishment of JİTEM, the Gendarmerie Intelligence

---

[20] National Security Archive, Electronic Briefing Book No. 368, "Memorandum for ARA/PPCP," June 1, 1998, p.3, at https://nsarchive2.gwu.edu//NSAEBB/NSAEBB368/docs/19980601.pdf (accessed November 2, 2018).

[21] National Security Archive, Electronic Briefing Book No. 223, Document 4, "Biographic Report—Colombia, Colonel Mario Montoya Uribe, Colombian Army, Director of Intelligence," July 1, 1998, at https://nsarchive2.gwu.edu/NSAEBB/NSAEBB223/19980701.pdf (accessed November 2, 2018).

[22] Mehmet Ali Kışlalı, *Güneydoğu: Düşük Yoğunluklu Çatışma* (Istanbul: Ümit, 1996), 222–3.

[23] Mehtap Söyler, *The Turkish Deep State: State Consolidation, Civil–Military Relations and Democracy* (London: Routledge, 2015), 101; Evren Balta Paker, "Dış Tehditten İç Tehdide: Türkiye'de Doksanlarda Ulusal Güvenliğin Yeniden İnşaası," in Evren Balta Paker and İsmet Akça (eds), *Türkiye'de Ordu, Devlet Ve Güvenlik Siyaseti* (Istanbul: Bilgi Üniversitesi, 2010), 414.

and Counter-Terrorism, the death squad that assaulted Kurdish civilians. Large pockets of the Turkish army connived with JİTEM and covered for it. However, the Turkish army also had officers in its ranks who were flatly against the paramilitary complex, in particular the JİTEM death squads. Former Turkish intelligence officer Hüseyin Oğuz alleged that there were serious conflicts among the various military institutions regarding these new paramilitary strategies.[24] Between 1991 and 1993, a significant number of high-ranking soldiers were either killed or died suspiciously, allegedly due to their opposition to these transformations.[25] The most prominent example of these was when Gendarmerie General Eşref Bitlis (1933–1993) died in a highly suspicious helicopter accident. The rumors that he was part of a clique that was against the paramilitarization of the state and was therefore liquidated have not abated ever since.[26]

Serb paramilitaries in the Yugoslav wars of dissolution had similar ambivalent relationships with the Bosnian Serb Army (VRS) or the Yugoslav National Army (JNA). Whereas none of these militaries were in their entireties against Serb paramilitaries in Croatia and Bosnia, strong opposition existed against them, for various reasons. The documents held in the archives of the International Criminal Tribunal for the Former Yugoslavia (ICTY) offer unique insights into these relations. For example, they demonstrate that the VRS did cooperate with Vojislav Šešelj's men (the *Šešeljevci*), even though as early as October 1991, an internal JNA report to the Command of the First Military District described how they engaged, criticizing the looting and "sadistic abuse" of civilians.[27] Commanders of Šešelj's detachments were later distinguished with the honorary Chetnik title *vojvoda*, which framed them in the tradition of Balkan social banditry. Men such as Branislav Gavrilović Brne commanded in the region of 100 to 200 men around Sarajevo, and his unit, much like other Chetnik groups, was heavily criticized by the VRS for abuse of civilians. In November 1992, Stanislav Galić,

[24] Emin Demirel and Ali Burak Ersemiz, *Ömrüm: Bir İstihbaratçı Askerin Anıları* (Istanbul: Lagin, 2010), 170–2.

[25] Ercüment İşleyen, "Eşref Bitlis Zinciri," *Milliyet*, February 17, 1994; Cumhuriyet Bürosu, "Özal'ın Ölümü İçin Araştırma Önergesi," *Cumhuriyet*, May 22, 2002.

[26] Adnan Akfırat, *Eşref Bitlis Suikastı: Belgelerle* (Istanbul: Kaynak, 1997).

[27] ICTY Šešelj case (IT-03-67), P00251, 3.

commander of the Sarajevo-Romanija Corps of the Bosnian Serb army, called them a "group of criminals whose actions damage the VRS reputation."[28] Negative attitudes toward paramilitaries were widespread. General Manojlo Milovanović, Chief of Staff of the VRS and close associate of General Ratko Mladić, openly aired his contempt for Arkan in the documentary *Jedinica* ("The Unit"). According to Milovanović, Arkan did not respect military authority and was only in it for the looting and self-aggrandizing.[29] There is no reason to dismiss these criticisms as facetious or disingenuous. The JNA and the VRS were armies that had ambitions to be and remain a professional, structured, professional or conscript army.

Of all the ICTY files, perhaps the Tolimir report is most relevant for understanding the relations between armies and paramilitaries. Colonel Zdravko Tolimir (1948–2016) of the 1st Krajina Corps Command of the VRS wrote a "strictly confidential" report entitled "Report on paramilitary formations in the territory of the Serbian Republic of BH." This unique and highly relevant report, dated July 28, 1992, offered an outline of paramilitary actions and violence, and mounted staunch opposition to their existence and excesses. Tolimir identified many different paramilitary groups, some with clear names such as Arkan's Tigers, Šešelj's Chetniks, or White Eagles, but others as a hodgepodge of twenty men "stealing chickens." He then listed the problems they caused: lack of unity, "law of the jungle," scattered nature, "hatred of non-Serbian peoples" (even calling them the "genocidal element among the Serbian people"), war profiteering and looting, following the VRS from behind instead of fighting, and frequent links between the paramilitaries and corrupt political leaderships. But despite being on the ground, even Tolimir did not have a complete overview of all groups, but found it difficult to wade through the murky waters of their existence. Tolimir then presented a list of those paramilitary groups he knew of, with different sizes, affiliations, backgrounds, and motives. His conclusion was crystal clear:

The presence and activity of paramilitary formations negatively affect the Serbian people in two ways: (1) by diminishing trust in the

---

[28] ICTY Mladić, Stanislav Galić report November 18, 1992, discussed on August 28, 2014.
[29] Filip Švarm, *Jedinica* (Documentary, 2006), Episode 2, at 29:20.

government and its capacity to deal with war profiteers, criminals and mass murderers; and (2) by immensely discouraging the fighting élan of SR BH Army members, often resulting in the abandonment of positions. Every armed Serb in BH must be placed under the exclusive command of the SR BH Army, or else he should be disarmed and legal measures taken.[30]

In this remarkable report, Tolimir made a comprehensive argument that was at once moral, political, and functional.

Even more remarkable was that the report induced his superior, General Ratko Mladić, to issue a clear order abolishing paramilitaries. Mladić wrote in a two-page order that "these unlawful formations act under the banner of opposition parties, declaring themselves to be Chetniks or guard units with the intention of evading the front lines." He then added that "plundering paramilitary formations" from the Federal Republic of Yugoslavia (FRY) were acting independently in the areas of VRS responsibility, "with the basic goal of extracting material, technical and other types of goods from the SR BiH." Mladić then summarized them as follows:

These gangs of looters parade around in the rear of the front, in inhabited areas and municipal centers together with local war profiteers and individuals from the authorities who provide them with legitimacy and shelter, with the basic goal of covertly using them to plunder national assets and in their struggle for power and internal conflicts among the Serbs.[31]

Finally, Mladić issued a seven-point order, which stipulated the disarming and disbanding of paramilitary units by August 15, 1992, the placing of all armed men under the unified command of the VRS, the banning of all paramilitary formations, groups, and individuals, and the prosecuting of "commanders and the relevant military territorial organs and organs of government who enable paramilitary organization and

---

[30] MICT Mladić case, 65ter03743, Tolimir report, July 28, 1992. See also ICTY, *The Prosecutor v Ratko Mladic*, Case No. IT-09-92-I, Pre-Trial Brief, February 24, 2012, at http://www.icty.org/x/cases/mladic/custom3/en/120224a.pdf (accessed February 14, 2019).

[31] MICT Mladic, 65ter03744, Mladić confidential order number 31, July 28, 1992.

evasion of recruitment and conscription in accordance with the SR BiH Law on the Army."[32]

These measures and exhortations did not seem to have a comprehensive impact. Well into the mid-1990s, paramilitary bosses continued to roam around and wreak havoc on their victims, mostly defenseless civilians, but occasionally even other security agencies. For example, in 1995, Arkan stopped a car near Prijedor carrying an officer of the VRS, insulted him, slapped him around, shaved his head, and robbed him. The VRS officer then went to complain to General Manojlo Milovanović, asking: "Can anyone beat VRS officers? Because I just got beaten up by Arkan."[33] It seemed as if Arkan was above any law, and local authorities and the VRS could only go as far as to arrest a few of his men.[34] Ratko Mladić was a ruthless, masculinist military leader who never shied away from asserting his authority and control, and he was a force to be reckoned with during wartime Bosnia. But even Mladić never really confronted someone like Arkan, despite the fact that the VRS under his command vastly outnumbered and outgunned the Serb Volunteer Guard (SDG/Arkan's Tigers). VRS generals like Mladić and Milovanović were missing the point—or they knew but acquiesced. Serb(ian) paramilitarism was never about muckraking gangsters only or even an institutional conflict between the Ministry of Defense and the Ministry of Interior (MUP). It was a much more complex beast, an entangled network of intelligence, politics, organized crime, and the presidency. As an informal emergency measure to defeat an enemy or achieve illegitimate objectives or objectives illegitimately, paramilitarism may have had detrimental effects on the army, such as undermining its morale, prestige, and legitimacy. But in the eyes of its organizers, it was worth it.

In no case of paramilitarism is the army or Ministry of Defense the sole, or even main, responsible agency for setting up or tacitly condoning paramilitary groups. Interior Ministries and their police and intelligence agencies are generally at least as involved, if not more. These ministries are widely seen as the keepers of "law and order," have access to weapons from police caches, and often are in control of the intelligence agencies, which are major actors in all examples of paramilitarism.

---

[32] Ibid.   [33] Filip Švarm, *Jedinica* (Documentary, 2006), Episode 2, at 29:20.
[34] ICTY Stanišić and Simatović case (IT-03-69), Nielsen report, 216.

In Argentina's Dirty War of the 1970s, paramilitary collusion and death squad activity were widespread, and tens of thousands of people disappeared and were executed. But despite the fact that Argentina had a strong army, it was not the Ministry of Defense that was responsible for most paramilitary violence. The Argentine Anti-Communist Alliance (AAA or Triple A), for example, assassinated hundreds of opposition civilians, specializing in kidnapping, torture, and executions of journalists, artists, lawyers, and academics. This organization was conceived at an October 1973 secret meeting, at which the then president, interior minister, and various provincial governors were present. The key organizers were Social Welfare Minister José López Rega and counter-insurgency expert police commissioner Alberto Villar, who together wove an entangled web between the ministry, police, and a host of other actors, including "army officers and police officers on active duty, but also discharged police officers, enlisted common criminals, and cadres of the right-wing Peronist Youth of the Argentine Republic (JPRA) and the quasi-fascist Peronist Trade Youth (JSP)."[35] Ton Robben adds to this that the AAA even included "firemen who deactivated bombs on duty and assembled them off-duty."[36]

The free press and critical media was one of the major targets of AAA hit squads, who assaulted the left-wing newspaper *El Mundo* frequently. One of its reporters, Ana Maria Guzzetti, had the courage to ask General Perón at a press conference about "fascist attacks of para-police groups." Perón lost his temper, threatened to sue her, and Guzzetti began receiving death threats. The AAA abducted her, and she was found, drugged and nearly beaten to death, six days later on a highway outside the city. The Interior Ministry finally closed *El Mundo*, and its premises were also firebombed to make sure it stayed closed.[37] López Rega died in 1989 while awaiting trial in prison, and so did Aníbal Gordon (in 1987).

---

[35] Donald C. Hodges, *Argentina's "Dirty War": An Intellectual Biography* (Austin: University of Texas Press, 2014), 173.

[36] Antonius Robben, *Political Violence and Trauma in Argentina* (Philadelphia: University of Pennsylvania Press, 2010), 137. Robben rightly argues that although both left-wing and right-wing assassination squads were highly violent, the latter had the force and legitimacy of the state behind them.

[37] Paul H. Lewis, *Guerrillas and Generals: The "Dirty War" in Argentina* (Westport, CT: Praeger, 2002), 94; Laura Di Marco, "La periodista que desafió a Perón," *La Nacion*, October 5, 2012.

Villar was assassinated by the leftist Montoneros guerrillas in 1974, but Eduardo Almirón, a major operative in AAA, was later found living a comfortable life in the Spanish coastal city of Valencia.[38] Many other assassins and torturers went free due to years of protection from higher office. The death squads that operated freely, rooting out "subversives" and "terrorists," did so due to the ministerial and police protection offered by Villar and López Rega.

In the pecking order of Interior Ministries, the police are rarely at the helm of power. Paramilitarism is much more often a product of intelligence agencies and the elusive webs some of their more powerful bosses cast across various bureaucracies, structures, and levels of government. This makes the phenomenon difficult to research to a level of required precision. But it is possible to paint a composite picture of various cases and reach some conclusions based on the overlap and contrasts between them. Despite differing political systems in which they operate, intelligence agencies share certain characteristics that predispose them to paramilitarism: their partial or complete secrecy regarding the targets of their surveillance, the hardly transparent and accountable nature of their budgets, their authority in the eyes of elected officials, their priority in situations of crisis and security risks, their unfettered and clandestine acquisition of confidential information building up to huge databases, and their general power as a result of a license to kill or detain. Paramilitarism benefits from one or more of these aspects of most intelligence agencies, especially their secretive nature, access to covert action, and ambivalent accountability.[39]

To grasp the relevance of these agencies, Turkey, Colombia, or Yugoslavia are again obvious choices to look into. However, without venturing into struggling democracies or the Global South, the United States is a good example of how intelligence organizations develop, promote, or condone paramilitary networks. The growth and proliferation of US intelligence agencies is legendary—to the point of being mythical in its supposed omniscience and omnipotence. From the 1930s on, American intelligence has grown exponentially. Indeed, so dramatic was

---

[38] Félix Martínez and Nando García, "El Jefe de la Triple A Vive en un Arrabal Valenciano," *El Mundo*, December 17, 2006.

[39] For a broad overview of relevant issues in intelligence studies, see Loch Johnson (ed.), *The Oxford Handbook of National Security Intelligence* (Oxford: Oxford University Press, 2010).

its growth that by 1964, researchers were criticizing "a massive, hidden apparatus, secretly employing about 200,000 persons and spending several billion dollars a year," which was all kept "out of public view and quite apart from the traditional political process."[40] By now, the United States disposes over at least fifteen intelligence agencies employing countless civilian and military personnel, at an estimated annual cost of $75 billion, which is more than all other intelligence budgets—much like the US' regular military budget. Hence, Timothy Melley has argued that "the covert sector has increasingly become a version of the state itself. It has its own bureaucracies (the intelligence services, shell companies), its own laws (NSC [National Security Council] memorandums, secret authorization directives, covert rules of engagement), and its own territories (remote airstrips, Guantánamo Bay, rendition sites)."[41] This industry, since World War II, has been responsible for much covert paramilitary activity in the Global South, especially Latin America (see Chapter 2). And much of it operates by collaboration between US intelligence agencies and Latin American security agencies.

Research on the Yugoslav wars, and in particular the Serbian state under Slobodan Milošević, strongly suggests that Milošević seems not to have fully trusted the army, and therefore set in motion the Serb paramilitary operation through the State Security Service (SDB), in particular its director Jovica Stanišić and his right-hand man Franko Simatović.[42] The duo was most likely responsible for the practical organizing of Serb paramilitarism in the 1990s, through an elaborate but impalpable infrastructure spanning the SDB, police, territorial defense units, and organized crime groups. From their power positions at the Interior Ministry (MUP), they oversaw paramilitarization well into the Kosovo war. For example, a 1999 order from MUP reads: "You shall register all volunteer and paramilitary units and their members and keep them under control in case that you might need to engage them."[43] According to their ICTY indictment, they were in charge of secret

[40] David Wise and Thomas Ross, *Invisible Government* (New York: Random House, 1964), 4.

[41] Timothy Melley, *The Covert Sphere: Secrecy, Fiction, and the National Security State* (Ithaca, NY: Cornell University Press, 2012), 5.

[42] For a thorough study of these relations, see Iva Vukušić, "Serb Paramilitaries and the Yugoslav Wars" (PhD thesis, Utrecht University, 2019).

[43] Interior Ministry dispatch no.Y0196342 to the headquarters of the Public Security Departments, March 24, 1999.

paramilitary units which were not legally authorized to undertake any of the operations they did. Serb paramilitarism demonstrates a powerful paradox: on the one hand, much of it was, as the proverbial underwater iceberg, invisible and unobservable, but at the same time it had the most profound impact on the onset and course of mass violence in Yugoslavia. It was imperceptible even to some of the closest observers of and actors in the war. General Manojlo Milovanović once met Stanišić in Serbia and testified later:

> Badza was in uniform and Stanišić in plain clothes. I asked General Panić who these people were. He told me that it was Stanišić—he only said that he was from the State Security Service, he did not say that he was the chief. I was astounded by Stanišić's knowledge about our situation in Podrinje. Some things he even knew better than I did. He knew who was fighting in which village, who was in command, who...I really was a bit amazed.[44]

Vojislav Šešelj, flamboyant and loquacious, confirmed in many of his media and court appearances that Stanišić and Simatović were the key controllers of the Serb paramilitary industry. Šešelj laid out the variety of paramilitary groups in Serbia, including his own, and added by saying that the idea of paramilitarism "was thought up by key persons from the State Security Service, including Franko Simatović, Frenki, and he was one of the persons who carried it out."[45] Although the ICTY acquitted them in 2013, then ordered a retrial through the United Nations Mechanism for International Criminal Tribunals (MICT), the extant prosecutorial files, witness statements, and declassified documents on the two spy bosses demonstrate the clearest possible picture of paramilitarism to date: a state's intelligence agency conniving and conspiring with other actors to set up paramilitary groups to commit illegitimate violence for political goals.

---

[44] General Manojlo Milovanović testifying in the Stanišić and Simatović ICTY case, on April 23, 2010, speaking about a meeting at Hotel Omorika, Mount Tara, Republic of Serbia. The meeting took place on January 23, 1993; see http://www.icty.org/x/cases/stanisic_sima-tovic/trans/en/100423ED.htm (accessed February 20, 2019).

[45] ICTY Šešelj case (IT-03-67), P17241, March 6, 2012, at www.icty.org/x/cases/seselj/trans/en/120306ED.htm (accessed February 20, 2019).

Serbian journalist Dejan Anastasijević characterized the network in which Stanišić and Simatović operated as the "military line" (*vojna linija*). His 2017 statement at the MICT is worth citing in full:

> I first heard the term *vojna linija* from General Aleksandar Vasiljevic, the former head of the JNA's intelligence and counter-intelligence agency, KOS. The term is generally used unofficially to describe an informal circle of police, military and state officials closely involved in preparations for the war and in conducting paramilitary operations. The *vojna linija* or military line manifested itself in 1990 and 1991 as a diffuse network of mostly MUP officials and some JNA officers loyal to Slobodan Milošević and the idea of Serbian supremacy in Yugoslavia. *This loose network of high-ranking officials loyal to Slobodan Milošević was established to bypass or undermine the decisions of official governmental, police and military bodies.* If these official bodies made decisions, issued orders or took actions antithetical to Slobodan Milošević's aims, members of the *vojna linija* were called upon to undermine these official decisions. In some cases, the *vojna linija* initiated actions that aimed to take control over various official institutions, to force the ouster of persons not loyal to Slobodan Milosevic within those institutions, or to initiate activity throughout the areas in the former Yugoslavia that would serve the aims of the *vojna linija* and Slobodan Milošević.[46]

This remarkable assessment matches quite closely the notions of the Turkish deep state and Colombian para-politics: it captures the informal and networked nature of paramilitarism, as well as its undermining impact on formal state institutions and decisions.

The view from Colombia is similar to that of Serbia. If the Colombian army's relations to the paramilitaries were ambivalent and fragmented, the country's intelligence agencies show a different picture. Declassified files on Military Intelligence General Iván Ramírez Quintero portray him as a highly intelligent spymaster who not only shared sensitive intelligence with pro-state paramilitaries, but also cultivated relationships

---

[46] MICT, File C0003462, Witness Information, Dejan Anastasijević, March 2 and 3, 2017, 9, emphasis added.

with drug traffickers, thereby functioning as the mainstay of the Colombian paramilitary project. Quintero received his intelligence training in the US in 1983, then commanded an intelligence unit of the army, which was disbanded because of overwhelming evidence it had carried out assassinations and forced disappearances in the 1980s and 1990s.[47] The declassified reports of the National Security Archive are useful in that they lay bare the nature of Quintero's ties with narcotraffickers, and paramilitary groups, and his irremovable power base in the Colombian military intelligence community. Apparently Quintero had surrounded himself with personally loyal subordinates, who collaborated with paramilitaries like the AUC to outsource violence they did not want traced back to them. Remarkably, once Quintero was removed from office in 1998, curbing paramilitarism became easier virtually overnight.[48] Major Colombian paramilitary bosses Salvatore Mancuso and Carlos Castaño observed that Quintero was their main conduit for information with officials in the Colombian state in general, and the intelligence services in particular. Much like Stanišić, paramilitarism would not have gained as much influence as it did in Colombia if this intelligence boss had not actively pursued a policy of collusion.

Northern Irish paramilitarism exemplifies the influence of intelligence agencies differently: in no way was the British government's Special Reconnaissance Unit as directly involved in setting up Loyalist paramilitarism as Serbia's SDB was. However, it is likely that ties existed, not necessarily as a top-down hierarchical process, but one of infiltration from below. Many journalistic and advocacy pieces, some sensationalist and speculative, others fairly credible, have been written over the collusion and cooperation between British intelligence and the Loyalist paramilitaries UVF and UDA. Most of these studies misunderstand Northern Irish paramilitarism as a well-oiled conspiracy that was intentionally designed to operate with uncanny precision.[49] Other books

---

[47] Douglas Farah and Laura Brooks, "Colombian army's third in command allegedly led two lives," *Washington Post*, August 11, 1998.

[48] National Security Archive, Electronic Briefing Book No. 166, Document 5, "Paramilitaries Massacre as Many as 50 in Norte de Santander," July 29, 1999, at https://nsarchive2.gwu.edu//NSAEBB/NSAEBB166/19990729.pdf (accessed November 1, 2018).

[49] Anne Cadwallader, *Lethal Allies: British Collusion in Ireland* (Cork: Mercier Press, 2013); Margaret Urwin, *A State in Denial: British Collaboration with Loyalist Paramilitaries* (Cork: Mercier Press, 2016).

suggest that the intelligence agencies were operating as legitimate institutions and that therefore all their actions were strictly within the democratic rule of law.[50] Both views are problematic. Despite functioning in a different socio-political environment than Serbia in the 1990s, Loyalist paramilitarism was a complex phenomenon fraught with internal contradictions. Loyalist paramilitaries penetrated British police and intelligence detachments and leaked sensitive information to their own gangs in Belfast and beyond. Journalist Martin Dillon examined these ties through interviews and files, and reached the conclusion that British intelligence was not hand-in-glove with Loyalist paramilitaries, but that "a number of men in the security forces were sympathetic to the Loyalist cause," and "that as late as 1975 policemen in the Shankill area were drinking in pubs which were the haunts of UDA and UVF units," and that "intelligence files ended up in a loyalist hands because of disgruntled officials of the intelligence."[51] Infiltration from below and individual collusion with paramilitaries was serious enough to allow paramilitarism space to operate and flourish.

Armies and intelligence agencies can cooperate in promoting paramilitarism, but there is often tension between the Ministry of Interior, representing police and state intelligence, and the Ministry of Defense, representing the army, special forces and military intelligence.[52] In the above cases, those agencies who were ultimately implicated in developing paramilitarism had individuals or groups with superior will and/or power to push through their agenda. Whoever ends up on top in the power struggle depends on their effectiveness in mobilizing power *beyond* their own institutions. Julie Mazzei has argued that during crises that foster armed mobilization, a certain split can occur between political and military elites, "where hard-liners find themselves in search of extra-institutional means of achieving their preferred ends."[53]

[50] Fred Holroyd and Nick Brubridge, *War without Honour: Military Intelligence in Northern Ireland* (London: Medium, 1989); Simon Cursey, *MRF Shadow Troop: The Untold True Story of Top Secret British Military Intelligence Undercover Operations in Belfast, Northern Ireland, 1972–1974* (London: Thistle, 2013).
[51] Martin Dillon, *The Dirty War: Covert Strategies and Tactics Used in Political Conflicts* (London: Routledge, 2016), 232, 252–4.
[52] Competition between agencies is often a cause for hiring private military contractors.
[53] Julie Mazzei, *Death Squads or Self-Defense Forces? How Paramilitary Groups Emerge and Challenge Democracy in Latin America* (Chapel Hill: University of North Carolina Press, 2009), 18.

Paramilitarism is a product of this search, an "escape valve," and since states have become highly complex and expansive organizations, the ways in which paramilitarism can emerge has also broadened and diversified; there are simply many more institutions to collude with. So the place and role of an army differs from case to case: sometimes a civilian government erects paramilitary structures against the army, sometimes a military government intentionally creates *security polyarchy* or *security heterarchy* within the state. Furthermore, in the wrangling between the police, army, and intelligence services, it is not necessarily any one of these that reigns supreme, but sub-sections like military intelligence that manage to stretch their arms into the illegitimate sphere for paramilitary power.[54] These "arms" represent different types of network structures that allow differing degrees of influence and connectivity. Collusion differs in type, as a sustained cooperative effort of certain factions to informally collude with one another in intelligence, police, and politics. Sometimes they are personal ties or tribal connections, then again patronage networks, or party affiliations, but for the illegitimate violence that is common in paramilitarism, criminal connections are most useful and influential.

The informal, personalized, hybrid, and dynamic networks that are both cause and consequence of paramilitarism have consequences for how we theorize the state. These networks that give rise to paramilitarism have been described in various national contexts in colorful emic terms: the "deep state" (*derin devlet*) in Turkey, the "military line" (*vojna linija*) in Serbia, the "regime" (*al-nizaam*) in Syria, "para-politics" (*para-política*) in Colombia, or "the process" (*el proceso*) in Argentina.[55] There are substantial differences between these forms of state formation. For example, a "deep state" is not the same as a "state within a state," which is when one security agency becomes so strong to the extent that it overpowers other security agencies disproportionately and begins operating independently within the same state. Paramilitarism can also not be

---

[54] In Turkey, it was the Gendarmerie Intelligence that was most influential; indeed, the acronym JİTEM stands for exactly that: "Gendarmerie Intelligence and Counter-Terrorism" (*Jandarma İstihbarat ve Terörle Mücadele*).

[55] *El Proceso de Reorganización Nacional*, often shortened to *el Proceso* ("the Process") was the National Reorganization Process that the Argentinian army launched to socially engineer a new Argentine society through a broad spectrum of violence against an equally broad spectrum of civilian targets.

reduced to interpretations of the state of exception.[56] Rather, these differing concepts refer to clusters or individuals within various security agencies who cooperate in establishing a network that is not part of the regular institutions of the state, but that has significant executive power and creates extra-institutional spaces of force and power that are not legally sanctioned. Despite real differences in shape and historical context, in a way they all refer to informal parastatal networks that have existed throughout the twentieth and twenty-first centuries. This has two consequences for a redefinition of the state in praxiological and para-institutional terms.

First and foremost, paramilitarism highlights the problem that if you *perform* the state, you *are* the state. Joel Migdal redefined the state through the dual and complementary notions that the state is shaped by both the *image* of a coherent, controlling organization, and "the actual *practices* of its multiple parts."[57] Much like "actually existing socialism," the sum of the practices that states are realistically able to pursue and achieve can be called "actually existing states," or the praxeology of states. It is not the aspiration of states, but the overlapping or contradictory authority, policies, and conduct that matter in understanding and defining paramilitarism. The lower-end interface of the state consists of bottom actors who are very often keenly aware that they are "performing stateness" or making public authority. Koen Vlassenroot's research on the Congolese state is a case in point: he argues that local warlords' claims to legitimacy, governance, and public authority "seems to be one of the principal objects of reference deployed by these actors to legitimate their claims, mainly because it still resonates with the social imaginaries of public order."[58] The praxiological approach is perhaps best summed up by the Syrian pro-regime paramilitaries, a shadowy set of

---

[56] Paramilitarism has been defined as the institutional embodiment of what Giorgio Agamben called "the state of exception." But Agamben wrote about the paradoxical suspension of democracy as a means of saving democracy, which does not apply well to most cases of paramilitary violence, in which paramilitary regimes pursue other objectives, such as maintaining privileges, securing regime continuity, or eliminating perceived threats illegitimately. See Giorgio Agamben, *State of Exception*, trans. Kevin Attell (Chicago, IL: University of Chicago Press, 2005).

[57] Migdal, *State in Society*, 15.

[58] Kasper Hoffmann and Koen Vlassenroot, "Armed Groups and the Exercise of Public Authority: The Cases of the Mayi-Mayi and Raya Mutomboki in Kalehe, South Kivu," *Peacebuilding* 2:2 (2014), 202–20.

para-institutional groups commonly referred to as *Shabbiha* ("Ghosts"), who were widely criticized for not holding public office as part of an official security agency. But the *Shabbiha* generally respond with their favorite slogan: "We are the state, man!" (*Nahna al-dawla, oulak!*).[59] Therefore, in order to examine how the paramilitary infrastructure is set up, one needs to infer it from the conduct (including the violence) that is carried out on the ground in the name of the state. The nature of these relationships may differ from case to case, but there are a few archetypes, such as hierarchical, heterarchical, trade-off, marriage of convenience, delegation, orchestration, and sanctioning. This brings us to the second pillar of state-sponsored paramilitarism: para-institutionality.

Paramilitary infrastructures may look like institutional duplication or supererogation, ingeniously crafted through and across the meshes of institutional oversight; but it is more than that. The term "para-institutionality" emerged from Colombian political discourse and was defined by Alfonso Palacio in 1991 as "a series of mechanisms of social regulation and conflict resolution that do not rely on formal constitutional or legal means, but are governed by informal arrangements and ad hoc mechanisms."[60] This twin-track condition allows for the coexistence of formal institutionalism on the one hand, and the extra-institutional use of force to pursue political interests on the other. Ballvé's research on Colombian paramilitarism demonstrates a similar pattern of how state formation is produced "through the convergence of narco-paramilitary strategies, counterinsurgency, and government reforms aimed at territorial restructuring through decentralization," which are not necessarily contradictory to assumptions of modern "institution building," but a determined effort to make spaces and populations governable—albeit in a deeply violent and exclusionary manner.[61] One could speak of a form of "paramilitary governance," in which states actively legitimize para-institutionality as legitimate state formation. Finally, Rivke Jaffe's definition of Jamaican para-institutionality applies to many other cases as well: "An emergent political formation in

---

[59] See Uğur Ümit Üngör, *Shabbiha: Assad's Paramilitaries and Mass Violence in Syria* (forthcoming, 2021).

[60] Jasmin Hristov, *Paramilitarism and Neoliberalism: Violent Systems of Capital Accumulation in Colombia and Beyond* (London: Pluto, 2014), 33.

[61] Teo Ballvé, "Everyday State Formation: Territory, Decentralization, and the Narco Landgrab in Colombia," *Environment and Planning D: Society and Space* 30:4 (2012), 603–22.

which multiple governmental actors—in this case, criminal organizations, politicians, police, and bureaucrats—are entangled in a relationship of collusion and divestment, sharing control over urban spaces and populations."[62] These conceptualizations of para-institutionality share two major features: patrimonial and brokerage relations running through the state, and performances of statehood through violence. We are not dealing with the false opposites of "weak" versus "strong" states, but if anything, with smart states.

Parties and Constituencies

Stacey Hunt expressed in a single sentence the pivot of paramilitarism: "Paramilitaries transcend the boundaries between state and society."[63] As a complex political interplay between state and society, paramilitarism is not strictly a state affair. On the contrary, in some cases it is non-state actors that take the initiative in organizing paramilitary groups and committing paramilitary violence. A wide range of societal (or "civil society") actors are often involved in various ways: political parties, labor unions, cultural associations, religious authorities, businesses, activist groups, charities, cooperatives, foundations, voluntary organizations, sports clubs, academia, tribes, and others. This includes, indeed, organized crime. In fact, few examples of paramilitary violence are truly effective and lasting with only state actors steering the process. The most efficient infrastructures of paramilitarism are those webs woven across not only different state agencies, but in and beyond civil society. Indeed, the functioning of para-institutionality is highly dependent on lower-ranking officials and officers who toe the line and recognize and share each other's aims. This section looks at political parties and communities, focusing on several countries and highlighting key connections and mechanisms of para-institutional and paramilitary activity.

Political parties are a major vehicle of social mobilization. Across the world, countless political parties with millions of active and passive

---

[62] Rivke Jaffe, "The Hybrid State: Crime and Citizenship in Urban Jamaica," *American Ethnologist* 40:4 (2013), 734–48.

[63] Stacey Hunt, "Rethinking State, Civil Society, and Citizen Participation: The Case of the Colombian Paramilitaries," *Behemoth: A Journal on Civilisation* 2:1 (2009), 64–87.

members operate in democratic and authoritarian regimes alike. For many people, political parties are the only way in which they are mobilized and politically active; membership or involvement often brings prestige, power, privilege, and prosperity. In societies with paramilitary activity, political parties that have taken over the state through either bullets or ballots, or a mix between those, often entertain their own party militias before and after the seizure of power. The National Socialist German Workers' Party (NSDAP or Nazi Party) and its SA (Brownshirts) and later the SS in 1920s and 1930s Germany is the most commonly cited (and egregious) example, but a closer look demonstrates many other parties with armed wings loyal to the party. From the National Liberation Movement (MLN) in Guatemala to Jobbík in Hungary, and from the MHP in Turkey to the Institutional Revolutionary Party (PRI) in Mexico, party militias are fairly widespread. When their political parties seize power, these militias often end up in powerful positions in the state's official coercive apparatuses, or remain in the shadows of para-institutionality, thereby continuing to exist, but as part of the infrastructure of paramilitarism. It also seems less relevant whether these parties are governing parties or opposition parties, as some examples clearly demonstrate. In both cases, illegal retention of arms caches and the ability to mobilize men in uniforms are powerful indicators of paramilitary activity. Examples can be given the world over.

The Iraqi Ba'ath party was a vanguard party based on secular nationalism with millenarian undertones, a movement that believed in a coming fundamental transformation of society through forceful action. This already gave it a fairly violent nature, but when it came under the influence of Saddam Hussein, from the 1970s on, its paramilitary wings multiplied and became more influential. Its "Popular Army" (al-Jaysh al-Shaabi) party militia terrorized the streets of Iraqi cities, and two other paramilitary wings, the "National Guard" (Haras al-Qawmi) and "Saddam's Men of Sacrifice" (Fedayeen Saddam) carried out assassinations and rioted against other political parties, especially the Iraqi Communist Party, and was backed by the CIA.[64] Once the Ba'ath Party

---

[64] Con Coughlin, *Saddam: His Rise and Fall* (New York: HarperCollins, 2005), 62–3, 197. A similar process occurred to the "Special Apparatus" (*Jihaz al-Khaas*), the Ba'ath party's intelligence organization. Saddam was in charge of it in the 1960s, and after the 1968 coup, he

came into power through a *coup d'état* on July 17, 1968, these militias transformed from a street-fighting gang to a militia dedicated to protecting the regime, both against internal opposition and against any coup attempt by the regular Iraqi army. Having seized the Iraqi state institutions, the Popular Army grew from a few thousand members in 1970 to an estimated 650,000 in 1987.[65] The fact that *al-Jaysh al-Shaabi* was subordinated to the party meant that it functioned not only as a reserve, but as an anti-army group to offset the power of the Ministry of Defense and offer the regime control of the civilian population in the interior rather than on military fronts. In other words, the militia was a coup-proofing device, as was the case for many paramilitary groups.[66]

In Colombia, party militias were profoundly influential in setting up paramilitary infrastructures, but differently from Iraq.[67] According to Álvaro, "the penetration of irregular armed groups into politics originated in the political and administrative decentralization process of the early 1980s, an opportunity that was exploited by guerrilla groups to initiate infiltration and take over local and regional power."[68] Specifically, paramilitary groups were involved in the assassination and election of a number of mayors, councilors, deputies, and parliamentarians, through which they influenced party politics from the municipal to the national level. Through this sustained support and coercion, paramilitary groups prescribed *and* precluded certain political parties from gaining power, thereby cementing strong networks of armed clientelism running through Colombian politics.[69] This skewed electoral processes; more importantly, some political parties were established *after* paramilitary

expanded it and integrated it with the existing Intelligence (*Mukhabarat*) system in Iraq: ibid., 85ff. See also Fayez al-Khafaji, *Al-Haras al-Qawmi wa Dawru al-Damawi fi al-Iraq* (Baghdad: Sutoor, 2015).

[65] Ibrahim Al-Marashi and Sammy Salama, *Iraq's Armed Forces: An Analytical History* (London: Routledge, 2008), 124–6.
[66] Konstantin Ash, "Threats to Leaders' Political Survival and Pro-Government Militia Formation," *International Interactions* 42:5 (2016), 703–28.
[67] Phillip McLean, "Colombia: Failed, Failing, or Just Weak?," *The Washington Quarterly* 25:3 (2002), 123–34.
[68] Miriam Álvaro, "La Parapolítica: la infiltración paramilitar en la clase política colombiana" (May 15, 2007), *Nuevo Mundo Mundos Nuevos*, at https://journals.openedition.org/nuevomundo/4636 (accessed February 28, 2019).
[69] Francisco Gutierrez Sanin, *Clientelistic Warfare: Paramilitaries and the State in Colombia (1982–2007)* (Oxford: Peter Lang, 2019).

groups became active in an area, giving birth to *parapolítica*, the phenomenon in which paramilitary bosses were running politics and parties to their liking.[70] The Colombian case most of all demonstrates that relations between parties and paramilitaries is not a simplistic top-down process of parties "buying muscle" from paramilitaries, but also the latter co-opting the former for their own interests. In several interviews, paramilitary bosses such as Vicente Castaño or Salvatore Mancuso openly stated that they had dozens of sympathizers in the Colombian Congress.[71]

In late 1980s Yugoslavia, political parties other than the Communist Party were gradually set up amidst the increasing ethno-political polarization. But it was paradoxically not Slobodan Milošević's ruling Socialist Party of Serbia (SPS) that was most entangled with paramilitaries. It was the new Serb(ian) parties that set up their own militias, including Radovan Karadžić's Serb Democratic Party (SDS) in Bosnia-Herzegovina and Vojislav Šešelj's Serbian Radical Party (SRS). Even Arkan set up a new party, the Party of Serbian Unity (SSJ). Zdravko Tolimir's incisive report on paramilitarism acknowledged this reality. Tolimir wrote that paramilitaries

> harm the reputation of both the authorities and the ruling party and create an impression among the population that the ruling party is pro-Chetnik, and that the paramilitaries are its exponents. However, a more detailed analysis of these formations shows beyond any doubt that their leaders, their core, and even all their members belong to opposition parties (SPO, SNO, SRS). Through the actions of party paramilitaries one gets the impression that the Serbian Democratic Party is losing its role and standing among the Serbian population...public actions of party armies are damaging the reputation of the ruling SDS.[72]

Whereas Milošević made a serious effort to distance himself from paramilitaries, Karadžić openly flirted with them and did not hide his

---

[70] Jorge Melo, "Los paramilitares y su impacto sobre la política colombiana," in Francisco Buitrago and León Zamosc (eds), *Al Filo del Caos: crisis política en la Colombia de los años 80* (Bogotá: Iepri y Tercer Mundo, 1990), 475–514.

[71] Álvaro, "La Parapolítica," 25.

[72] MICT Mladić case, 65ter03743, Tolimir report, July 28, 1992, 2.

involvement with them in any way. For him, they were Serb patriots whose shady backgrounds were irrelevant or of secondary concern.[73] Secret documents from the 1990s reveal how Karadžić's political party took power in Bosnia in collusion with paramilitaries. In December 1991, the SDS leadership drew up a top secret document entitled "For the organization and activity of organs of the Serb people in Bosnia-Herzegovina in extraordinary circumstances." The document laid out a strategy for the takeover of municipalities, and, according to James Gow, "the creation of shadow governments and para-governmental structures through various 'crisis headquarters.'"[74] A political party was now itself acting as a paramilitary group.

Finally, a particularly destructive example of party militias can be seen in the Rwandan genocide of 1994. From the beginning of the civil war in 1990 on, the two leading parties, the National Republican Movement for Democracy and Development (MRND) and Coalition for the Defence of the Republic (CDR), established party militias drawn up from mostly Hutu youth. The MRND commanded the *Interahamwe* ("Those who work together"), and the CDR the more extreme and violent *Impuzamugambi* ("Those with the same goal"). They became mostly known as the main perpetrators of the Rwandan genocide, but their history before 1994 is equally relevant to understand paramilitarism and party politics in Rwanda.[75] A painstaking analysis by André Guichaoua demonstrates that these militias could exist due to party support, financing, and training.[76] Rwandan President Juvenál Habyarimana, himself of the MRND party, supported their existence from December 1991 on, thereby providing legitimacy, as their membership rose from thousands to tens of thousands, and they donned uniforms and badges.[77] Then, gradually, they began taking over the public sphere by controlling neighborhoods in Kigali. Being a member of either militia was fun and

---

[73] For example, there exists only one photo of Milošević and Arkan together, standing inadvertently and awkwardly at a funeral, but there are several public photos of Karadžić with Arkan.

[74] James Gow, *The Serbian Project and Its Adversaries: A Strategy of War Crimes* (Montreal: McGill-Queen's University Press, 2003), 122–3.

[75] Luke Fletcher, "Turning *Interahamwe*: Individual and Community Choices in the Rwandan Genocide," *Journal of Genocide Research* 9:1 (2007), 25–48.

[76] André Guichaoua, *From War to Genocide: Criminal Politics in Rwanda, 1990–1994* (Madison, University of Wisconsin Press, 2015).

[77] Mathieu Ngirumpatse, *La tragédie rwandaise: l'autre face de l'histoire* (n.p.: n.p., 1999), 69.

brought power, status, access to alcohol, and enabled Hutu identity. Their members, young men, would party at Kigali nightclubs and cafés, training with weapons such as machetes, hoes, axes, clubs, and bows and arrows. During the June 1992 peace negotiations between the Rwandan government and the rebel Rwandan Patriotic Front (RPF), they rampaged through Kigali, beating up Tutsis and looting shops. Gradually, paramilitarism began to be anchored in the Rwandan state, and their influence metastasized to the prefecture, other parties, soldiers, retired officers, local sponsors, and the influential *conseils de securité préfectoraux*.[78] Since the militias were not legally recognized, nobody was really accountable for their actions; transgressors and offenders would get away with crimes thanks to patronage within the parties. Édouard Karemera, one of the main organizers of the *Interahamwe*, reorganized them only when it became clear that the militia began harassing Hutus as well. But by then, it was May 1994, and the genocide was well underway.[79] Within years, paramilitarism had transformed a number of unorganized rowdy boys' groups hanging around football clubs, into a well-organized network of genocide perpetrators.

All in all, political parties have been influential in paramilitarism, but in different ways: in some cases, they set up their own militias who later controlled a formal security service; in other cases they were set up by a ruling party against the army; and again in other cases, they were the private armies of politicians bent on holding power. But political parties do not only revolve around the party activists and leadership. They have constituencies, including members, and wider communities in which they operate. The conduct of these communities is just as important to an understanding paramilitarism as the decisions of the party leadership. From large-scale ethnic communities down to tribes, and further down to families and individuals, paramilitarism is affected by and can affect all of these primary social ties. Furthermore, civil society organizations such as sports clubs and labor unions have also contributed to paramilitarism. Their hierarchical stratification, group identity, strong solidarity, and masculinity may give them a proclivity, or perhaps lower thresholds, to violence.

---

[78] Guichaoua, *From War to Genocide*, 126–34.   [79] Ibid., 258.

Ethnic communities and tribes are a case in point. Many paramilitary groups are largely drawn from particular ethnic communities in particular areas, such as Serbs from Eastern Bosnia, Uzbeks from northern Afghanistan, Chechens from northern Chechnya, or Alawites from the Syrian coast. This is neither to say that these communities are predetermined to militarize, nor that they are "martial races." However, over a longer period of time (decades, generations), for various reasons political violence has deeply affected them: politicizing identities, deepening threat perceptions, pursuing narrow ethnic agendas, and thereby paving the way for even longer and deeper conflicts. Emil Souleimanov's study of Chechen tribes who ended up supporting the Russian government as paramilitaries draws a similar picture for Chechnya. Moscow's "Chechenization" policy attempted to eliminate the local Chechen resistance by using the Kadyrov clan as proxy human resources. Souleimanov demonstrates "the crucial importance of cultural knowledge understood in an ethnographic sense in terms of patterns of social organization, persisting value systems, and other related phenomena."[80] Even though this paramilitarization of Chechens appears like empowerment of these tribes, most often they are not in fact. In Guatemala, paramilitaries drawn from indigenous Mayan communities were given surrogacy, not agency, and were just as powerless toward the end of the conflict as they were in the beginning.[81] After all, these community-based paramilitaries operated within the strictures of the state and could hardly transform their militarization into political power. Their militarization did, however, change power and economic relations *within* the community and affected them profoundly; a cursory look into Chechen, Afghan, or Kurdish society would confirm that. Furthermore, when states "flip" insurgents and turn them against their insurgent brethren as paramilitaries, they not only split such movements, as in Kashmir, Peru, Chechnya, Kurdistan, and Sri Lanka, but those defectors who end up joining the state often turn out to be most effective pro-state paramilitaries.[82]

---

[80] Emil Souleimanov, "An Ethnography of Counterinsurgency: Kadyrovtsy and Russia's Policy of Chechenization," *Post-Soviet Affairs* 31:2 (2015), 91–114.
[81] Marcia Esparza, *Silenced Communities: Legacies of Militarization and Militarism in a Rural Guatemala Town* (New York: Berghahn, 2018).
[82] Paul Staniland, "Between a Rock and a Hard Place: Insurgent Fratricide, Ethnic Defection, and the Rise of Pro-State Paramilitaries," *Journal of Conflict Resolution* 56:1 (2012), 16–40.

Tribes, led by chieftains and clan leaders, are among Migdal's famous "strongmen," and in many cases of paramilitarism were crucial. In a thorough study of warlords in Afghanistan, Antonio Giustozzi discusses the "incipient warlordism" among southern Pashtun tribes. Warlordism can be seen as paramilitarism minus the state (in that all paramilitary bosses are warlords as well). Considering the fluctuating status of the Afghan state in recent history, certain tribal attributes were prone to paramilitarization, such as hierarchical structures, honor codes, loyalty, patronage structures, and patrimonialism. When a weakening Afghan state failed in its military leadership, and foreign states began supporting militias, tribes would fill the void as tribal chieftains fashioned themselves into warlords.[83] Tribes also play a key role in the Turkish–Kurdish conflict. The early Turkish nation state, although it employed a strongly anti-tribal political discourse, did not seek to monopolize violence universally. Rather, it instrumentalized structures of violence outside of the formal state system by enlisting tribes selectively and opportunistically. Tribal groups continued to play an important role in shaping state institutions in the transition from empire to nation state. This recrudesced into the tribal auxiliaries or "village guards" (*köy korucuları*), tens of thousands of armed Kurdish men, who the Turkish state deployed in an effort to fight the PKK, in order to draw Kurdish support for the state, and offer local knowledge. Some tribal chieftains became members of parliament, which buttressed their relations with the state and power in the government.[84] Postcolonial modern republics such as Iraq also relied on tribal paramilitaries; for example, Saddam Hussein enlisted Arab tribes in the "Tribal Army" (*Jaish al-Asha'ir*), an auxiliary force. These groups started as counter-insurgency forces due to their mobilizational capacity, since there are many very large Iraqi tribes, but gradually became the tribal "interface" of the Iraqi state, functioning as the main interlocutors between local communities and the state.[85] This created the paradoxical situation of a modern republic

---

[83] Antonio Giustozzi, *Empires of Mud: War and Warlords in Afghanistan* (London: Hurst, 2012), 35ff.

[84] Şemsa Özar, *Geçmişten Günümüze Türkiye'de Paramiliter bir Yapılanma: Köy Koruculuğu Sistemi* (Diyarbakır: DİSA, 2013).

[85] Lisa Blaydes, *State of Repression: Iraq under Saddam Hussein* (Princeton, NJ: Princeton University Press, 2018), 287.

relying on pre-modern tribal social formations and thereby promoting feudalization. All in all, communities and tribes are effective actors for paramilitarism because they can identify and track people due to their familiarity with local languages, geography, and culture; they can extract information; they have geographic and political knowledge; they can offer a temporary solution to win battles and conflicts; and they can offer technologies of rule. However, they do run the risk of deepening societal contrasts (in communities) and entrenching feudalization (for tribes).

Beyond communities and tribes, paramilitarism is also relevant at the level of kinship. Many paramilitary groups are either set up by a nuclear or extended family, or consist of influential relatives. In Colombia, Alvaro Uribe and his cousin Mario led a paramilitary group, and the three Castaño brothers Vicente, Fidel, and Carlos did likewise. Kinship relations are intensive and impactful, and can be potentially either very constructive or very destructive. In these examples, private, intimate conflicts between siblings (such as love, sex, property, hierarchy, jealousy, bonding, fear, protection) were amplified through political conflicts and the wide availability of arms. For example, Carlos Castaño published a book, outlining his vision of how "self-defense units" like the AUC were formed in response to the state's incapability of defending hardworking landowners like his father. Revenge for his father's losses was a major motive for the three brothers.[86] In the Eastern Bosnian town of Višegrad, two cousins, Milan and Sredoje Lukić, formed a paramilitary group and ran a reign of terror during the war. The duo committed several massacres, including burning alive over one hundred people, and playing a prominent role in the ethnic cleansing of the town. Milan had two more brothers, one who was killed while police tried to arrest Milan, and another who faced trial in Serbia for war crimes. Another distant cousin, Sreten Lukić, was a high official in the Serbian police, and from his position in Belgrade attempted to protect Milan during the war by lobbying for him.[87] The internal structure of the Piqueteros, militant neighborhood unions that can function as

---

[86] Carlos Castaño, *Colombia, siglo XXI: Las Autodefensas y la paz* (n.p.: Editorial Colombia Libre, 1999).

[87] Milan Lukić later wrote a memoir during his imprisonment by the ICTY: see Milan Lukić, *Confession of the Prisoner of the Hague* (Belgrade: M. Lukić, 2011).

pro-government militias in Argentina, is marked by clientelist relations (which is quite common) but also by personal and family relationships that in some cases date back over twenty years.[88] The Chechen example of the Kadyrovtsy exemplifies this best: a paramilitary group named after the very family that leads and staffs it.

Finally, paramilitaries are individuals. At the micro level, it is relevant how and why particular types of individuals become involved in para-military groups. Yet answering these questions is no easy task, since the variation across cases and diversity within the cases is significant. However, there are some assumptions we can identify. The notion that members of large groups do not act in accordance with a common inter-est unless motivated by personal gain (whether economic or social) is just as valid for paramilitaries as it is for other social organizations.[89] One of the Serb recruits of the Scorpions famously said: "I loved three things in life, and I am going to share them with all of you. I loved, and I am going to be vulgar because that is the kind of man I am... I loved pussy, the rifle, and the state and I still stand by that. That has to be clear to all."[90] Along similar lines, Zdravko Tolimir indiscriminately described their membership as follows:

> They are mostly composed of individuals of low moral quality, and in many cases of persons previously prosecuted for crimes and offences and even convicted for crimes of murder, robbery, larceny and the like. Very often, such units have in their ranks pathological criminals whom the conditions of war and general lawlessness have brought to the fore.[91]

There was certainly an element of truth to this (see Chapter 3), but it was also a simplistic and reductionist depiction as the membership base was more diverse. There is no particular profile and almost anyone

---

[88] Manwaring, *Gangs*, 43.

[89] Mancur Olson, *The Logic of Collective Action* (Cambridge, MA: Harvard University Press, 2009), 34.

[90] Slobodan Medić Boca, Scorpions commander, statement in court. Transcript of the audio recording, February 22, 2006, trial at County Court in Belgrade, War Crimes Department, 45.

[91] MICT Mladić case, 65ter03743, Tolimir report, July 28, 1992. See also ICTY, *The Prosecutor v Ratko Mladic*, Case No. IT-09-92-I, Pre-Trial Brief, February 24, 2012, at http://www.icty.org/x/cases/mladic/custom3/en/120224a.pdf (accessed February 14, 2019).

seems to be able to get involved: at one end of the spectrum, some have PhDs, at the other end many are illiterate; and there is a broad range of actors in between. However, it does seem that most members of paramilitary groups have little exposure to foreign cultures, are habitually or chronically unemployed, and are fairly uneducated, both in terms of formal education and civic education—what in German is called *politische Bildung*. Only further biographical research, both individually and collectively, could clarify the profiles, motives, and experiences of these men.

The documentary *The Act of Killing* depicts the former paramilitary killer Anwar Kongo from Indonesia in vivid detail. We see a vain, shallow, and narcissistic monoglot who has never left his country and does not realize how genocide is perceived in the outside world (he says: "outsiders"). His social environment consists mostly of idolaters, right-wing Indonesian vigilantes, and Suharto regime apologists and propagandists—all of whom are steeped in nationalism and sexism. In front of the cameras, they mutually reinforce the moral landscape of the 1965 genocide, continuously and repeatedly convincing each other that what happened was a necessary act of national self-defense against the threat of communism. The film presents him as a perpetrator in a broad societal context, and it is not hard to imagine how he could have gotten involved in paramilitary violence, having been thoroughly socialized in this violent moral universe, in which mass murder is good, the victims have no humanity, and democracy is only a barely tolerable means. At the same time, he affectionately teaches his grandchildren to be honest and respectful, for example when he explains them to be gentle with a handful of ducklings at a pond. Paramilitaries such as Anwar Kongo share characteristics with other criminals, even perpetrators, but what makes them unique is the particular paramilitary infrastructure that empowered/empowers them.

Finally, one category of individuals that has not received enough comparative attention is the businessperson. The involvement of corporations such as Chiquita in paramilitarism has been well-researched. But individual businessmen also get caught up in paramilitary activities, in various ways. For example, in Colombia, the civilian sponsors of paramilitary activity included business owners like ranchers, plantation owners, and miners. The presence of large landholdings, particularly those owned by narcotraffickers, has been a strong indicator of paramilitarism. One US State Department report sums up the involvement of businessmen in paramilitarism as follows:

> Those with the money to buy their own 'justice'—wealthy landowners, cattle ranchers, emerald miners, business owners, and narcotraffickers—hire armed vigilantes to protect their lives and their property. Some of these 'self-defense' groups are simply that; others [at] the opposite end of the spectrum have become death squads.[92]

Consequently, some researchers have argued that paramilitarism is a violent defense of the economic status quo and a form of oppression of the working class and peasantry.[93] Whereas this Marxist interpretation might be valid for the Colombian case, in other case (such as Serbia, Sudan, or Syria), paramilitarism actually empowered working-class people and led to upward social mobility for many of them. The Rwandan example demonstrates that these interpretations can coexist: Hutu businessmen like Désiré Murenzi, director of Petrorwanda and MRND member, recruited *Interahamwe* militias from the Loisirs football team supporters, and also IDPs. He financed them through his business, donations, and rent. The boys enjoyed the perks of the *Interahamwe*: free transport, travel to/in Kigali, influential contacts, free beer after rallies, and membership "permitted survival by means of petty criminality, since it protected members de jure or de facto from prosecution."[94] This demonstrates that, indeed, pro-status quo businessmen funded paramilitaries, but it was also mostly disadvantaged working-class youth who joined them. The broader argument here is that paramilitarism is not just top-down state-orchestrated, nor only bottom-up grassroots, but that the interrelationships between these forms the complex interaction and *intreccio* (Aldo Civico) that builds the paramilitary infrastructure. Communities with collective identity fears,

---

[92] National Security Archive, Electronic Briefing Book No. 368, "Memorandum for ARA/PPCP," June 1, 1998, 3, at https://nsarchive2.gwu.edu//NSAEBB/NSAEBB368/docs/19980601.pdf (accessed March 14, 2019).
[93] Lesley Gill, *A Century of Violence in a Red City: Popular Struggle, Counterinsurgency, and Human Rights in Colombia* (Durham, NC: Duke University Press, 2016).
[94] Guichaoua, *From War to Genocide*, 125, 132, 136–9.

tribes with structural proclivities, and individuals prone to recruitment all form the architecture of paramilitarism.[95]

Committing Violence

Paramilitarism is about committing violence, in particular violence against civilians. Paramilitaries, as studied in this book, have been most often deployed as counter-insurgency forces, and as such have been responsible for murdering civilians the world over. Three massacres demonstrate well how that violence was embedded in the paramilitary infrastructure of the respective states: the Bahia Portete massacre in northern Colombia (April 18, 2004), the Cizre massacre in southeastern Turkey (March 21, 1992), and the Trnovo massacre in eastern Bosnia and Herzegovina (July 17, 1995). All three were eminently paramilitary massacres, committed with the backing of the respective para-institutional establishment. Their timing, forms, and causes reflect not only the when, how, and why, but also various elements of organization highlighted in the previous section, including variations and differences.

Colombia witnessed a number of large-scale, brutal paramilitary massacres from the 1990s to the 2000s. Several of these have received international attention and gained notoriety for their brutality and scale, such as the Mapiripán massacre, the Putumayo massacre, or the El Aro massacre—almost all committed by the AUC.[96] One of the most "instructive" massacres was that of Bahía Portete, in Colombia's north-ernmost tip, which is mostly inhabited by the Wayúu indigenous people. On April 18, 2004, paramilitaries of the "North Bloc" of the AUC, carried out a massacre of this settlement, killing twelve (mostly women), kidnapping thirty-three more, and forcibly displacing over 500 people. The Bahía Portete massacre is instructive for two distinct reasons: first, because of the paramilitaries' use of different forms of violence, including torture, rape, murder, expulsion, and forced disappearance, which

---

[95] The metaphor of "architecture" is taken from Kate Ferguson, *Architectures of Violence: The Command Structures of Modern Mass Atrocities, from Yugoslavia to Syria* (London: Hurst, 2018).
[96] Human Rights Watch, *Breaking the Grip? Obstacles to Justice for Paramilitary Mafias in Colombia* (New York: Human Rights Watch, 2008), 52ff.

means it was more than a "mere" instance of mass killing. Second, because of the identities of the perpetrators: the responsible killers were the subordinates of AUC commander Rodrigo Tovar Pupo (a.k.a. "Jorge40"), who was at the heart of the parapolítica scandal.[97] The massacre was carried out as revenge for a local incident which reflected broader problems: a local Wayúu family kidnapped an employer in a private conflict, but the AUC was broadly hostile to the Wayúu coastal population, accusing them of trafficking and smuggling, and allied to the FARC. According to the platform Verdad Abierta, the Bloque Norte's ambition was to cleanse the coast of the potentially disloyal population and take control of a port for all types of illegal traffic. Furthermore, there were intra-Wayúu conflicts on hand as well: one of the organizing perpetrators was José María Barros Ipuana (Chema Bala), himself a Wayúu.[98]

The violence was diverse, brutal, and effective. That day, about 150 paramilitaries entered the village, went through several ranches door-to-door, rounded up unarmed civilians, and executed them. The killers were not murdering at random but came prepared, carrying "a death list" (una lista de la muerte).[99] The killing was conducted by shooting with AK-47s or burning alive, but most victims were hacked to death or decapitated with machetes and axes. An eyewitness later reported in an interview:

I could see, I saw her when they killed her [Diana], they took her down, she was tied with her hands back and they killed her at the side of the road when they got her out of the vehicle. They killed her with a blunt iron, they put her on her back and they hit her with the bar behind her head, her head was opened and then she was cut on the ground with a small chain saw (una motosierra pequeña).[100]

---

[97] "Jorge 40," Rodrigo Tovar Pupo profile, Verdad Abierta, at http://www.verdadabierta.com/victimarios/ los-jefes/691-perfil-rodrigo-tovar-pupo-alias-jorge-40 (accessed March 18, 2019).

[98] Carlos Arturo Salamanca, "Bahía Portete, la masacre y el ritual: Violencia masiva, mediaciones y practices transversales de memoria en La Guajira," Antípoda: Revista de Antropología y Arqueología 21 (2015), 121–43.

[99] For an elaborate discussion of the Bahía Portete massacre, including eyewitness testimony and analysis, see Grupo de Memoria Histórica, La masacre de Bahía Portete: Mujeres Wayúu en la mira (Bogotá: Semana, 2010), 80.

[100] Ibid., 58.

The paramilitaries also committed torture and sexual violence, for example by cutting off sexual organs such as women's breasts, before and after death. They also kidnapped thirty-three people, including two young girls (5 and 7 years old), none of whom were ever heard of again, and all of whom were likely killed but must be officially considered "forcibly disappeared." Finally, they destroyed the clinic, desecrated the cemetery and the Wayúu's sacred stones, and issued the population an ultimatum of twenty-four hours to leave the area.[101]

Much like other AUC massacres in Colombia, the Bahía Portete massacre, too, is highly relevant in furthering an understanding of paramilitarism. First and foremost, the massacre demonstrates very clearly the alliance and collusion between the paramilitaries and the state's official security apparatus, especially the army division stationed there. The day before the massacre, an officer from the Colombian army's Cartagena Battalion transported the paramilitaries to the area in two cars and passed, without problem, several checkpoints. Débora Barros Fince, a Wayúu indigenous woman who survived the massacre, noted in an interview that her uncle was terrified and wanted to contact the authorities:

He called up the Cartagena Battalion in Riohacha on his cell phone. It's almost impossible to believe. He told them, "There are some men here who are paramilitaries, and they are threatening to kill everyone, to destroy the community. We need you to send some troops here." And they said "Yes, we know. We are preparing to send some troops over." So what happened? A half hour later he got a call on his cell phone. The paramilitaries told him they were going to kill him, that they were going to cut him to pieces. They said a whole lot of things to him. We were just paralyzed when we found out they had called him like that.[102]

---

[101] Aviva Chomsky, *Linked Labor Histories: New England, Colombia, and the Making of a Global Working Class* (Durham, NC: Duke University Press, 2008), 271–2, 287–91.

[102] Fince and other survivors fled across the Venezuelan border to Maracaibo, where they reported the massacre. Colombian Vice President Francisco Santos stated to the press that the communities had returned to Bahía Portete swiftly after, but the survivors vowed never to trust the Colombian army again. See "It Seems Impossible to Believe," *Cultural Survival* (December 2004), at www.culturalsurvival.org/publications/cultural-survival-quarterly/it-seems-impossible-believe-survivor-describes-massacre (accessed March 18, 2019).

A second relevant aspect is the politically expedient use of co-ethnics in paramilitarism (like in Kurdistan or Chechnya), who were first utilized and then disposed of. Chema Bala was one of the local indigenous leaders who had a prehistory of illicit trade and drug trafficking in the region. Research demonstrated that he contacted the Bloque Norte, made a deal with Jorge40, and orchestrated the massacre. After the massacre, he and his men were thrown to the wolves by the higher-ranking paramilitaries and convicted in 2007. Jorge40 went free.[103] A third key feature was the nature of the violence: not only did the paramilitaries commit various forms of violence (torture, killing, rape, expulsion), but there was also no attempt to hide or dispose of the victims' bodies. On the contrary, they were tortured and exhibited in public, and their bodies left lying in open places, often near their homes or on intersections of busy roads. These dynamics are telling: the state was not weak, but so powerful that it could allow or enable gangs involved in organized crime to function as a justification of its own continuation. In other words, the state first created a temporary bogeyman, and then eliminated it, never to address the deeper sources of their violence.[104] These peculiarities of the massacre do not render it unique at all; they are traits we can find in other massacres as well.

During the Yugoslav wars, Serb paramilitaries committed a wide range of violence: torture, sexual violence, incarceration, and several important, brutal massacres, such as those in Višegrad, Ovčara, and of course Srebrenica. One massacre stands out from the others for its notoriety. On July 17, 1995, members of the Serb paramilitary unit "Scorpions" executed six young Bosnian Muslim men and boys in broad daylight near the village of Trnovo, south of Sarajevo.[105] The perpetrators shot the victims in the back and in the head, and then moved on as a unit, which was its general modus operandi. The massacre was a covert operation by the Scorpions, who were around Srebrenica to support Bosnian Serb forces, as they were contracted specifically for this

---

[103] "Condenados dos wayuu por masacre de Bahía Portete," *El Heraldo*, August 31, 2012.

[104] In a similar vein, *Los Pepes* were very effective paramilitary actors, because they were a criminal group that the state embraced to get rid of Pablo Escobar.

[105] The Scorpions unit was headed by Slobodan Medić, and the victims of the massacre were Safet Fejzić (17), Azmir Alispahić (17), Sidik Salkić (36), Smail Ibrahimović (35), Dino Salihović (16), and Juso Delić (25).

job. The Trnovo massacre was relevant for several reasons. First, the perpetrating paramilitary group, the Scorpions, was under the direct command of the Serbian Interior Ministry, in a rare but not uncommon case of relatively unconcealed ties. Second, the massacre can be seen as part of the broader Srebrenica massacre, since the victims had been brought to Trnovo almost 200 kilometers from the Srebrenica area in the immediate aftermath of the fall of the enclave. Third, as a novelty in the era before YouTube and smartphones, the perpetrators themselves videotaped the massacre, and the footage provides undeniable evidence and depiction of paramilitary violence.[106] Finally, the perpetrators were convicted in court, some for genocide, due to the evidential value of the videotape. The Trnovo massacre was unique among the three examples discussed here for two reasons: the video recordings, and in that some justice was delivered.

The length of the footage is not known, and is rumored to be between twenty-six minutes and possibly as long as two hours. It starts with a scene in which a Serbian Orthodox priest blesses the militiamen before they embark on their mission. The footage then cuts to a truck standing on an unknown, leafy country road, on a sunny day, as six young men are ordered, amid heavy insults, to get off the truck and lay down on the ground, with their hands tied behind their back. The faces of the fairly young, possibly teenage men are bloated from beatings, and their clothes are dirty, with some possibly having soiled themselves. Laying in the ditch, two of the Scorpions taunt the men: one asks them if he ever "fucked" (*prcao*), and when the boy answers no, the Scorpion scoffs, "well, you won't," casting an inexorable fate on all of them. A second man then shoots over their heads to scare them, or to perform a mock execution. The perpetrators, with short hair and wearing red berets, are smoking and joking among themselves, before they order four of the victims to walk up a hill, where they are lined up one by one in the tall grass, and sprayed in the back with automatic weapons. The last two men are then untied and made to carry the others to a pit, before being executed themselves in a small building. The killers continue their

---

[106] For the story of how the videotape was obtained by human rights activist Nataša Kandić, and ended up in the hands of Serbian prosecutors, see Ivan Zveržhanovski, "Watching War Crimes: The Srebrenica Video and the Serbian Attitudes to the 1995 Srebrenica Massacre," *Journal of Southeast European and Black Sea Studies* 7:3 (2007), 417–30.

banter and calmly walk off, as the scene ends, according to the cameraman because the camera's battery ran out. The following scene shows the unit lying in the grass under some trees, roasting a piglet, relaxing and drinking.

The Trnovo massacre is as instructive as the Bahía Portete massacre, but for different reasons. First of all, it is a crystal-clear depiction of paramilitaries committing violence on civilians, even if some fought on the fronts against combatants. Tolimir had reported that the paramilitaries did not fight on the fronts, but rather were mostly "operating behind the lines of the regular SR BH Army units, looting and burning property and killing the innocent population."[107] The Trnovo massacre indeed demonstrates this well, as the footage shows a heavily armed paramilitary unit executing a group of emaciated and exhausted men. Second, throughout the month of July, police reports clearly identified the Scorpions as a unit of the Serbian MUP.[108] In other words, the Scorpions were not a local, bottom-up Bosnian Serb unit, but one that fell directly under the supervision of Milošević's mastermind of paramilitarism, Jovica Stanišić. Third, the fact that the video cassette was copied and circulated among the Scorpions for a decade as a memento, demonstrates that the violence they commit is a deeply meaningful event to paramilitaries. Even though the executions were cold-blooded and performed matter-of-factly, they cast a long shadow on the perpetrators' afterlives. Fourth, the massacre also attests to the widely held racism and cruelty of paramilitaries. Throughout the video, the Scorpions make nationalist comments, taunt, insult, and mock their victims' alleged Muslim identities, and it is clear that they share an imaginary of Bosnian Muslims as the fundamental Other. Finally, as Iva Vukušić rightly points out: "What is particularly interesting about this unit is that the members often originated from the same town, and were relatives, friends and acquaintances long before the war. That, according to one member, brought a special sense of closeness to the unit."[109]

---

[107] MICT Mladić case, 65ter03743, Tolimir report, July 28, 1992, 2.

[108] See the documentation available at http://srebrenica.sense-agency.com/assets/Uploads/hr-7-03-skorp-mupsrbije-en.pdf and http://srebrenica.sense-agency.com/assets/Uploads/hr-7-05-skorpioni-smjena-en.pdf (both accessed March 20, 2019).

[109] Iva Vukušić, "Nineteen Minutes of Horror: Insights from the Scorpions Execution Video," *Genocide Studies and Prevention* 12:2 (2018), 35–53, at 39.

In the conflict between the Turkish state and the Kurdistan Workers' Party (PKK), which militarized in 1984 and escalated in the 1990s, para-military units were widely active in the field. The 1990s stand out for particularly intensive and extensive violence against civilians committed by the secretive JİTEM (Gendarmerie Intelligence Organization), a product of Turkey's "deep state" configurations—or what is discussed in this chapter as para-institutional structures. JİTEM was involved in counter-insurgency operations against the PKK, including widespread violence against civilians: assassinations, disappearances, torture, sexual violence, material and environmental destruction, and several import-ant massacres of civilians. Among these, the Cizre massacre of March 21, 1992 stands out for its relevance: it happened on the celebration of Newroz (the Kurdish New Year)—eighteen people were killed, dozens wounded, over one hundred arrested, and the aftermath was followed by silence and repression, both journalistically and legally. The massacre was the paramilitaries' response to the public celebration of Newroz by the town's population. As the celebrations turned into a demonstration, the security forces intervened and violently chased and dispersed the townsfolk with armored vehicles, randomly killing and arresting civil-ians in the process.[110] The massacre was followed by a general curfew for Cizre, but this only facilitated the paramilitaries in removing people from their houses and making them disappear. The longer aftermath was therefore much more deadly, and over fifty people were killed in the following days, over one hundred people were disappeared, and count-less numbers arrested and tortured.

The massacre received significant media coverage because the domes-tic and foreign media had taken up positions in the Kadıoğlu Hotel, and reported on it. Furthermore, the celebration and demonstration, as well as the paramilitaries' initial violent intervention were videotaped.[111] The footage is eighteen minutes long, and shows the paramilitaries storming and dispersing the demonstration. Some paramilitaries wear civilian clothes, leather jackets, and ski masks, but others are uniformed and

[110] For a thorough study of paramilitarism in Turkey, see Ayhan Işık, "Paramilitarism, Organized Crime, and the State in Turkey in the 1990s" (unpublished PhD thesis, Utrecht University, 2019), especially ch. 5 on Cizre.
[111] "1992 Cizre Newrozu ilk kez yayınlanan görüntüler," at www.youtube.com/watch?v=ROqnwlymgEc (accessed March 21, 2019).

armed with M-16s. Some of them have moustaches hanging over the side of their lips, a feature associated with right-wing Turkish-nationalist culture. Women shriek and children scamper as the paramilitaries disembark from the armored vehicles and run to grab any young men. Scuffles ensue, the paramilitaries beat people, round them up, and shove them in the armored vehicles. The footage constitutes a unique piece of evidence because Turkish paramilitaries are undisguisedly visible, indeed personally recognizable, and one can witness forced disappearances live in action, as many arrestees disappeared without a trace.[112] Whereas some disappeared, others were killed. A court case that was launched years later, noted that the detainees were taken from Cizre in white Renault vehicles, killed with Kalashnikov rifles or a pistol, and buried in shallow graves "8–10 centimeters below the ground surface."[113] Others were "only" arrested and tortured. JİTEM arrested the young Kurdish girl, Berîvan, and took her to its station in Cizre. Berîvan later remembered:

> They took me to the torture floor. They tortured me such that…to be frank I don't know how to tell it. They tortured me in a horrible way. 17–18 days *strappado*…cold water…electricity…they pulled my finger nails. They burnt me across my body. "As long as you confess," they said. They tortured me in a very bad physical way. They continued until I was paralyzed. One of my hands and one foot became paralyzed…Every 10 minutes they would take a break. They would get tired (*diwastîna*).[114]

Berîvan made it out alive. Many other detainees who were arrested by JİTEM were said to have committed suicide, and their bodies were delivered to their families.

A close look at the Cizre massacre offers many pointers about paramilitarism. First, much like other cases, the paramilitaries committed

---

[112] See the forced disappearances database of the Hafıza Merkezi NGO on Cizre, at http://www.zorlakaybetmeler.org/ (accessed March 21, 2019).

[113] "Bir Ölüm ve Yıkım Mekanı Olarak Şırnak," at http://hakikatadalethafiza.org/bir-olum-ve-yikim-mekani-olarak-cemal-temizozun-sirnaki (accessed March 21, 2019).

[114] See Aydın Orak's documentary "Destaneka Serhildanê, Bêrîvana Cizîrî," minutes 13:15–15:20, at https://archive.org/details/CIZRELRBERVAN (accessed March 21, 2019).

various forms of violence. Second, it is relevant for its aftermath, in that the violence empowered the paramilitaries and led to a certain "paramilitary governance," as the government and state institutions more or less abandoned the town to JİTEM's rule. The two key members of the military and administrative bureaucracy in Cizre were Cemal Temizöz, a commander of JİTEM, and Kamil Atağ, tribal chieftain of the village guards and mayor of Cizre from 1994 to 1999. The duo not only commanded the paramilitary groups in Cizre, but also determined the political and administrative climate in Cizre from the massacre onward. The massacre was followed by generic impunity, but even when there were dead bodies and witnesses to the killings, some murders were never cleared up. For example, the courts dismissed the case of one journalist who was killed in broad daylight in front of dozens of people, because allegedly the empty casings of the bullets could not be found. The murder was shelved as a case of an "unknown perpetrator" (*faili meçhul*).[115] Third, and finally, the attackers' identities were surrounded by typical para-institutional ambiguity: some were recognizable, others were not. Some looked like armed civilians, others did not. The production of this type of ambiguity brings us to a central and complex problem of paramilitarism: deniability.

Deniability: A Nod and a Wink

Paramilitarism exists in the secretive "nooks and crannies" of the state. It is a covert phenomenon that forces us to reflect on secrecy and clandestinity, but also raises the problem of denial and deniability.[116] Indeed, many books on paramilitarism carry in their titles the terms denial or deniability, which demonstrates the general awareness and relevance of

---

[115] "Raporda, 8 Gazeteciyi Çete Öldürdü İddiası," *Hürriyet*, February 22, 1998.

[116] Deniability is not only a political-sociological concept but also a rhetorical strategy in propositional logic, as well as a philosophical concept. For example, Žižek's adage for ideological disavowal is "I know very well . . . but just the same . . . ." See Douglas Walton, "Plausible Deniability and Evasion of Burden of Proof," *Argumentation* 10:1 (1996), 47–58; Slavoj Žižek, *Looking Awry: An Introduction to Jacques Lacan through Popular Culture* (Cambridge, MA: MIT Press, 1992), 27–35.

the topic.[117] Some scholars have even defined deniability as the constitutive element of paramilitarism; Mazzei, for example, explicitly defined paramilitarism as a strategy that enables states to avoid appearing as direct sponsors of violence.[118] States can disavow any linkage with these shadowy organizations by claiming they were private groups committing violence on their own volition. Deniability is considered necessary not only for domestic reasons (electorate, institutions), but also for international reasons, including the threat of foreign intervention, monitoring by NGOs, the UN, international criminal tribunals, the EU, and "sanction-busting" to circumvent embargos. The more press exposure and foreign criticism the killings receive, the more categorical the denials become internally (through a press ban) and externally (e.g. toward ambassadors and diplomats), even if early on in the setting up of paramilitary forces there can be public expressions of approval. Furthermore, paramilitarism, as constructed in para-institutional networks, is relatively easy to deny, because it is most often organized incoherently and inconsistently, so that responsibility is fractured across various levels and agencies of the state anyway. The institutional infrastructure of a state's covert spaces, for example hyper-compartmentalization or psychological warfare, are very serious barriers to certain forms of public knowledge, including transparency over deniable violence. So how is plausible deniability even researchable, empirically and theoretically? Deniability has been widely postulated in paramilitarism, but how does it function, if not exactly, then at least approximately?

First and foremost, we must recognize that deniability and denial are closely related: the former is a way to accelerate and facilitate the latter, since denial does not follow the violence, but is part of it, and even precedes it—such as in denial of intentions. Therefore, one must begin a discussion of deniability with a healthy dose of skepticism toward the official position of the state involved, and *infer* it, not only from spoken or written disavowals or denials, but also from acts of commission, and,

[117] Urwin, *A State in Denial*; Maria McFarland Sánchez-Moreno, *There Are No Dead Here: A Story of Murder and Denial in Colombia* (New York: Public Affairs, 2018); Cheryl Lawther, *Truth, Denial and Transition: Northern Ireland and the Contested Past* (London: Routledge, 2018); Bruce Campbell and Arthur Brenner (eds), *Death Squads in Global Perspective: Murder with Deniability* (London: Palgrave, 2002).

[118] Mazzei, *Death Squads or Self-Defense Forces?*, 203.

importantly, acts of omission. Due to the paradox of official secrecy but public knowledge, it is best approached in a bottom-up, ethnographic manner, by starting with the victims and survivors who emphatically claim that the paramilitaries *are* the state, and then to piece together the evidence to test or prove that claim. In any case, it can only be researched in a circumspect way with close attention to detail, and informed extrapolation. Despite these difficulties, deniability plays a role in all cases and forms of paramilitarism, and can be conceptually unpacked in two directions: first, as part and parcel of the broader covert strategies of a state, and second, as a form of violent, coded performance by the state.

Of course, secrecy is an entirely normal process in state affairs, especially in the security services. Covert actions are part of this process, although security services and intelligence agencies also operate overtly. Mark Lowenthal distinguishes covert action in terms of level of violence and degree of plausible deniability, and has argued that there are four basic categories: propaganda, political and economic activities, coups, and paramilitary operations, the latter comprising "inherently the most violent covert actions, and consequently they offer the lowest likelihood of plausible deniability for the government involved."[119] Bruneau and Dombroski claimed that "[t]he larger the paramilitary operation, the less likely it is to provide the cover of plausible deniability for the sponsoring state."[120] Paramilitarism often begins to "fester" first in states' existing domains of secrecy, especially the intelligence agencies. However, at various levels of government, political and administrative groups and networks can deliberately develop secret forms of para-institutional power. McGovern coined an important term when he concluded that the British government was actively "creating *spaces of deniability*" in Northern Ireland—"spaces" not only understood in territorial terms.[121] McFate even argues that plausible deniability allows the government "*to hide secrets from itself*, especially official oversight mechanisms," and

[119] Mark Lowenthal, *Intelligence: From Secrets to Policy* (Washington: CQ Press, 2003), 129–31.
[120] Thomas Bruneau and Kenneth Dombroski, "Reforming Intelligence: The Challenge of Control in New Democracies," in Thomas Bruneau and Scott Tollefson (eds), *Who Guards the Guardians and How: Democratic Civil–Military Relations* (Austin: University of Texas Press, 2006), 152.
[121] Mark McGovern, *Counterinsurgency and Collusion in Northern Ireland* (London: Pluto Press, 2019), 5, emphasis added.

that deniability "fosters moral hazard among decision makers."[122] This is where secrecy can promote deniability, as it is about preventing undesired consequences. In different states and countries, not all secret spaces exist to protect and promote paramilitarism, but all paramilitarism flourishes in spaces of secrecy.

A second problem is related to how states "perform violence," in that a counter-insurgency, a civil war, or peacetime repression is always carried out in front of both domestic and foreign audiences. As the state organizes and enacts violence, so the audiences watch and judge. In a seminal volume on death squads, Bruce Campbell related plausible deniability mainly to the circumventing of international and domestic norms:

> One major factor for the use of death squads lies in the need of states to deny that they are breaking established norms of behavior. The modern state is bound by a whole range of internal and external norms that place strict limits on a state's range of options—if respected. Only death squads and other covert means provide plausible deniability of state involvement in violent acts.[123]

James Ron's interpretation of deniability supplements this approach; focusing on Serb paramilitaries, he has noted that when "human rights monitors seek to limit state violence to create a better world, they may sometimes simply drive the violence underground."[124] Paramilitarism studies are concerned with the inner workings of that process of "taking the violence underground." In order to not overtly break national and international norms, governments can "perform" paramilitarism to these audiences by setting up elaborate para-institutional structures, but nevertheless still committing the violence deemed necessary. The state is thereby covertly signaling in a coded performativity to the victims: "Yes,

---

[122] Sean McFate, *The Modern Mercenary: Private Armies and What they Mean for World Order* (Oxford: Oxford University Press, 2017), 56, emphasis added.

[123] Bruce Campbell, "Death Squads: Definition, Problems, and Historical Context," in Bruce Campbell and Arthur Brenner (eds), *Death Squads in Global Perspective* (London: Palgrave Macmillan, 2000), 12.

[124] James Ron, "Territoriality and Plausible Deniability: Serbian Paramilitaries in the Bosnian War," in Campbell and Brenner (eds), *Death Squads*, 308.

it *is* us, and you can do nothing about it, nobody will believe you."[125] This structures and shapes the violence: the use of forced disappearances, for example, is a consequence of the authorities' attempt to maintain plausible deniability. After all, if there is no body, there is no crime, and if there is no crime, there is no perpetrator.[126]

For these reasons, in her study of pro-state paramilitary violence in Brazil, Martha Huggins argues that a new methodology should be developed of how to approach and study these processes. She suggests relying on the work of undercover journalists and court testimonies.[127] This should be supplemented with leaks, wiretapped materials, and protected (anonymous) sources. These methods can go a long way in exposing the secrecy of regimes that deploy paramilitaries in an attempt to "manufacture ambiguity." Examples of this practice abound. In the Philippines of the mid-1980s, the informal support by the Aquino administration for "vigilantism" (as pro-state paramilitaries were called there) was expressed in officials' public, verbal manifestations of support for vigilantism. In other words, "the search for evidence of government backing beyond policy formulation and implementation highlights the import of signals of support other than legislated policy."[128] Another example of condoning militias was the Turkish Deputy Prime Minister Tansu Çiller's famous comment only three weeks after the Susurluk scandal: "Anyone who shoots a bullet or takes a bullet for the sake of this nation, for the sake of the country, for the sake of the state, is always remembered with respect by us. They are honorable."[129] These informal practices of governance by government officials provide encouragement to paramilitary formation.

---

[125] In some cases, the paramilitaries themselves will confess or boast of their direct ties with the state, as the Russian–Ukrainian example of Wagner, or some Shabbiha militias in Syria demonstrate.

[126] Robben, *Political Violence and Trauma in Argentina*, 320.

[127] Martha K. Huggins, "From Bureaucratic Consolidation to Structural Devolution: Police Death Squads in Brazil," *Policing and Society* 7:4 (1997), 207–34.

[128] Eva-Lotta Hedman, "State of Siege: Political Violence and Vigilante Mobilization in the Philippines," in: Bruce Campbell & Arthur Brenner (eds.), *Death Squads in Global Perspective: Murder With Deniability* (New York: St Martin's Press, 2000), 125–51, at 134–5.

[129] "Çiller: Abdullah Çatlı şerefli," *Milliyet*, 27 November 1996: "Bu millet uğruna, ülke uğruna, devlet uğruna kurşun atan da yiyen de her zaman bizim için saygıyla anılır. Onlar şereflidirler..." The Susurluk scandal was the car crash, on November 3, 1996, near the town of Susurluk, in which the deputy chief of the Istanbul Police Department, a Member of Parliament who led a powerful Kurdish tribe, and a top mafia boss and leader of the Grey Wolves were in the same vehicle. See Chapter 3.

Manufacturing ambiguity is often a stated objective during and after the commission of the violence, even though we can infer from the patterns of violence who the likely perpetrators could/must have been. Examples of blatant denial and (exposed) deniability abound in each and every case of paramilitarism. Indonesian state officials were quick to frame the assassinations of people labeled criminals in the early 1980s as "mysterious shootings" (*penembakan misterius*).[130] The Turkish government argued the similar targeted killings of prominent Kurdish individuals was carried out by "unknown assailants" (*faili meçhul*). The Guatemalan government in the 1980s not only denied any institutional connection and responsibility for its paramilitary patrols, but also claimed that the patrols were local groups spontaneously created to protect towns from insurgents. In other words, abolishing them would violate the constitutional guarantee of freedom of association.[131] The Mexican government went even farther, by not only denying the violence committed by the paramilitary White Guards that operated in southernmost Chiapas state in the mid-1990s, but even denying altogether the existence of the groups themselves.[132] The Indian security service deliberately released Muslim men from prison on the precondition that they kill human rights activists in Kashmir; the killers would then either disappear or be killed themselves. Thus, Kashmiri human rights advocate Dr. Abdul Ahad Guru was killed by a Hizb-ul-Mujahidin (an Islamist party) member, who was later eliminated himself.[133] This type of framing furthered the notion that these were intra-ethnic rivalries, criminal score-settling, and in any case not the government's making. After the violence, too, ambiguity and cloaking remain a prime objective of the government. For example, the German Freikorps were officially disarmed and disbanded in 1920, but many recast themselves as labor associations, shooting clubs, security firms, sporting societies, or other

---

[130] Justus van der Kroef, "'Petrus': Patterns of Prophylactic Murder in Indonesia," *Asian Survey* 25:7 (1985), 745–59.
[131] Kay Warren, "Death Squads and Wider Complicities: Dilemmas for the Anthropology of Violence," in Jeffrey Sluka (ed.), *Death Squad: The Anthropology of State Terror* (Philadelphia: University of Pennsylvania Press, 2000), 227.
[132] Joel A. Solomon, *Implausible Deniability: State Responsibility for Rural Violence in Mexico* (New York: Human Rights Watch, 1997), 42.
[133] *The Human Rights Crisis in Kashmir: A Pattern of Impunity* (New York: Human Rights Watch, 1993), 136–7.

"civil society" organizations that effectively were a dormant infrastructure for paramilitarism.[134] In Argentina, the Triple A paramilitary death squads were generally believed to have been organized behind Perón's back and without his knowledge.[135] But Robben claimed that "[w]hether or not the AAA had the approval of Perón is a moot question given the liberty with which López Rega and his death squads operated. Perón did nothing to stop them."[136] In other words, Peron's act of omission was more telling than the Triple A's acts of commission. In Northern Ireland, declassified documents from the British military intelligence archives show an official toleration of Loyalist paramilitary violence and infiltration of the local security forces with the explicit clause of "maximum plausible deniability" in the British government's relations with the Ulster Defence Regiment (UDR).[137] In this case, the perpetrating government built in mechanisms of deniability well before the violence was even carried out. In Turkey, successive governments denied that the government was ever involved in violence against civilians, including through paramilitaries. The story got really interesting when lower-ranking paramilitaries who defected, began to expose and uncover the very links that the state had denied for so long. The infamous paramilitary killer Abdulkadir Aygan said, for example, that the state was using them and discarding them like a napkin, but that there was no denying their orchestration. He also denied his own responsibility, which was ironic, because the state used him and others precisely for deniability.[138] The Turkish examples show that controlling the spread of embarrassing information leaked by the rank and file is of utmost importance in maintaining credible deniability. But the most instructive examples of deniability are from the USA, Colombia, Serbia, Sudan, and Russia.

---

[134] Robert Gerwarth & John Horne (eds.), *War in Peace: Paramilitary Violence after the Great War* (Oxford: Oxford University Press, 2012).
[135] Donald C. Hodges, *Argentina's "Dirty War": An Intellectual Biography* (Austin: University of Texas Press, 2014), 173.
[136] Robben, *Political Violence and Trauma in Argentina*, 138.
[137] Paul O'Connor and Alan Brecknell, "British Counterinsurgency Practice in Northern Ireland in the 1970s: A Legitimate Response or State Terror?," in Scott Poynting and David Whyte (eds), *Counter-Terrorism and State Political Violence: The 'War on Terror' as Terror* (London: Routledge, 2012), 58–9.
[138] I am grateful to Dr. Yeşim Yaprak Yıldız, whose PhD research on paramilitary repentants and defectors examined the problem of deniability by the paramilitary killers themselves: see Yeşim Yaprak Yıldız, "(Dis)avowal of State Violence: Public Confessions of Perpetrators of State Violence against Kurds in Turkey" (PhD dissertation, University of Cambridge, 2019).

Successive United States governments have erected smokescreens of deniability, from the Bay of Pigs to Vietnam, into Iraq and beyond. Already during the Bay of Pigs invasion, US officials spoke of the importance of deploying "deniable operators" in order to control future scenarios: if the paramilitary operation worked out, it would be a suc-cess that did not trace back; if the operation failed, there would be no backlash or censure. Paramilitarism was a win-win situation.[139] But it went beyond the Cold War, from US interventions in Latin America in order to support right-wing authoritarians such as General Pinochet to the "War on Terror." As Rebecca Sanders has summarized US policies: "Through omission and commission, plausible denial facilitated intelli-gence activities that violated other countries' sovereignty, promoted anti-democratic forces, engaged in paramilitary violence, or was impli-cated in illegal, immoral, or hypocritical behaviors."[140] Deniability made an unexpected and serious comeback at the beginning of the twenty-first century, when in the aftermath of the September 11 attacks on the USA, President George W. Bush signed a Memorandum of Notifications authorizing the CIA to launch an aggressive and ambitious covert-action plan to annihilate terrorism. Jane Mayer has characterized it most elo-quently in a study of the "War on Terror":

The proposed finding included the inauguration of secret paramili-tary death squads authorized to hunt and kill prime terror suspects anywhere on earth. A week earlier, these deaths would have been classified as illegal assassinations. Under the new legal analysis, such killings were sanctioned as acts of national 'self-defense'... a secret war, fought not by the military, with its well-known legal codes of conduct and a publicly accountable chain of command, but instead in the dark by faceless and nameless CIA agents following commands unknown to the American public... To give the President deniabil-ity, and to keep him from getting his hands dirty, the finding called for the President to delegate blanket authority to [George] Tenet to

---

[139] Alan Axelrod, *Mercenaries: A Guide to Private Armies and Private Military Companies* (Washington, DC: CQ Press, 2013), 175.

[140] Rebecca Sanders, "(Im)plausible Legality: The Rationalisation of Human Rights Abuses in the American 'Global War on Terror,'" *International Journal of Human Rights* 15:4 (2011), 605–26.

decide on a case-by-case basis whom to kill, whom to kidnap, whom to detain and interrogate, and how.[141]

The US CTC Special Operations unit was like the accumulation of a century of American covert paramilitarism, broadly authorized to assassinate real and alleged Islamist militants. The way that its members joked among themselves that "if they weren't carrying out black operations for the CIA they'd probably be robbing banks" spoke well to the intimacy between organized crime and paramilitarism.[142] Deniability played a major role in discussions surrounding torture of terror suspects, as Sanders argued: "The demand for denial evinces awareness of the distinction between legality and illegality and the risk of sanction, embarrassment, and blowback that might accompany the latter."[143]

The Indonesian state, with its long tradition in militia violence, also has a long track record of deniability. Geoffrey Robinson, who has studied Indonesian militias across the country's history, wrote about the 1965 genocide, that the Suharto regime created militias to sustain the essentialist and orientalist myths of a crazed Indonesian population running amok. The claims of popular and spontaneous violence were "deliberate lies concocted and spread by the very army officers who orchestrated the killings."[144] In Joshua Oppenheimer's documentaries *The Act of Killing* and *The Look of Silence*, not only did the militiamen who perpetrated the genocide openly confess that they massacred scores of civilians, but in some segments even recognized that they had been mobilized as deniable operators. One member of the paramilitary units recounted about the army: "They waited at the road with the truck. They didn't come down here [to the riverbank] … They called this 'the people's struggle' so they kept their distance. If the army was seen doing [the killing] the world would be angry."[145] Throughout the 1970s and 1980s, the Suharto regime kept paramilitary thugs on retainer and used them whenever it needed them. During the 1999 East Timor conflict, the

---

[141] Jane Mayer, *The Dark Side: The Inside Story of How the War on Terror Turned into a War on American Ideals* (New York: Doubleday, 2008) 39.

[142] Ibid., 40.   [143] Sanders, "(Im)plausible Legality."

[144] Geoffrey Robinson, *The Killing Season: A History of The Indonesian Massacres, 1965–66* (Princeton, NJ: Princeton University Press, 2018), 163.

[145] Joshua Oppenheimer, *The Look of Silence*, at 0:59.

Indonesian army again encouraged the activities of pro-government militias to create the illusion of internecine conflict or anarchy, into which it then could conveniently step to restore order. In his examination of those militias in the Indonesian historical context, Robinson lends weight to deniability as am explanatory factor:

> [L]ike all semi-official forces, locally-recruited militias afforded Portuguese, Dutch, and Indonesian authorities a measure of deniability for acts of extreme violence that violated legal and moral norms. This is unlikely to have been a major preoccupation of the Portuguese and Dutch during colonial times. But for the Dutch in 1945–49, and for Indonesia in 1974–75, and in the 1990s, as international attention focused increasingly on Indonesia's poor human rights record, such plausible deniability was vitally important.[146]

Traditions of deniability were molded in the slipstream of traditions of paramilitarism. As a government allied with the West, the Suharto regime never abandoned deniability. Much like Turkey, as a consequence of decades of denial, Indonesia has not been able to face its history of genocide and paramilitary violence.

In Colombia, denial of paramilitarism or of paramilitary–state relations dates back decades as well. Already in the 1980s, the army had continuously denied any links with paramilitaries, and argued that those groups arose on their own volition and initiative.[147] The 1990s and 2000s were they heyday of paramilitarism in Colombia, and the deeper the entanglement became, the more sophisticated the denial. During the Colombian presidential elections of 2002, opposition contender Horacio Serpa accused Álvaro Uribe of drawing support from paramilitaries, but Uribe flatly denied it.[148] In his memoirs, Uribe emphatically and repeatedly denied the notion that he had entertained any relationships with paramilitaries as "usual baseless allegations"

---

[146] Geoffrey Robinson, "People's War: Militias in East Timor and Indonesia," *South East Asia Research*, 9:3 (2001), 271–318, at 315.

[147] Melo, "Los paramilitares y su impacto sobre la política colombiana," in Leal and Zamosc (eds), *Al Filo del Caos*.

[148] Robert T. Buckman (ed.), *The World Today: Latin America 2013* (New York: Rowman & Littlefield, 2013), 148.

and "lies."[149] He also portrayed himself as a defender of Colombian state institutions against paramilitaries who "controlled, or had penetrated, elements of our institutions," including courts, local administrations, and security forces. He also added that he had never heard of paramilitary bosses such as Rodrigo Tovar Pupo or Carlos Mario Jiménez. Uribe then continued to argue specifically about DAS that it had been infiltrated by paramilitaries, that he had attempted to reform it but failed, concluding:

> The armed forces, the analysts, the general population, and I were unaware of the size and penetration of the terrorist organizations that operated in our democracy...A third of the country was under the reign of the paramilitaries...We pursued the paramilitary bosses with the same vigor with which we pursued senior leaders of the FARC and ELN.[150]

This was one of the clearest examples of denial of collusion by a former head of state. This contradicted a litany of criticisms that he had developed warm relations with paramilitaries (even if only based on mutual loathing of socialism and communism), and that many of his aides had been subject to judicial investigations for paramilitary links. But even a top paramilitary boss like Carlos Mauricio García Fernández (a.k.a. "Doble Cero") could deny state involvement, arguing that because they were self-financed, the state had nothing to do with them: "Paramilitaries don't exist in Colombia, because paramilitaries are armed groups at the edge of the law. They are like the government's and state's dark or secret forces."[151]

Analysts of the Yugoslav wars have cogently argued that plausible deniability was a major element of Serbia's interventions in Bosnia. Tom Naylor wrote that "irregular forces provided Belgrade with deniability by taking the heat for ethnic cleansing campaigns and for looting."[152] James Ron argued that Serb paramilitaries were created to circumvent territorial restrictions on Serbian state action: "The very fact that the

---

[149] Alvaro Uribe Velez, *No Lost Causes* (New York: Celebra, 2012), 175.
[150] Ibid., 179–80.   [151] Civico, *The Para-State*, 168.
[152] Tom Naylor, *Patriots and Profiteers: Economic Warfare, Embargo Busting, and State-Sponsored Crime* (Montreal: MQUP, 2008), 351.

Serbian leadership's responsibility is difficult to prove suggests that secrecy and plausible deniability are what made the ethnic cleansing policy feasible, appropriate, and cost-effective for the Serbian regime in 1992–93."[153] Indeed, during the war, Borisav Jović, Milosević's close associate and Socialist Federal Republic of Yugoslavia (SFRY) president in 1990–1, explained that the emerging Serb statelets must have their own official armed forces. Jović claimed that in a meeting with Milosević, they agreed that in case of Bosnian independence, the Yugoslav army could not afford to be seen as an occupying force. Therefore, a distancing device was needed.[154] The façade of distancing and persistent deniability could then be lifted by 1999 for Kosovo, since it was legally in Serbia. The notion of deniability then shifted to the type of involvement, and the violence against civilians. The Serbian example demonstrates very well how manufacturing ambiguity was outright formulated as one of the main goals of paramilitarism. Unit members were not only instructed to remove insignia before operations, but they were temporarily renamed, relocated, integrated, or subordinated to local army groups and paid as freelancers. These acts not only created distance, but also minimal mutual involvement between the state and the paramilitaries. The purpose of this manufactured ambiguity was to shield the Serbian government from criticism, sanctions, and criminal prosecution.[155] Furthermore, secrecy and deniability was also entirely clear to the paramilitaries themselves. One former Unit for Anti-Terrorist Action (JATD) member testified at the ICTY that when he joined the unit, he noted a strict atmosphere of secrecy. He was also plainly told not to discuss his work anywhere and quickly understood that he had joined a special unit of the state security, referring to it as "a kind of paramilitary branch of the DB [state security]." For months, his employment papers were not arranged.[156] The same held true for Arkan: despite the broad censure against him, no decisive measures were ever taken.

[153] James Ron, *Frontiers and Ghettos: State Violence in Serbia and Israel* (Berkeley: University of California Press, 2003), 57.

[154] Susan L. Woodward, *Balkan Tragedy: Chaos and Dissolution after the Cold War* (Washington, DC: Brookings Institution Press, 1995), 458.

[155] Vukušić, "Serb Paramilitaries." See also Kari van der Ploeg, "Outsourcing Genocide: Plausible Deniability and the Use of Paramilitary Groups during the Yugoslav Wars from 1991 to 1995" (unpublished MA thesis, University of Amsterdam, 2013).

[156] ICTY Stanišić and Simatović, JF-48, June 15, 2010.

In the big picture of global paramilitarism, Slobodan Milošević was to be the undisputed master of denial, dissimulation, and deception of international and domestic public opinion, as well as courts of justice, when it came to Serbian state collusion with paramilitaries. During the war, he regularly denied that Serb paramilitarism was in any way connected to his government. In 1997, NATO Secretary General Javier Solana accused Milošević of infiltrating Serbian secret forces into Bosnia, but the Serbian president flatly denied the assertions.[157] Milošević generally used at least two middlemen for the paramilitary strategy: Stanišić and Simatović, who in their turn had one middleman for the operation. At one meeting, Milošević refers to the paramilitaries as "wild brigades," implying that they were in no way backed, directed, or supported by the state.[158] Whereas Radovan Karadžić was often seen in the company of paramilitaries, on multiple occasions ostentatiously with Arkan himself, Milošević wisely kept his distance from the units and their commanders. There are no historical records of any conversation between Milošević and Arkan, and the only known moment in which they are both present is at the 1997 funeral of middleman Radovan "Badža" Stojičić. A monochrome photo taken there is a perfect allegory for paramilitarism, as it shows them in the same frame, doubtlessly unintended, as Milošević stares uncomfortably ahead while Arkan seems to creep up behind him, standing in his shadow.[159] But all in all, much like a mafia boss scared of incriminating himself, Milošević ran the whole operation verbally through intermediaries, according to statements by insiders. After the war, it was no surprise that his ICTY case (and that of Stanišić and Simatović) were difficult trials for the Office of the Prosecutor. The prosecutors attempted to lay bare the paramilitary web that the men had spun through Serbian state institutions, but they largely failed to expose it, and Milošević died before his verdict was announced.

Sudan is a particularly illuminating case of deniability. From the genocide in Darfur to the repression of the 2019 demonstrations, the

[157] Louis Sell, *Slobodan Milosevic and the Destruction of Yugoslavia* (Durham, NC: Duke University Press, 2003), 173.

[158] Vukušić, "Serb Paramilitaries."

[159] See the image at http://news.bbc.co.uk/2/hi/europe/1485142.stm (accessed March 28, 2019).

regime of Sudanese President Omar al-Bashir resorted to blanket denial of the paramilitary violence it launched and supported. Starting with the Janjaweed militia in Darfur, al-Bashir has systemically denied any Sudanese government involvement in arming, protecting, and directing the Arab militias against Darfuri rebel groups and civilians. He retorted that foreigners "fabricated and exaggerated" the conflict, adding: "Yes, there have been villages burned, but not to the extent you are talking about. People have been killed because there is war. It is not in the Sudanese culture or people of Darfur to rape. It doesn't exist. We don't have it."[160] The al-Bashir regime resorted to deception when denial did not convince the international, and to the extent it mattered, domestic audiences. It paraded ordinary criminals arrested before the rebellion as Janjaweed and executed them as a demonstration of the rule of law. It organized sham disarmament ceremonies, for example on August 27, 2004, the UN Special Representative witnessed 300 men in the Darfur border town of Geneina lay down their weapons. But the weapons were simply handed back to them the next day.[161] On March 4, 2009, the International Criminal Court issued an arrest warrant for al-Bashir based on an indictment of war crimes and crimes against humanity in Darfur. Al-Bashir was never arrested, but should it ever get to a trial, legally ascertaining his connections to the Janjaweed will prove difficult.

It was no surprise then that when mass demonstrations broke out in Sudan in 2019, al-Bashir's response was a recognizable, time-tested blend of tasking paramilitaries with violent repressions of the mass demonstrations. By now, the Janjaweed had been renamed with the ostensibly respectable title Rapid Support Forces (RSF), but it was still run by the same ruthless general Mohammad Hamdan Dagalo (a.k.a. Hemedti). The RSF beat, killed, tortured, and raped demonstrators, dumped their bodies into the Nile, and what had worked in Darfur over a decade ago now seemed to be working in the heart of Khartoum. But there were two major differences this time: first, there were smartphones for coordinating, recording, and documenting, and the outrage over the violence only galvanized the demonstrators and Arab public opinion.

---

[160]   NBC News, March 20, 2007.
[161]   Julie Flint and Alex de Waal, *Darfur: A New History of a Long War* (London: Zed Books, 2008), 145.

The outpouring of digital material resulted in detailed media reports on the RSF geo-located prisons, identification of militia members and their crimes through video analysis, and the exposing of links between the intelligence services, police, and paramilitaries.[162] Second, the genocide in Darfur demonstrated the spatial compartmentalization of paramilitarism: Janjaweed brutality had been a well-known fact to Darfuris but had occurred far from the capital. Once the same militias began killing and raping in the streets of Khartoum with impunity, ordinary Sudanese were confronted with the brutality of their government and this in turn helped them understand and imagine the Janjaweed's conduct in Darfur.[163] Persistent mass demonstrations finally impelled the Sudanese army to oust Bashir on April 11, 2019. But a cosmetic change of the regime, in which Bashir would disappear, but the complex web of army, paramilitary units, and intelligence services would persist, was unacceptable to most Sudanese demonstrators, who were profoundly aware of the para-institutional nature of the Bashir regime. When second-in-command General Awad Ibn Ouf took the reins to preside over a two-year transitional period, protesters called for the sacking of General Dagalo and the end of the "deep state" (العميقة الدولة).[164]

From 1990 on, the Russian Federation was at war in Chechnya twice, and in both wars it employed paramilitary proxies. During the first war (1994–6), the Russian government outsourced violence to paramilitaries covertly, but during the second war (1999–2006) it did so overtly. According to Biberman, the shift can be explained through the changes in Russian public attitudes toward the war, as deniability became unnecessary.[165] When Russian paramilitaries bearing no insignia ("little

---

[162] BBC Africa, "Sudan's Secret Hit Squads," February 13, 2019, at https://www.bbc.com/news/av/world-africa-47216487/what-happens-inside-sudan-s-secret-detention-centres; Kaamil Ahmed, "How Sudan's Militiamen Filmed their Deadly Assault on Protesters," *Middle East Eye*, July 16, 2019, at https://www.middleeasteye.net/news/rsf-khartoum-how-sudan-feared-militia-janjaweed-filmed-deadly-assault-protesters (both accessed September 7, 2019).

[163] Hamza Hendawi, "Out of the Darfur desert: the rise of Sudanese general Mohammed Hamdan Dagalo," *The National*, April 29, 2019, at https://www.thenational.ae/world/africa/out-of-the-darfur-desert-the-rise-of-sudanese-general-mohammed-hamdan-dagalo-1.855219 (accessed May 1, 2019); Declan Walsh, "Sudan ousted a brutal dictator; his successor was his enforcer," *New York Times*, June 15, 2019, at http://www.nytimes.com/2019/06/15/world/africa/sudan-leader-hemeti.html (accessed September 7, 2019).

[164] *Deutsche Welle*, "هل ما تزال الدولة العميقة تحكم في السودان؟," April 16, 2019.

[165] Yelena Biberman, "Violence by Proxy: Russia's Ex-Rebels and Criminals in Chechnya," in Bettina Koch (ed.), *State Terror, State Violence: Global Perspectives* (Wiesbaden: Springer, 2016), 135–50.

green men") informally invaded Crimea in the spring of 2014, Russia tried to deny its undeclared, "hybrid war" against Ukraine.[166] At a press conference on March 5, 2014, Russian President Vladimir Putin responded to a question about the identities of the armed forces that had seized the Crimea and denied that they were Russian soldiers. With his typically stoic look, Putin said: "They are not there" (их там нет).[167] But the facts on the ground, close investigative research, and the attitudes of the paramilitaries themselves gradually deflated official Russian denials, and ultimately debunked them permanently. Bellingcat conclusively exposed that it *was* Russian paramilitary operatives that had occupied Crimea and Eastern Ukraine.[168] After years of very precise research, the Dutch public prosecutor's office published an elaborate report, incontrovertibly establishing that it was pro-Russian forces that had used a Russian army anti-aircraft missile to shoot down Malaysia Airlines flight MH-17, a good example of the unintended consequences of deniable violence.[169] From Crimea to the Donbass to Syria, a large number of Russian men fought as mercenaries, labeled by the Kremlin as "volunteers." But the leaders of the private military company Wagner were employed by the Russian Ministry of Defense, Spetsnaz, or Main Intelligence Directorate (GRU), and the military hardware that was used was official Russian army material. Wagner fighters were paid thousands of dollars, were prohibited from using social media or speaking about their operations, and were decorated with medals by the Minister of Defense himself—or by Wagner's commander Dimitriy Utkin.[170] As Russian deniability ultimately became untenable, it slowly shifted away from deniability, although never fully acknowledging that its armed

[166] For a discussion of Russian "hybrid war" (гибридная война), see Mark Galeotti, *Hybrid War or Gibridnaya Voina? Getting Russia's Non-Linear Military Challenge Right* (London: Routledge, 2016).

[167] Constantine Pleshakov, *The Crimean Nexus: Putin's War and the Clash of Civilizations* (New Haven, CT: Yale University Press, 2017), 120.

[168] "Wagner Mercenaries with GRU-issued Passports," *Bellingcat*, January 30, 2019, at https://www.bellingcat.com/news/uk-and-europe/2019/01/30/wagner-mercenaries-with-gru-issued-passports-validating-sbus-allegation/ (accessed March 16, 2019).

[169] The research was fully published on the website of the Dutch public prosecutor's office: see https://www.om.nl/onderwerpen/mh17-crash/ (accessed March 29, 2019).

[170] "Peskov confirms the presence of Dimitriy Utkin at a reception in the Kremlin," *RBK*, December 15, 2016, at https://www.rbc.ru/politics/15/12/2016/585278bb9a7947efc948945b (accessed January 22, 2018).

forces were officially fighting in Ukraine.[171] What had started with the pro-Putin hashtag #ихтамнет (#They'reNotThere), ended with the disgruntled fighters responding with their own appropriately sarcastic hashtag #НасТутНет (#We'reNotHere).[172] General levels of discontent among the Russian forces were sharpened by feelings of being unappreciated and uncared for, as well as by a wave of inexplicable (but likely Russian government-organized) liquidations of Wagner combatants after the fighting.[173] The problems for Russian state deniability demonstrate the difficulty in maintaining it in the current digital information age, and the difficulty the principal has in controlling its agents after paramilitarism actions.

The 2019 demonstrations in Hong Kong against the Chinese extradition bill were a prime example of failed deniability. As hundreds of thousands of Hong Kong residents poured into the streets to protest the bill, the government's response became increasingly violent. On Sunday July 21, 2019, demonstrators were violently attacked by men in white t-shirts, who pursued and beat the protesters with metal rods and sticks at a metro station. The government of Chief Executive Carrie Lam quickly denied that they were government-hired thugs, but it was an unconvincing attempt at deniability. Not only was this not the first time the Hong Kong government had deployed the triads, but the police was strangely very late in responding, the conduct of the thugs was suspiciously coordinated, and their proven ties to pro-Chinese businessmen did not leave much doubt about who they were working for.[174] In a joint statement, the protesters denounced the "collusion" between the Hong Kong police and pro-Beijing triads, arguing that the government had clearly outsourced the repression of the protests to the triads in order to

---

[171] Graeme Herd, "Crimea as a Eurasian Pivot in 'Arc of Conflict': Managing the Great Power Relations Trilemma," in Matt Killingsworth, Matthew Sussex, and Jan Pakulski (eds), *Violence and the State* (Oxford: Oxford University Press, 2016), 107–27, at 112.

[172] Halya Coynash, "Kremlin-Sponsored Mercenaries go to International Criminal Court to prove Russia is Deploying in Ukraine & Syria," December 4, 2018, at http://khpg.org/en/index.php?id=1543252935 (accessed March 14, 2019).

[173] Jack Losh: "Is Russia Killing Off Eastern Ukraine's Warlords?," *Foreign Policy*, October 25, 2016, at https://foreignpolicy.com/2016/10/25/who-is-killing-eastern-ukraines-warlords-motorola-russia-putin/ (accessed January 22, 2019).

[174] Louisa Lim, "The thugs of mainland China," *The New Yorker*, October 8, 2014, at https://www.newyorker.com/news/news-desk/thugs-mainland-china-hong-kong-protests (accessed September 7, 2019).

appear uninvolved.[175] Placed in its proper historical and political context, it appeared that even a strong state like China relied on deniable actors, as long as evasion of state responsibility was desirable, and Hong Kong civil society was too robust to bend or break.[176]

As a historical process, it is unclear what the future of deniability is, but it has a fairly clear direction. Already in the 1970s, Richard Helms, the US Director of Central Intelligence, held the position that plausible deniability was a *sine qua non* of any covert action, but recognized that it was becoming moot due to the spread of better public knowledge and the expanded requirements for oversight and notification. What was sustainable in the 1950s has become much more difficult in the 1970s or 1990s, let alone in the 2010s.[177] As a political phenomenon, deniability is inconsistent and diverse. Sometimes states rely on deniability, sometimes they do not; some individuals or acts they deny and hide, others they do not; sometimes deniability is prominent during a conflict, sometimes it is used *ex post facto*. But there are certain constants as well: deniability is not only a political and legal distancing device, but above all a moral distancing process. The examples of the USA and Sudan demonstrate that both authoritarian and democratic states use deniability. Also, deniability has different objectives, and can be intended to obscure the territorial and/or jurisdictional responsibility, the forms of violence, or the systematism of violence. Whatever its changing nature, whenever states are involved in violence against civilians, deniability in some shape or form appears.

Conclusions

Alfonso Cuarón's powerful film *Roma* (2018) depicts daily life in Mexico in the 1970s and is a unique representation of paramilitarism in cinema. The backdrop of the movie consists of the 1968 student movement in

[175] Holmes Chan, "'Servants of Triads': Hong Kong democrats claim police condoned mob attacks in Yuen Long," *Hong Kong Free Press*, July 22, 2019, at https://www.hongkongfp.com/2019/07/22/servants-triads-hong-kong-democrats-claim-police-condoned-mob-attacks-yuen-long (accessed September 7, 2019).

[176] Lynette Ong, "'Thugs-for-Hire': Subcontracting of State Coercion and State Capacity in China," *Perspectives on Politics* 16:3 (2018), 680–95.

[177] Mark M. Lowenthal, *Intelligence: From Secrets to Policy* (London: Sage, 2014), 241.

Mexico and their violent repression by a youth combat group known as the "Falcons" (*Halcones*), a paramilitary group surreptitiously organized by the dominant Mexican political party, the PRI (Partido Revolucionario Institucional). The PRI's aim was to resist and repress socialism and communism, prevent the spread of student protests and riots, and to maintain "order." On June 11, 1971, several hundred *Halcones*, armed to the teeth, attacked over 10,000 demonstrating university students in Mexico City, massacring 120 students as the police stood by and watched.[178] The example of the *Halcones* epitomizes paramilitarism: influential men in the security forces from a dominant political party used the opportunities of state agencies to weave a para-institutional network of militias and commit a deniable massacre to maintain the political status quo and send an unmistakable signal to society. *Roma* is not only very effective in the way that it portrays the *Halcones* and paramilitarism in Mexico, but the movie is also a cinematographic success for depicting paramilitarism as an elusive but vital side plot. Throughout the movie, the viewer is gradually overcome by the creeping feeling that the para-institutionality undergirding the *Halcones* is as imperceptible as it is influential. Films like *Roma* reach beyond the limits of what judicial or scholarly investigations can offer. They allow us to imagine the complexity of paramilitarism, which, even if it is depicted for one country, is a universal phenomenon.

Like two octopuses ensnared in a deadly embrace, paramilitaries and the state feed off each other. Geoffrey Robinson has concluded that "different configurations of state power may facilitate the emergence of different kinds of militia formation."[179] The way that paramilitarism is organized in Colombia, for example, differs from that in Northern Ireland or Kenya. However, paramilitary systems have much in common as well. Whether we assume Aldo Civico's concept *intreccio* or Jasmin Hristov's term *interpenetration*, this chapter has argued that the organization of paramilitarism is a deeply complex affair that concerns a triangle of relationships between various state agencies, political parties,

---

[178] Kate Doyle, "The Corpus Christi Massacre" (June 10, 2003), The National Security Archive, at https://nsarchive2.gwu.edu/NSAEBB/NSAEBB91/mexstu-38.pdf (accessed March 31, 2019).
[179] Robinson, "People's War," 316.

and communities.[180] These relationships are dialectical in that they mutually influence each other: a state can form paramilitary groups, and paramilitary groups can shape a state. This chapter has discussed how most paramilitary infrastructures that have been actively built or tacitly condoned, have often begun in the state's broad coercive apparatuses, including its armed intelligence agencies. These patrimonial and patronage networks through, across, and beyond state agencies, exhibit several important features that have made paramilitarism possible. First, these networks can "flex and wane" according to conditions, can take on hierarchical and heterarchical shapes, and can be organized by a political party or a civil society organization in order to provide control over key state positions and resources. Second, these networks can be cultivated through informal connections that are common in various communities, such as tribes, extended families, and co-ethnics. These relationship types help explain the capacity of political actors to maintain paramilitary networks.

This chapter has interpreted paramilitarism as a praxiological phenomenon that is a consequence of para-institutional constellations. Para-institutionality refers to the tension between formal institutionalism on the one hand, and the extra-institutional development of powerful, informal networks on the other hand. The praxis of paramilitarism then is key to understand the phenomenon: states should not only be defined by what they *say* they are, but primarily by what they actually *do*. These approaches allow us to see paramilitarism as an extension of Mann's infrastructural state power or Migdal's state social control, as it can reach into off-limit and out-of-bounds spaces and shape social realities that are normally illegal and illegitimate. At the same time, the state and its interpenetration with paramilitaries is not a static phenomenon, but a dynamic and often contradictory process, and therefore transformations of the state profoundly influence paramilitarism, and vice versa. To start with, this concerns global changes to the state, since

---

[180] Civico, *The Para-State*, 21ff.; Hristov, *Paramilitarism and Neoliberalism*, 157–62, in particular at 159: "While the state's coercive apparatus extends into civil society by involving civilians in its security operations, the second process enables paramilitary power to exercise influence and control over the functioning of these institutions and the outcomes of their actions. It is then a question of controlling not only the means of violence but also most spaces inside the state. We may call this process the paramilitarization of the state or, alternatively, the institutionalization of paramilitarism."

global integration of nation states alters state-level politics: "If interstate relationships are becoming more important, then state decisions and practices are constrained by their relationships with other states."[181] In other words, even within the same state, para-institutionality and inter-penetration would look very different across the decades, since the range of what is possible changes. As the number of legal conventions and forms of accountability change, so do the increasingly extra-legal parastate structures. Many paramilitary leaders were acutely aware of these transformations and bent them to their advantage. In his book, Colombian AUC boss Carlos Castaño defined paramilitarism as an "anti-subversive political-military movement exercising the right to legitimate self-defense *that demands transformations of the State, but does not fight against it*."[182] Castaño did not specify what type of trans-formations he had in mind, but two major types stand out: paramilitar-ies "going rogue," and paramilitaries launching a takeover of the state. Both are related to changing forms of relative autonomy.

After extended periods of empowerment, paramilitaries can turn their backs on the state and develop significant forms of autonomy. Further privatization can mean that they begin working for themselves, as in the case of warlords who turn into private military contractors. They can begin pursuing their own political and economic agendas, no longer heeding their patrons in the state. At some point they can gener-ate non-violent jobs and even provide public goods.[183] Alternatively, they turn their guns to protect their power bases or suppress truth and justice-seeking politicians. In his memoirs, the South African President F. W. De Klerk admitted that the paramilitary units who functioned under apartheid

> soon acquired a high degree of autonomy and often carried out operations on their own initiative. They became a law unto themselves. They recruited some agents who were criminals... At some further

---

[181] Jackie Smith and Hank Johnston (eds), *Globalization and Resistance* (New York: Rowman & Littlefield, 2002), 208.

[182] Carlos Castaño, *Colombia, siglo XXI: Las Autodefensas y la paz* (n.p.: Editorial Colombia Libre, 1999): "Definir las Autodefensas Unidas de Colombia como un movimiento político-militar de carácter anti-subversivo en ejercicio del derecho a la legítima defensa que reclama transformaciones del Estado, pero no atenta contra él." Emphasis added.

[183] Hunt, "Rethinking State," 74.

stage, probably about the time that I became president, these murky elements in the undercover structures of the security forces began to formulate their own policy.[184]

The assassinations of Serbian Prime Minister Zoran Đinđić and likely poisoning of Turkish President Turgut Özal shed light on the problem of "blowback." In some cases, such as Iraq or Chechnya, they capture or become the state.[185] Their attitude toward the state becomes more antagonistic, as they no longer merely wish to ensure their own survival but focus on capturing (parts of) the state. Once created and unleashed, each passing day solidifies their social structure and cohesion, and it becomes increasingly difficult to unmake them, especially after they have committed very intimate forms of violence. Nevertheless, despite these transformations, their political vulnerabilities hardly change. They remain heterogeneous and uncoordinated, dependent on their bases and sources of power, vulnerable economically and militarily, and inexperienced politically. Only if their vulnerabilities can be leveraged and the competition between them checked, can demobilization and reintegration begin to be a topic of discussion. After paramilitarism, we mostly see infighting, insubordination, franchising, fractioning, and spoiling peace processes.[186]

Existing discussions of paramilitary violence have argued a range of differing, sometimes contradictory, arguments in a literature that does not yet show any signs of consensus. Some have argued that paramilitarism is developed by weak states as a less violent last resort for counterinsurgency purposes, as a consequence of which levels of violence against civilians generally decrease.[187] A slightly different rendering of the weak state argument posits that structural conditions of state weakness offer opportunities for paramilitaries to pursue private agendas and

---

[184] Frederik de Klerk, *The Last Trek: A New Beginning* (London: Macmillan, 1998), 123.

[185] Coughlin, *Saddam*, 100, 107.

[186] Sasha Lezhnev, *Crafting Peace: Strategies to Deal with Warlords in Collapsing States* (Lanham, MD: Lexington Books, 2006); "Las AUC fueron una alianza criminal de ejércitos privados," *Verdada Abierta*, June 10, 2017, at https://verdadabierta.com/las-auc-fueron-una-alianza-criminal-de-ejercitos-privados (accessed February 10, 2018).

[187] David Mason and Dale Krane, "The Political Economy of Death Squads: Toward a Theory of the Impact of State-Sanctioned Terror," *International Studies Quarterly* 33:2 (1989), 175–98.

commit mass killings.[188] Others have suggested that having civilians enlist in pro-state paramilitary groups is an effective strategy to separate local insurgents from local civilians, which reduces indiscriminate violence, but at the same time breeds resentment and conflict within local communities and increases counter-insurgent violence against the insurgents who have been picked out.[189] Research on a key issue that influences the levels of violence, intelligence gathering, indicates that political and military leaders subcontract control and repression to militias due to their local intelligence skills necessary to "read" the civilian population.[190] This leads to lower levels of indiscriminate violence against civilians and more precise applications of violence. Finally, varying levels of violence have also been explained through discipline and control. Some have argued that the deployment of pro-state militias increases human rights violations due to deficiencies in training and lack of state control.[191] But other research has challenged these findings and argues that governments make strategic, if brutal, decisions about when to use militias against which civilians, and how. In this reading of paramilitarism, delegating "shameful" violence against civilians is a deliberate policy that serves illegitimate government agendas and builds cohesion within militias.[192] Whereas all of these interpretations have merit and incrementally expand our understanding, paramilitary violence is a broad, historically and culturally varying phenomenon that cannot be reduced to a single overarching explanation or theory.

This chapter has examined paramilitary violence through a comparison of three massacres. The three cases demonstrate that violence developed along three axes: tight secrecy before the massacre, which caught the victims by surprise, brutality during the massacre, with civilians

---

[188] Ariel Ahram, "The Role of State-Sponsored Militias in Genocide," *Terrorism and Political Violence* 26:3 (2014), 488–503.

[189] Govinda Clayton and Andrew Thomson, "Civilianizing Civil Conflict: Civilian Defense Militias and the Logic of Violence in Intrastate Conflict," *International Studies Quarterly* 60:3 (2016), 499–510.

[190] Kristine Eck, "Repression by Proxy: How Military Purges and Insurgency Impact the Delegation of Coercion," *Journal of Conflict Resolution* 59:5 (2015), 924–46.

[191] Neil Mitchell, Sabine Carey, and Christopher Butler, "The Impact of Pro-Government Militias on Human Rights Violations," *International Interactions* 40:5 (2014), 812–36.

[192] Dara Kay Cohen and Ragnhild Nordås, "Do States Delegate Shameful Violence to Militias? Patterns of Sexual Violence in Recent Armed Conflicts," *Journal of Conflict Resolution* 59:5 (2015), 877–98; Jessica Stanton, "Regulating Militias: Governments, Militias, and Civilian Targeting in Civil War," *Journal of Conflict Resolution* 59:5 (2015), 899–923.

being targeted with violence reminiscent of organized crime methods,[193] and selective but often widespread impunity after the violence. All three massacres were denied by the then ruling governments in the three states. Allegedly, they argued, the Colombian army, the Serbian Interior Ministry, or the Turkish gendarmerie had nothing to do with the violence—"allegedly," because astute observers then and more recently have seen through the thick smokescreen of deniability. Whether paramilitary violence is an efficacious strategy for maintaining a political order is questionable, since it is a deeply destructive, "negative" form of violence, in that the main goal is to secure short-term victory through human destruction.[194] But whether this perpetuates the state's power or undermines it remains to be seen, and in most cases it seems to have had deeply ambivalent effects: the strengthening of domestic state power, but the loss of international legitimacy and stature. Hannah Arendt's argument that "violence can destroy power" may apply especially to paramilitarism since its violence eradicates the victims and inflicts trauma on them, instead of maintaining power over them.[195] Finally, paramilitary violence has always been a method and means of messaging and signaling. Much like how mafias want people to know what happens to those who do not pay, so too, paramilitary violence is a performance of messaging, by utilizing violence to convey a broader message to society.

---

[193] Robinson argues that the most violent and bellicose of the militias were those who were associated with the *preman*-type thugs of the 1990s. The involvement of criminals in paramilitaries shapes the forms of violence committed: kneecapping, torture, and rape are all typically criminal forms of violence, this time under a political guise: see Robinson, "People's War," 315.

[194] Rosenbaum and Sederberg, "Vigilantism," 559.

[195] Hannah Arendt, *On Violence* (New York: Harcourt, Brace, Jovanovich, 1969), 56.

5

Conclusion

The Complexity of Paramilitarism

An Iraqi Epilogue: "We are all Hashd"

On June 13, 2014, Grand Ayatollah Ali al-Sistani issued a rare fatwa for the mass mobilization of Iraqi men against the Islamic State of Iraq and Syria. Sistani, a major authority in the Shia world, proclaimed the "collective duty" (*wajib kifa'i*) of Iraqi men to defend the nation from ISIS' threat: "Therefore, it is incumbent on citizens able to carry weapons and fight the terrorists, to defend their country, their people, and their holy sites, they should volunteer to serve in the security forces (القوات الأمنية) for this holy purpose."[1] Sistani's fatwa followed the Iraqi government's pursuit of paramilitary mobilization. Initially, the ruling Dawa Party government was against the proliferation of paramilitaries, but the emergence of ISIS changed its attitude. When the Iraqi army collapsed in June 2014, Prime Minister Nouri al-Maliki signed a decree to establish the Commission for the Popular Mobilization Forces (PMF)—which became the shorthand umbrella group "Popular Mobilization" (*al-Hashd al-Shaabi*), Hashd for short.[2] Although Sistani's fatwa was intended to motivate men to join the regular security forces and was not a fiat for paramilitarization, the two decrees legitimized at least seven pre-existing paramilitary units and sanctioned several new ones.[3] Consequently, long-standing Shia paramilitary groups could now operate in total freedom and transparency, and approximately 100,000 men rallied under

---

[1] See the decree at https://www.sistani.org/arabic/archive/24918/ (accessed April 25, 2019).
[2] See the official website at http://al-hashed.net/ (accessed April 25, 2019).
[3] Some of the pre-existing paramilitary groups were the Badr Organization, Asa'ib Ahl al-Haqq, Kata'ib Hezbollah, Kata'ib Sayyid al-Shuhada, Harakat Hezbollah al-Nujaba, Kata'ib al-Imam Ali, and Kata'ib Jund al-Imam.

the new banner of the Hashd. The new Prime Minister Haider Al-Abadi's government struggled to control the Hashd, but rather than integrating it into the army, it legitimized the PMF as a "state-affiliated" force.[4]

The formation of the Hashd was officially a flagrant violation of the 2005 Iraqi constitution (Article 9, Paragraph B), which prohibited "the formation of military militia outside the framework of the armed forces."[5] But after years of systemic corruption, sectarian clientelism, politicization of the state bureaucracy, and the ingrained cultures of patronage and "loyalty over merit" within Iraqi state institutions (including the security forces), the Iraqi state proved incapable of warding off a threat like ISIS. However, it would be a fallacy to see the Hashd and the Iraqi state as opposing, fundamentally contradictory forces. In a way, Iraq in 2014 was no different from Colombia, Serbia, or Turkey in the 1990s: para-institutional structures emerged in a set of overlapping and competing networks that had armed groups under their command. Indeed, the Hashd can best be seen as a para-institutional function and reflection that is broadly symptomatic of the post-2003 Iraqi state. As Haddad argued: "From Badr to the Peshmerga to the Jaysh al-Mahdi to the Awakening Councils and on to the various paramilitary groups that dot Iraq's security, political, and criminal landscapes, such groups have been a permanent fact of post-2003 Iraq."[6] In this perspective, the Hashd were not a new phenomenon, but represented a strong sense of continuity in Iraq's "paramilitary state."[7] Earlier ostensibly pacifying attempts at "demobilization" had often brought adverse effects. For example, already in 2004, the Badr Organization agreed to dissolve and integrate into the Interior Ministry, but not only did the militia perpetuate a group of fighters separate from the official armed forces, "it also ensured that those fighters sent into the ministry remained loyal to the paramilitary

---

[4] Renad Mansour and Faleh Jabar, *The Popular Mobilization Forces and Iraq's Future* (Washington, DC: Carnegie Endowment, 2017).

[5] See the 2005 Iraqi constitution at https://www.constituteproject.org/constitution/Iraq_2005.pdf?lang=en (accessed April 25, 2019).

[6] Fanar Haddad, "Understanding Iraq's Hashd Al-Sha'bi: State and Power in Post-2014 Iraq," *The Century Foundation* (March 5, 2018), at https://tcf.org/content/report/understanding-iraqs-hashd-al-shabi/ (accessed April 25, 2019).

[7] For example, one of the most powerful militias, Muqtada al-Sadr's Mahdi Army (*Jaysh al-Mahdi*), grew out of the process of demobilized Iraqi soldiers rallying around new concepts of statehood in post-2003 Iraq. See Amir Taha, "Turning Ex-Combatants into Sadris: Explaining the Emergence of the Mahdi Army," *Middle Eastern Studies* 55:3 (2019), 357–73.

group." As a result, half a generation later, the Badr Organization and the Hashd in a broader sense, ended up infiltrating and controlling the ministry, from the top echelons down to the feared Federal Police.[8]

The faces of this new Iraqi state were not Saddam's many intelligence bosses that had characterized and terrorized Baathist Iraq, but paramilitary leaders that enjoyed immense power. For example, Qais al-Khazali, head of the Asa'ib Ahl al-Haq group, celebrated the widespread popularity of the Hashd and proposed that it should branch out beyond the security sector and take on other state functions. "We are all Hashd," he concluded.[9] Another powerful example of a paramilitary leader is Hadi al-Ameri, former minister of transportation, member of parliament, and veteran of the Supreme Council for Islamic Revolution in Iraq (SCIRI). After 2003, al-Ameri set up the Badr Organization, the main pro-Iranian paramilitary group in Iraq whose power extends well beyond military affairs.[10] A final example is Abu Mahdi al-Muhandis, who had long-standing ties to Iran's Revolutionary Guard in the 1980s, and after 2003 became a member of parliament for the Dawa Party, and deputy chairman of the Hashd Commission. Abu Mahdi started the Kata'ib Hezbollah, the Iraqi pendant of the Lebanese Hezbollah, which is listed as a terrorist group by the USA.[11] All of these old and new paramilitary groups have fought battles against the US army, ISIS, and Syrian rebel groups. But they have also arrested, assassinated, and massacred civilians in residential areas across Syria and Iraq, and are therefore dreaded especially by Sunni communities, who consider most Shi'ite militias as occupying armies—even if there are notable but inconsistent exceptions such as the Sadr loyalists' conduct in Samarra.[12] But Sunni communities are not the only ones to dread these groups. Having defeated ISIS militarily, most Hashd fighters returned to their hometowns in the south and began operating as a parallel state, to the extent

[8] Renad Mansour, "Reining in Iraq's Paramilitaries Will Just Make Them Stronger," *Foreign Policy*, July 9, 2019, at https://foreignpolicy.com/2019/07/09/reining-in-iraqs-paramilitaries-will-just-make-them-stronger/ (accessed September 10, 2019).

[9] Haddad, "Understanding Iraq's Hashd Al-Sha'bi."

[10] Geneive Abdo, *The New Sectarianism: The Arab Uprisings and the Rebirth of the Shi'a–Sunni Divide* (Oxford: Oxford University Press, 2017), 28.

[11] See their official website at http://www.kataibhezbollah.com/ (accessed April 25, 2019).

[12] Thanassis Cambanis, "Nation Building at Gunpoint." *The Atlantic*, May 10, 2019, at https://www.theatlantic.com/international/archive/2019/05/samarra-sunni-city-shia-militias-iraq/588772/ (accessed September 10, 2019).

that in the southern mostly Shi'ite city of Basra, there were widespread protests against them, with local activists blaming the Hashd for killing two dozen protesters on September 8 and 9, 2018.[13]

Much of Iraqi paramilitarism bears the imprint of Iranian paramilitarism and transnational influence, embodied by Qasem Suleimani, a Major General in the Revolutionary Guards and commander of the Iranian Quds Force. Suleimani's aims were driven by a complex mix of Iranian nationalism, anti-Israeli and anti-American geopolitical considerations, revanchism for the Iran–Iraq war, and unmistakably sectarian appropriations.[14] The consequences for Syria and Iraq are serious, and his deep influence and powerful imperative continue to be felt in the vast lands between Beirut and Tehran.[15] In the twenty-first century, both Syria and Iraq, countries with fairly parallel histories and dynamics of state and society, collapsed into violent conflicts that differed significantly.[16] Iraq was occupied from abroad; Syria experienced a grassroots uprising. One central factor became and has remained prominent in both countries as they imploded in civil war: paramilitarism. There are clear differences between the cases: Syria is still a security state, where the various intelligence agencies reign supreme and Russia supports the Syrian army as a powerful foreign backer. But there are similarities as well: strong Iranian influence, empowerment of paramilitaries due to the persistent conflicts, and sectarianization due to the conduct of pro-government militias. Both countries' recent pasts attest to the importance of paramilitarism: it is here to stay and we have to deal with it.

The Shadow of the State

If one had to use a metaphor to characterize paramilitarism, it would be the solar eclipse. It is the temporary alignment of different actors with

[13] Mansour, "Reining in Iraq's Paramilitaries."

[14] Dexter Filkins, "The Shadow Commander," *The New Yorker* (September 23, 2013), at https://www.newyorker.com/magazine/2013/09/30/the-shadow-commander (accessed April 25, 2019).

[15] For a comprehensive overview of Shi'ite militias in Lebanon, Syria, and Iraq, see Phillip Smyth, "The Shia Militia Mapping Project" (May 2019), at https://www.washingtoninstitute.org/policy-analysis/view/the-shia-militia-mapping-project (accessed September 10, 2019).

[16] For a concise but deft analysis of both countries' descent into violence, see William Harris, *Quicksilver War: Syria, Iraq and the Spiral of Conflict* (Oxford: Oxford University Press, 2018).

different agendas that nevertheless, in that moment or period in time, produces vectors of violence against a particular group(s). Just like the sun, the moon, and the earth each have their own separate courses and paths, during an eclipse they are aligned and cast a shadow. That shadow is not always intended and by themselves they cannot produce it, but the eclipse generates it nevertheless. In particular moments and under particular constellations, state officials, paramilitaries, and organized crime together cast this "shadow of the state." This book has examined several lines of research germane to paramilitarism: its global history, criminal connections, and arrangements within the state. It has argued that whereas the forces of paramilitarism proliferated over time, so have counterforces: states' capacities have expanded over time due to increasingly intricate links with civil society actors (including organized crime), and have exploited sophisticated possibilities to conceal paramilitary violence; but at the same time, concealment of paramilitary violence has become more possible due to increased international interaction between states and human rights monitoring of states, as well as domestic forces of truth-seeking journalism and the sensitivities of electorates.

Historically, paramilitarism has changed between the early modern age and the twenty-first century. The relationships between states and paramilitaries have persisted, subject to modernization. The *condottieri* of the fifteenth century differ from the sectarian militias of the twenty-first, but militias can *gravitate* around a state, whose magnetism can draw them in and push them away in various ways. This persistence is due to two processes. First, state formation is not a linear progress from premodern states with chaotic security to well-ordered modern monopolies of violence, but it is a volatile and reversible process. Second, even under the surface of ostensibly uniform monopolies of violence, there is often a patchwork of institutions, jurisdictions, and agencies at work. Throughout history, political elites have understood very well the benefits of outsourcing particular forms of violence. Mazzei argued that the historical willingness of a state to use paramilitary repression is "likely to provide the paramilitary groups with a sense of legitimacy in continuing tactics that have been successfully used in the past."[17] Robinson,

---

[17] Julie Mazzei, *Death Squads or Self-Defense Forces?* (Chapel Hill: University of North Carolina Press), 209.

who has studied Indonesian militias across the country's history, wrote about the 1999 East Timor militias:

> The militias that seemed to sprout like mushrooms in 1999 were neither spontaneous expressions of a timeless traditional pattern, as Indonesian officials have claimed, nor simply a modern-day fabrication of the Indonesian army, as critics have suggested. While it is certainly true that the militias received support from Indonesian authorities in 1999, their repertoires, technologies, and modes of organization borrowed heavily from models and antecedents deeply rooted in East Timorese and Indonesian history.[18]

Interestingly, the Global South was often ahead of Europe in many ways: the examples of Indonesia in the 1960s and Guatemala in the 1980s demonstrate that neither Northern Ireland nor Serbia were unique in their trajectories of paramilitarism. Finally, both within national histories and the wider historical trajectory of global paramilitarism, a clear direction is suggested: as states' violent capacity increased, so did the international human rights regime and democratic internal pressure. The result was no linear growth or decline of paramilitarism, but an increasing ability of states to engage in *concealment* of paramilitarism.[19]

This book has also looked at crime and criminalization. It has argued that state–crime relations are not a relic of the past, but that banditry is very much alive, just in modern capitalist incarnation. It is quite common for governments, cornered in (civil) wars, to contact criminals and "strongmen" for various purposes, in particular sensitive tasks of violent threat neutralization. During crises these people are contacted, empowered, covered, and afterwards often disposed of. Mobilization for violence and the types of violence are organized crime's expertise,

---

[18]   Geoffrey Robinson, "People's War: Militias in East Timor and Indonesia," *South East Asia Research* 9:3, 271–318, at 313.

[19]   Rejali has shown that the twentieth century saw the development of coercive interrogation techniques specially designed to leave behind no evidence or identifiable traces. Paramilitarism is its counterpart as it follows a similar path in the same period: increasing interdependence and interpenetration between states, proliferation of transnational ties, emancipation of citizens, and most importantly, human rights monitoring and electoral accountability, necessitated the concealment of illegitimate violence by states through the development of paramilitary infrastructures. See Darius Rejali, *Torture and Democracy* (Princeton, NJ: Princeton University Press, 2009).

because their recruitment also often runs through personal connections. Seeing paramilitaries as merely criminals de-politicizes them, as "narcos," "bosses," and "dons" often want to be part of ruling capitalist elites and wield influence over both electoral democratic politics and authoritarian orders. Finally, criminals were clearly involved in paramilitarism in Yugoslavia, Turkey, and Chechnya, but more research is needed to determine whether the groups were typical, necessary, and sufficient, to qualify as paramilitarism in general.

The issue of criminal entanglements enabling and fostering parastatal structures highlights the problem of historical continuities of paramilitarism. Since the 1990s, there has been regular discussion in various media outlets (not to mention by the paramilitaries themselves) that Chechen, Turkish, and Serbian paramilitaries were modern manifestations of older organizations or deeper "cultures of paramilitarism." While these allusions were often based on hastily written, essentialist, or misconstrued uses of history, the persistent problem of paramilitarism in these societies did raise questions about continuities that spanned their histories. Were certain societies or states prone to paramilitarism? Did they have habits, routines, legacies, mentalities, or norms that led to recrudescence? And if so, how? Or is it mostly the imagination of the paramilitaries themselves, who model their militias after historical examples? The problem of continuities or recrudescence is best viewed through the perspective of the concept of path dependence, the notion that "particular courses of action, once introduced, can be virtually impossible to reverse" and lead to a certain "lock-in" in the historical and political development of states—such as the above example of the Badr Organization in Iraq.[20] Whereas this concept offers explanatory value, only thorough diachronic studies of paramilitarism in one society can provide conclusive answers to the above questions. The same can be said about societies that do *not* have traditions of paramilitarism, or, societies in which paramilitarism comes to an end. These issues remain the task of future research.

The book has also examined the organization, morphology, infrastructure, or "architecture" of paramilitarism with and within the

---

[20] Paul Pierson, "Path Dependence, Increasing Returns, and the Study of Politics," *American Political Science Review* 94:2 (2000), 251–67.

state. Various scholars have studied these relationships as *intreccio* or "interpenetration," but it must be added that these are processes that change across time and assume different shapes. This interpenetration is influenced not only by the will of state officials, but also by external forces, the course of the conflict, and by the endogenous nature of paramilitary–state relations: the longer paramilitarism develops and entrenches itself in a state, the more established a tradition of paramilitarism becomes, and the more difficult it is to extricate it from this intricate system. Also, paramilitaries need the state for many reasons, for example to legalize looted movable and immovable properties—much like a major long-term goal of organized crime is to become a legal enterprise. The book has also argued that paramilitarism is a praxiological and performative phenomenon. Para-institutionality refers to the tension between formal institutionalism on the one hand, and the extra-institutional development of powerful, informal networks on the other hand. Paramilitarism is also performative, in that paramilitary violence conveys a broader message into society by announcing to both its victims and the public that the violence is set up not to be traced back to the state.

The state has been central to this book. Classic weak state approaches have been critiqued, most notably through the example of Colombia, which expanded its coercive apparatus throughout the twentieth century and was anything but weak when it actively created paramilitary groups. Indeed, most states that have actively built or tacitly condoned paramilitary infrastructures command a broad coercive apparatus, including armed intelligence agencies, military police, and support troops. For lack of a better term, we have been dealing with smart, or shrew states. In any case, the Weberian state does not apply as a descriptive but a normative model.[21] The corrective of the literature has departed from widespread misunderstandings that most states themselves actually make or allow paramilitarism, and are not simply reacting to strongmen building a power base for themselves. Whether this can be called "perverse state formation" or an extension of "infrastructural state power" or "state social control" can be debated.[22] But the net result

---

[21] Louise Andersen, Bjørn Møller, and Finn Stepputat (eds), *Fragile States and Insecure People? Violence, Security, and Statehood in the Twenty-First Century* (New York: Palgrave Macmillan, 2007), 12.

[22] Jenny Pearce, "Perverse State Formation and Securitized Democracy in Latin America," *Democratization* 17:2 (2010), 286–306.

is that paramilitarism has allowed the state to reach into spaces and shape social realities that are normally illegal, illegitimate, off-limits, or out of bounds. This "flexing and waning" has alternated between empowerment and disempowerment of paramilitaries. Finally, paramilitarism has often been explained with the argument of groups defending the political and economic status quo. But the status quo argument has clear limits and needs further development, as some regimes that use paramilitaries do want to transform society, such as in the Serb ethnic cleansing campaigns, the Filipino anti-crime agenda, or the Iraqi sectarianization policies. Furthermore, paramilitary forces are not static in their defense of the status quo, but use their empowerment by the state (for the sake of the status quo) to transform state–society relations.

A key argument in this book is that states have not just *down*contracted but also *up*contracted violence: as much as they formed groups top-down, they could also allow bottom-up vigilantism and popular mobilization, with the similar result that paramilitarism became sanctioned. The magnetism of the state is such that even in the case of "independent" militias, the state looms large, when it allows, condones, turns a blind eye to, or in other ways makes militia activity possible. Staniland characterized these relationships cogently: "mainstream politicians build armed wings, states collaborate with militias against common foes, police ignore private counterinsurgency armies, militaries tacitly share sovereignty with insurgent enemies, and warlords place their loyalists inside state security forces."[23] Tolerating groups as an attempted force multiplier facilitates plausible deniability, especially when the macro-ideological context allows militias to act *in the spirit of* the ideology. This way, no direction or coordination is needed, as the state allows the violence to happen. Feldman uses the term "mimesis" to convey this phenomenon.[24] Strictly speaking, this is not state-sponsored violence and prosecutors would have difficulties pinning state officials down on particular acts. However, condoning violence through tacit consent or watching passively is a de facto endorsement by the state, which has major impact on public perceptions of paramilitarism. The argument

---

[23] Paul Staniland, "States, Insurgents, and Wartime Political Orders," *Perspectives on Politics* 10:2 (2012), 243–64, at 243.
[24] Allen Feldman, *Formations of Violence: The Narrative of the Body and Political Terror in Northern Ireland* (Chicago, IL: University of Chicago Press, 1991), 41.

that paramilitarism is about paramilitaries hiding behind the state has a clear flipside: to maintain the façade of popular support for the state, the state can also hide behind paramilitaries. This book has argued that, as a temporary workaround, paramilitarism can be an act of commission as much as it can constitute an act of omission.

The Future of Paramilitarism

Paramilitarism poses at least three potential problems for the state: fragmentation, devolution, and crime.

Paramilitarism potentially fragments the state. Hristov has argued that the Latin American state has claimed its legitimacy not from a monopoly of the means of violence, but from its lack thereof. The disorder that allegedly ensues from violence, such as crime and youth gangs, has provided justification for imposing order via extreme measures.[25] In virtually all cases examined for this book, paramilitarism has fragmented the state: it has turned ministries against each other, and deepened informal patronage networks running through state bureaucracies. It has also made state violence less accountable, thereby also fracturing society and radicalizing victimized communities and pitting them against pro-state communities. Indeed, in some cases, spreading complicity was the explicit objective of state officials: paramilitary violence had the function of tying certain groups to the political elites, slicing sharp cleavages in society and state. Even after Milošević was long gone, the paramilitaries were stuck with his legacy of war crimes. In this way, paramilitarism makes its effects felt decades after the actual violence, posing dilemmas for transitional justice mechanisms such as the feasibility of disarming, demobilizing, and reintegrating policies.[26]

Second, paramilitarism devolves state power, usually temporarily, but sometimes permanently. Paramilitaries are not just instruments of the state, but forge mutually beneficial relationships, and in some cases and

---

[25] Jasmin Hristov, *Paramilitarism and Neoliberalism: Violent Systems of Capital Accumulation in Colombia and Beyond* (London: Pluto, 2014), 32.

[26] Chris Alden, Monika Thakur, and Matthew Arnold, *Militias and the Challenges of Post-Conflict Peace: Silencing the Guns* (London: Zed Books, 2011).

periods, paramilitaries have even dominated the state, at various levels: local, municipal, provincial, or federal. The state might create or allow paramilitary groups to be loyal to the state, but training, combat, and violence makes them loyal to their immediate commanders. This is a paradoxical situation that reflects the age-old principal–agent dilemma, but also pertains to how paramilitaries themselves imagine the state. The consequences of devolution have a deep impact on the nature and status of the state, which has been negotiating its tasks, through incremental transfers to the private sector, including aspects of the security sector.[27] These complex patterns of subcontracting and outsourcing of violence, as one of many services that states have been subcontracting out, is not the end of the state, but certainly a temporary retreat or devolution of it.[28] This has even led some researchers to simply accept paramilitarism as an alternative to classical state-building projects to provide safety and security.[29]

Finally, paramilitarism criminalizes in many ways: criminals seize and keep political power, and politicians do not desist from using criminal means. In all paramilitary arrangements, crime is influential, but in the most extreme cases, crime becomes tantamount to governance or the very continuation of the state by other means. Murder, torture, threats, trafficking, theft, extortion, kidnappings, and assassinations become established practice in societies suffering from paramilitarism, thereby influencing the state but also popular culture.[30] The longer paramilitarism lasts, the easier young, rural, and/or unemployed men can become initiated, inducted, and employed. Experiencing excitement, proving toughness, breaking everyday routines, and exercising power otherwise impossible are motives that are likely to exist among young men. Exorcising criminal ties and practices from those offices and

---

[27] Saskia Sassen, *Territory, Authority, Rights: From Medieval to Global Assemblages* (Princeton, NJ: Princeton University Press, 2008), 237.

[28] Martin van Creveld, *The Rise and Decline of the State* (Cambridge: Cambridge University Press, 1999); Susan Strange, *The Retreat of the State: The Diffusion of Power in the World Economy* (Cambridge: Cambridge University Press, 1996); Robert Bunker and Pamela Bunker, "The Modern State in Epochal Transition: The Significance of Irregular Warfare, State Deconstruction, and the Rise of New Warfighting Entities beyond Neo-Medievalism," *Small Wars & Insurgencies* 27:2 (2016), 325–44.

[29] Ariel Ahram, "Learning to Live with Militias," *Journal of Intervention and Statebuilding* 5:2 (2011), 175–92.

[30] Colin Knox, "'See No Evil, Hear No Evil': Insidious Paramilitary Violence in Northern Ireland," *British Journal of Criminology* 42:1 (2002), 164–85.

agencies of the state that have relied on them, has proven to be an exceptionally difficult process for many states.

One thing is certain. From the war in Eastern Ukraine, to "weekend paramilitaries" in Poland and Slovakia, to flirtations in Bosnia, and their entrenchment in Syria, paramilitarism is here to stay.

Select Bibliography

Ahram, Ariel (2011), "Learning to Live with Militias," *Journal of Intervention and Statebuilding* 5:2, 175–92.

Ahram, Ariel (2011), *Proxy Warriors: The Rise and Fall of State-Sponsored Militias*. Stanford, CA: Stanford University Press.

Ahram, Ariel (2014), "The Role of State-Sponsored Militias in Genocide," *Terrorism and Political Violence* 26:3, 488–503.

Alden, Chris, Monika Thakur, and Matthew Arnold (2011), *Militias and the Challenges of Post-Conflict Peace: Silencing the Guns*. London: Zed Books.

Aliyev, Huseyn (2016), "Strong Militias, Weak States and Armed Violence: Towards a Theory of 'State-Parallel' Paramilitaries," *Security Dialogue* 47:6, 498–516.

Ash, Konstantin (2016), "Threats to Leaders' Political Survival and Pro-Government Militia Formation," *International Interactions* 42:5, 703–28.

Ballvé, Teo (2012), "Everyday State Formation: Territory, Decentralization, and the Narco Landgrab in Colombia," *Environment and Planning D: Society and Space* 30:4, 603–22.

Barkey, Karen (1994), *Bandits and Bureaucrats: The Ottoman Route of State Centralization*. Ithaca, NY: Cornell University Press.

Berenschot, Ward (2011), *Riot Politics: Hindu–Muslim Violence and the Indian State*. London: Hurst.

Biberman, Yelena (2019), *Gambling with Violence: State Outsourcing of War in Pakistan and India*. Oxford: Oxford University Press.

Biberman, Yelena (2016), "Violence by Proxy: Russia's Ex-Rebels and Criminals in Chechnya," in Bettina Koch (ed.), *State Terror, State Violence: Global Perspectives*. Wiesbaden: Springer, 135–50.

Billingsley, Phil (1988), *Bandits in Republican China*. Stanford, CA: Stanford University Press.

Blok, Anton (1972), "The Peasant and the Brigand: Social Banditry Reconsidered," *Comparative Studies in Society and History* 14, 494–503.

Bobrovnikov, Vladimir (2007), "Bandits and the State: Designing a 'Traditional' Culture of Violence in the Russian Caucasus," in Jane Burbank, Mark Von Hagen, and A. V. Remnev (eds), *Russian Empire: Space, People, Power, 1700–1930*. Blooomington: Indiana University Press, 239–67.

Böhmelt, Tobias and Govinda Clayton (2018), "Auxiliary Force Structure: Paramilitary Forces and Progovernment Militias," *Comparative Political Studies* 51:2, 197–237.

Bridenthal, Renate (2017), *The Hidden History of Crime, Corruption, and States*. New York: Berghahn Books.

Briquet, Jean-Louis and Gilles Favarel-Garrigues (eds) (2010), *Organized Crime and States: The Hidden Face of Politics*. New York: Palgrave.

Briscoe, Ivan and Pamela Kalkman (2016), *The New Criminal Powers: The Spread of Illicit Links to Politics across the World and How it can be Tackled*. The Hague: Clingendael Institute.

Bunker, Robert and Pamela Bunker (2016), "The Modern State in Epochal Transition: The Significance of Irregular Warfare, State Deconstruction, and the Rise of New Warfighting Entities beyond Neo-Medievalism," *Small Wars & Insurgencies* 27:2, 325–44.

Cadwallader, Anne (2013), *Lethal Allies: British Collusion in Ireland*. Chester Springs, PA: Dufour Editions.

Campbell, Bruce and Arthur Brenner (eds) (2000), *Death Squads in Global Perspective*. New York: Palgrave Macmillan.

Carey, Sabine and Neil Mitchell (2017), "Pro-Government Militias," *Annual Review of Political Science* 20, 127–47.

Carey, Sabine, Neil Mitchell, and Will Lowe (2013), "States, the Security Sector, and the Monopoly of Violence: A New Database on Pro-Government Militias," *Journal of Peace Research* 50:2, 249–58.

Çelik, Selahattin (1998), *Verbrecher Staat: Der "Susurluk-Zwischenfall" und die Verflechtung von Staat, Unterwelt und Kontrerguerilla in der Türkei*. Frankfurt am Main: Zambon.

Center for the Study of Democracy (2004), *Partners in Crime: The Risks of Symbiosis between the Security Sector and Organized Crime in Southeast Europe*. Sofia: CSD.

Chambliss, William (1989), "State-Organized Crime," *Criminology* 27:2, 183–208.

Civico, Aldo (2016), *The Para-State: An Ethnography of Colombia's Death Squads*. Berkeley: University of California Press.

Clayton, Govinda and Andrew Thomson (2016), "Civilianizing Civil Conflict: Civilian Defense Militias and the Logic of Violence in Intrastate Conflict," *International Studies Quarterly* 60:3, 499–510.

Cockayne, James (2016), *Hidden Power: The Strategic Logic of Organized Crime*. Oxford: Oxford University Press.

Cohen, Dara and Ragnhild Nordås (2015), "Do States Delegate Shameful Violence to Militias? Patterns of Sexual Violence in Recent Armed Conflicts," *Journal of Conflict Resolution* 59:5, 877–98.

Colás, Alejandro and Bryan Mabee (eds) (2010), *Mercenaries, Pirates, Bandits, and Empires: Private Violence in Historical Context*. New York: Columbia University Press.

Curott, Nicholas and Alexander Fink (2012), "Bandit Heroes: Social, Mythical or Rational?," *American Journal of Economics and Sociology* 71:2, 470–97.

Davis, Diane and Anthony Pereira (eds) (2003), *Irregular Armed Forces and their Role in Politics and State Formation*. Cambridge: Cambridge University Press.

Del Vecchio, Giorgio (1965), "Der Staat als Verbrecher," *Archiv für Rechts- und Sozialphilosophie* 51:2, 161–5.

Diehl, James (1977), *Paramilitary Politics in Weimar Germany*. Bloomington: Indiana University Press.

Dillon, Martin (2016), *The Dirty War: Covert Strategies and Tactics Used in Political Conflicts*. London: Routledge.

Dowdle, Andrew (2007), "Civil Wars, International Conflicts and Other Determinants of Paramilitary Strength in Sub-Saharan Africa," *Small Wars & Insurgencies* 18:2, 161–74.

Dziedzic, Michael (ed.) (2016), *Criminalized Power Structures: The Overlooked Enemies of Peace*. New York: Rowman & Littlefield.

Eck, Kristine (2015), "Repression by Proxy: How Military Purges and Insurgency Impact the Delegation of Coercion," *Journal of Conflict Resolution* 59:5, 924–46.

Ero, Comfort (2000), "Vigilantes, Civil Defence Forces and Militia Groups: The Other Side of the Privatisation of Security in Africa," *Conflict Trends* 1, 25–9.

Esparza, Marcia (2018), *Silenced Communities: Legacies of Militarization and Militarism in a Rural Guatemala Town*. New York: Berghahn Books.

Esparza, Marcia, Daniel Feierstein, and Henry Huttenbach (eds) (2009), *State Violence and Genocide in Latin America: The Cold War Years*. London: Routledge.

Felbab-Brown, Vanda (2016), "Hurray for Militias? Not So Fast: Lessons from the Afghan Local Police Experience," *Small Wars & Insurgencies* 27:2, 258–81.

Feldman, Allen (1991), *Formations of Violence: The Narrative of the Body and Political Terror in Northern Ireland*. Chicago, IL: University of Chicago Press.

Ferguson, Kate (2018), *Architectures of Violence: The Command Structures of Modern Mass Atrocities, from Yugoslavia to Syria*. London: Hurst.

Fletcher, Luke (2007), "Turning *Interahamwe*: Individual and Community Choices in the Rwandan Genocide," *Journal of Genocide Research* 9:1, 25–48.

Fraenkel, Ernst (1941), *The Dual State: A Contribution to the Theory of Dictatorship*. New York: Oxford University Press.

Frazer, Chris (2006), *Bandit Nation: A History of Outlaws and Cultural Struggle in Mexico, 1810–1920*. Lincoln: University of Nebraska Press.

Galeotti, Mark (2013), *Russian Security and Paramilitary Forces since 1991*. Oxford: Osprey.

Gerlach, Christian (2010), *Extremely Violent Societies: Mass Violence in the Twentieth-Century World*. Cambridge: Cambridge University Press.

Gerwarth, Robert and John Horne (eds) (2012), *War in Peace: Paramilitary Violence after the Great War*. Oxford: Oxford University Press.

Gill, Lesley (2016), *A Century of Violence in a Red City: Popular Struggle, Counterinsurgency, and Human Rights in Colombia*. Durham, NC: Duke University Press.

Gill, Lesley (2004), *The School of the Americas: Military Training and Political Violence in the Americas*. Durham, NC: Duke University Press.

Gingeras, Ryan (2010), "Beyond Istanbul's 'Laz Underworld': Ottoman Paramilitarism and the Rise of Turkish Organised Crime, 1908–1950," *Contemporary European History* 19, 215–30.

Giustozzi, Antonio (2012), *Empires of Mud: War and Warlords in Afghanistan*. London: Hurst.

Godson, Roy (ed.) (2003), *Menace to Society: Political–Criminal Collaboration around the World*. London: Transaction.

Green, Penny and Tony Ward (2004), *State Crime: Governments, Violence and Corruption*. London: Pluto Press.

Gutierrez Sanin, Francisco (2019), *Clientelistic Warfare: Paramilitaries and the State in Colombia (1982–2007)*. Oxford: Peter Lang.

Haggar, Ali (2007), "The Origins and Organization of the Janjawiid in Darfur," in: Alex de Waal (ed.), *War in Darfur and the Search for Peace*, Cambridge, MA: Harvard University Press, 113–39.

Handelman, Stephen (1995), *Comrade Criminal: Russia's New Mafiya*. New Haven, CT: Yale University Press.

Heyman, Josiah (ed.) (1999), *States and Illegal Practices*. New York: Berg.

Hobsbawm, Eric (2000 [1969]), *Bandits*. London: Weidenfeld and Nicolson.

Hodges, Donald (2014), *Argentina's "Dirty War": An Intellectual Biography*. Austin: University of Texas Press.

Hoffmann, Kasper and Koen Vlassenroot (2014), "Armed Groups and the Exercise of Public Authority: The Cases of the Mayi-Mayi and Raya Mutomboki in Kalehe, South Kivu," *Peacebuilding* 2:2, 202–20.

Hristov, Jasmin (2014), *Paramilitarism and Neoliberalism: Violent Systems of Capital Accumulation in Colombia and Beyond*. London: Pluto Press.

Huggins, Martha (1997), "From Bureaucratic Consolidation to Structural Devolution: Police Death Squads in Brazil," *Policing and Society* 7:4, 207–34.

Huggins, Martha (ed.) (1991), *Vigilantism and the State in Modern Latin America: Essays on Extralegal Violence*. Westport, CT: Praeger.

Hughes, Geraint (2016), "Militias in Internal Warfare: From the Colonial Era to the Contemporary Middle East," *Small Wars & Insurgencies* 27:2, 196–225.

Human Rights Watch (1996), *Colombia's Killer Networks: The Military–Paramilitary Partnership and the United States*. New York: Human Rights Watch.

Hunt, Stacey (2009), "Rethinking State, Civil Society, and Citizen Participation: The Case of the Colombian Paramilitaries," *Behemoth: A Journal on Civilisation* 2:1, 64–87.

Işık, Ayhan (2019), "Paramilitarism, Organized Crime, and the State in Turkey in the 1990s." PhD thesis, Utrecht University, Department of History.

Jaffe, Rivke (2013), "The Hybrid State: Crime and Citizenship in Urban Jamaica," *American Ethnologist* 40:4, 734–48.

Jenss, Alke (2015), "From Coexistence and Complementarity to Confrontation? Colombian Paramilitaries, their Successors and their Relation to the State," *Sicherheit und Frieden/Security & Peace (S+F)* 33:4, 206–11.

Jentzsch, Corinna, Stathis Kalyvas, and Livia Schubiger (2015), "Militias in Civil Wars," *Journal of Conflict Resolution* 59:5, 755–69.

Kalyvas, Stathis (2015), "How Civil Wars Help Explain Organized Crime—and How They Do Not," *Journal of Conflict Resolution* 59:8, 1517–40.

Kalyvas, Stathis (2006), *The Logic of Violence in Civil War*. Cambridge: Cambridge University Press.

Kan, Paul Rexton (2019), *The Global Challenge of Militias and Paramilitary Violence*. Cham: Palgrave.

Karstedt, Susanne (2014), "Organizing Crime: The State as Agent," in Letizia Paoli (ed.), *The Oxford Handbook of Organized Crime*. Oxford: Oxford University Press, 303–20.

Kauzlarich, David, Christopher Mullins, and Rick Matthews (2003), "A Complicity Continuum of State Crime," *Contemporary Justice Review* 6:3, 241–54.

Kelly, Robert (ed.) (1986), *Organized Crime: A Global Perspective*. Totowa, NJ: Rowman & Littlefield.

Killingsworth, Matt, Matthew Sussex, and Jan Pakulski (eds) (2016), *Violence and the State*. Oxford: Oxford University Press.

Knox, Colin (2002), " 'See No Evil, Hear No Evil': Insidious Paramilitary Violence in Northern Ireland," *British Journal of Criminology* 42:1, 164–85.

Koliopoulos, John (1987), *Brigands with a Cause: Brigandage and Irredentism in Modern Greece 1821–1912*. Oxford: Oxford University Press.

Kupatadze, Alexander (2012), *Organized Crime, Political Transitions and State Formation in Post-Soviet Eurasia*. London: Palgrave.

Lawther, Cheryl (2018), *Truth, Denial and Transition: Northern Ireland and the Contested Past*. London: Routledge.

Lezhnev, Sasha (2006), *Crafting Peace: Strategies to Deal with Warlords in Collapsing States*. Lanham, MD: Lexington Books.

Lippmann, Walter (1931), "Underworld: Our Secret Servant," *Forum* 85, 1–4.

López, Fernando (2016), *The Feathers of Condor: Transnational State Terrorism, Exiles and Civilian Anticommunism in South America*. Cambridge: Cambridge Scholars.

Lund, Joshua (2011), "The Poetics of Paramilitarism," *Revista Hispánica Moderna* 64:1, 61–7.

Lupsha, Peter (1996), "Transnational Organized Crime versus the Nation-State," *Transnational Organized Crime* 2, 21–48.

Lyall, Jason (2010), "Are Coethnics More Effective Counterinsurgents? Evidence from the Second Chechen War," *American Political Science Review* 104:1, 1–20.

McCauley, Martin (2014), *Bandits, Gangsters and the Mafia: Russia, the Baltic States and the CIS since 1991*. London: Routledge.

McCoy, Alfred (2016), "Covert Netherworld: An Invisible Interstice in the Modern World System," *Comparative Studies in Society and History* 58:4, 847–79.

McFarland Sánchez-Moreno, Maria (2018), *There Are No Dead Here: A Story of Murder and Denial in Colombia*. New York: Public Affairs.

McGovern, Mark (2019), *Counterinsurgency and Collusion in Northern Ireland*. London: Pluto Press.

McKenzie, Jeffrey (1995), *The 'Black' Terrorist International: Neo-Fascist Paramilitary Networks and the 'Strategy of Tension' in Italy, 1968–1974*. Ann Arbor, MI, UMI Dissertation Service, UMI Number: 9529217.

McSherry, Patrice (2005), *Predatory States: Operation Condor and Covert War in Latin America*. Lanham, MD: Rowman & Littlefield.

Manwaring, Max (2012), *Gangs, Pseudo Militaries, and Other Modern Mercenaries: New Dynamics in Uncomfortable Wars*. Norman: University of Oklahoma Press.

Mappes-Niediek, Norbert (2011), *Balkan-Mafia: Staaten in der Hand des Verbrechens— Eine Gefahr für Europa*. Berlin: Ch. Links Verlag.

Mason, David and Dale Krane (1989), "The Political Economy of Death Squads: Toward a Theory of the Impact of State-Sanctioned Terror," *International Studies Quarterly* 33:2, 175–98.

May, Ronald (1992), *Vigilantes in the Philippines: From Fanatical Cults to Citizens' Organizations*. Mānoa: University of Hawai'i at Mānoa.

Mazzei, Julie (2009), *Death Squads or Self-Defense Forces? How Paramilitary Groups Emerge and Challenge Democracy in Latin America*. Chapel Hill: University of North Carolina Press.

Melo, Jorge (1990), "Los paramilitares y su impacto sobre la política colombiana," in Francisco Leal and Leon Zamosc (eds), *Al Filo del Caos: crisis política en la Colombia de los años 80*. Bogotá: Iepri y Tercer Mundo, 475–514.

Menjívar, Cecilia nd Néstor Rodríguez (eds) (2005), *When States Kill: Latin America, the U.S., and Technologies of Terror*. Austin: University of Texas Press.

Meyers, Jeff (2017), *The Criminal–Terror Nexus in Chechnya: A Historical, Social, and Religious Analysis.* New York: Lexington Books.

Migdal, Joel, Atul Kohli, and Vivienne Shue (eds) (1994), *State Power and Social Forces: Domination and Transformation in the Third World.* Cambridge: Cambridge University Press.

Milicevic, Aleksandra (2004), "Joining Serbia's Wars: Volunteers and Draft-Dodgers, 1991–1995." PhD thesis, University of California, Los Angeles.

Mitchell, Neil, Sabine Carey, and Christopher Butler (2014), "The Impact of Pro-Government Militias on Human Rights Violations," *International Interactions* 40:5, 812–36.

Morrison, Kenneth (2010), "The Criminal State Symbiosis and the Yugoslav Wars of Succession," in Alejandro Colas and Bryan Mabee (eds), *Mercenaries, Pirates, Bandits and Empires.* London: Hurst, 159–86.

Naylor, Tom (2008), *Patriots and Profiteers: Economic Warfare, Embargo Busting, and State-Sponsored Crime.* Montreal: MQUP.

Ngunyi, Mutahi and Musambayi Katumanga (2014), *From Monopoly to Oligopoly of Violence.* Nairobi: UNDP.

Nielsen, Christian Axboe (2012), "War Crimes and Organized Crime in the Former Yugoslavia," *Suedosteuropa-Mitteilungen* 52:3, 6–17.

Ong, Lynette (2018), "'Thugs-for-Hire': Subcontracting of State Coercion and State Capacity in China," *Perspectives on Politics* 16:3, 680–95.

Özar, Şemsa (2013), *Geçmişten Günümüze Türkiye'de Paramiliter bir Yapılanma: Köy Koruculuğu Sistemi.* Diyarbakır: DiSA.

Pansters, Wil (ed.) (2012), *Violence, Coercion, and State-Making in Twentieth-Century Mexico.* Stanford, CA: Stanford University Press.

Papazian, Taline (2016), *L'Arménie à l'épreuve du feu: Forger l'état à travers la guerre.* Paris: Karthala.

Pearce, Jenny (2010), "Perverse State Formation and Securitized Democracy in Latin America," *Democratization* 17:2, 286–306.

Porteux, Jonson (2013), "Police, Paramilitaries, Nationalists and Gangsters: The Processes of State Building in Korea." PhD dissertation, University of Michigan, Department of Political Science.

Poynting, Scott and David Whyte (eds) (2012), *Counter-Terrorism and State Political Violence: The 'War on Terror' as Terror.* London: Routledge.

Punch, Maurice (2012), *State Violence, Collusion and the Troubles: Counter Insurgency, Government Deviance and Northern Ireland.* London: Pluto Press.

Rangel, Alfredo (ed.) (2005), *El Poder Paramilitar.* Bogotá: Planeta.

Reno, William (1999), *Warlord Politics and African States.* Boulder, CO: Lynne Rienner.

Robinson, Geoffrey (2001), "People's War: Militias in East Timor and Indonesia," *South East Asia Research* 9:3, 271–318.

Rolandsen, Øystein (2007), "Sudan: The Janjawiid and Government Militias," in Morten Bøås (ed.), *African Guerrillas: Raging against the Machine.* Boulder, CO: Lynne Rienner, 151–70.

Romero, Mauricio (ed.) (2007), *Parapolítica: la ruta de la expansión paramilitar y los acuerdos políticos.* Bogotá: Intermedio.

Ron, James (2003), *Frontiers and Ghettos: State Violence in Serbia and Israel.* Berkeley: University of California Press.

Rosenbaum, Jon and Peter Sederberg (1974), "Vigilantism: An Analysis of Establishment Violence," *Comparative Politics* 6:4, 541–70.

Scheper-Hughes, Nancy (2004), "Parts Unknown: Undercover Ethnography of the Organs-Trafficking Underworld," *Ethnography* 5:1, 29–73.

Schlichte, Klaus (2010), "Na krilima patriotism/On the Wings of Patriotism: Delegated and Spin-Off Violence in Serbia," *Armed Forces & Society* 36:2, 310–26.

Schulte-Bockholt, Alfredo (2006), *The Politics of Organized Crime and the Organized Crime of Politics: A Study in Criminal Power.* New York: Lexington Books.

Silke, Andrew (2000), "Drink, Drugs, and Rock'n'Roll: Financing Loyalist Terrorism in Northern Ireland," *Studies in Conflict and Terrorism* 23:2, 107–27.

Slatta, Richard (1990), "Banditry as Political Participation in Latin America," *Criminal Justice History: An International Annual* 11, 171–87.

Slatta, Richard (2004), "Eric J. Hobsbawm's Social Bandit: A Critique and Revision," *A Contracorriente* 2, 1–30.

Sluka, Jeffrey (ed.) (2000), *Death Squad: The Anthropology of State Terror.* Philadelphia: University of Pennsylvania Press.

Šmída, Tomáš and Miroslav Mareša (2015), "'Kadyrovtsy': Russia's Counterinsurgency Strategy and the Wars of Paramilitary Clans," *Journal of Strategic Studies* 38:5, 650–77.

Solomon, Joel (1997), *Implausible Deniability: State Responsibility for Rural Violence in Mexico.* New York: Human Rights Watch.

Souleimanov, Emil (2015), "An Ethnography of Counterinsurgency: Kadyrovtsy and Russia's Policy of Chechenization," *Post-Soviet Affairs* 31:2, 91–114.

Söyler, Mehtap (2015), *The Turkish Deep State: State Consolidation, Civil–Military Relations and Democracy.* London: Routledge.

Staniland, Paul (2012), "Between a Rock and a Hard Place: Insurgent Fratricide, Ethnic Defection, and the Rise of Pro-State Paramilitaries," *Journal of Conflict Resolution* 56:1, 16–40.

Staniland, Paul (2015), "Militias, Ideology, and the State," *Journal of Conflict Resolution* 59:5, 770–93.

Staniland, Paul (2012), "States, Insurgents, and Wartime Political Orders," *Perspectives on Politics* 10:2, 243–64.

Stanton, Jessica (2015), "Regulating Militias: Governments, Militias, and Civilian Targeting in Civil War," *Journal of Conflict Resolution* 59:5, 899–923.

Stewart, Christopher (2008), *Hunting the Tiger: The Fast Life and Violent Death of the Balkans' Most Dangerous Man.* New York: Thomas Dunne Books.

Taha, Amir (2019), "Turning Ex-Combatants into Sadris: Explaining the Emergence of the Mahdi Army," *Middle Eastern Studies* 55:3, 357–73.

Tar, Usman (2005), "The Perverse Manifestations of Civil Militias in Africa: Evidence from Western Sudan," *Peace, Conflict and Development* 7, 135–73.

Thomson, Janice (1994), *Mercenaries, Pirates, and Sovereigns: State-Building and Extraterritorial Violence in Early Modern Europe.* Princeton, NJ: Princeton University Press.

Tilly, Charles (1985), "War Making and State Making as Organized Crime," in Peter Evans et al. (eds), *Bringing the State Back In*. Cambridge: Cambridge University Press, 169–86.

Tsoutsoumpis, Spyros (2017), "'Political Bandits': Nation-Building, Patronage and the Making of the Greek Deep State," *Balkanistica* 30:1, 37–64.

Üngör, Uğur Ümit (2012), "Rethinking the Violence of Pacification: State Formation and Bandits in the Young Turk Era, 1914–1937," *Comparative Studies in Society and History* 54:4, 746–69.

Urwin, Margaret (2016), *A State in Denial: British Collaboration with Loyalist Paramilitaries*. Cork: Mercier Press.

Utas, Mats (ed.) (2012), *African Conflicts and Informal Power: Big Men and Networks*. London: Zed Books.

Valencia, León (ed.) (2007), *Parapolítica: la ruta de la expansión paramilitar y los acuerdos políticos*. Bogotá: Intermedio.

Van der Kroef, Justus (1985), "'Petrus': Patterns of Prophylactic Murder in Indonesia," *Asian Survey* 25:7, 745–59.

Volkov, Vadim (2002), *Violent Entrepreneurs: The Use of Force in the Making of Russian Capitalism*. Ithaca, NY: Cornell University Press.

Von Lampe, Klaus (2015), *Organized Crime: Analyzing Illegal Activities, Criminal Structures, and Extra-Legal Governance*. London: SAGE.

Voronin, Yuriy (1997), "The Emerging Criminal State: Economic and Political Aspects of Organized Crime in Russia," in Phil Williams (ed.), *Russian Organized Crime: The New Threat?* London: Frank Cass, 53–62.

Vukušić, Iva (2019), "Serb Paramilitaries and the Yugoslav Wars." PhD thesis, Utrecht University, Department of History.

Waldron, Arthur (1991), "The Warlord: Twentieth-Century Chinese Understandings of Violence, Militarism, and Imperialism," *American Historical Review* 96:4, 1073–100.

Yang, Guobin (2016), *The Red Guard Generation and Political Activism in China*. New York: Columbia University Press.

Yaprak Yıldız, Yeşim (2019), "(Dis)avowal of State Violence: Public Confessions of Perpetrators of State Violence against Kurds in Turkey." PhD dissertation, University of Cambridge.

Zveržhanovski, Ivan (2007), "Watching War Crimes: The Srebrenica Video and the Serbian Attitudes to the 1995 Srebrenica Massacre," *Journal of Southeast European and Black Sea Studies* 7:3, 417–30.

Websites

Paramilitarism, Organized Crime, and the State: https://paramilitarism.org.

The Pro-Government Militias Database: https://militias-guidebook.com.

The Shia Militia Mapping Project: https://www.washingtoninstitute.org/policy-analysis/view/the-shia-militia-mapping-project.

US National Security Archive files on Colombia: https://nsarchive.gwu.edu/project/colombia-project.

Verdad Abierta: http://www.verdadabierta.com/.

Bibliographic Overviews

Beede, Benjamin (2018), "Semi-Military and Paramilitary Organizations," *Oxford Bibliographies*, at http://www.oxfordbibliographies.com/abstract/document/obo-9780199791279/obo-9780199791279-0100.xml.

Malejacq, Romain (2017), "Pro-Government Militias," *Oxford Bibliographies*, at http://www.oxfordbibliographies.com/view/document/obo-9780199743292/obo-9780199743292-0213.xml.

Case Files

ICTY Šešelj case (IT-03-67).
ICTY Stanišić and Simatović case (IT-03-69).
MICT Mladić case, 65ter03743.

Index